CAMBRIDGE TEXTS IN THE
HISTORY OF POLITICAL THOUGHT

*The Early Political Writings of
the German Romantics*

CAMBRIDGE TEXTS IN THE HISTORY OF POLITICAL THOUGHT

Series editors

RAYMOND GEUSS

Lecturer in Social and Political Sciences, University of Cambridge

QUENTIN SKINNER

Professor of Political Science in the University of Cambridge

Cambridge Texts in the History of Political Thought is now firmly established as the major student textbook series in political theory. It aims to make available to students all the most important texts in the history of western political thought, from ancient Greece to the early twentieth century. All the familiar classic texts will be included but the series does at the same time seek to enlarge the conventional canon by incorporating an extensive range of less well-known works, many of them never before available in a modern English edition. Wherever possible, texts are published in complete and unabridged form, and translations are specially commissioned for the series. Each volume contains a critical introduction together with chronologies, biographical sketches, a guide to further reading and any necessary glossaries and textual apparatus. When completed, the series will aim to offer an outline of the entire evolution of western political thought.

For a list of titles published in the series, please see end of book.

The Early Political Writings of The German Romantics

EDITED AND TRANSLATED BY

FREDERICK C. BEISER

Indiana University, Bloomington

CAMBRIDGE
UNIVERSITY PRESS

Published by the Press Syndicate of the University of Cambridge
The Pitt Building, Trumpington Street, Cambridge CB2 1RP
40 West 20th Street, New York, NY 10011–4211, USA
10 Stamford Road, Oakleigh, Melbourne 3166, Australia

First published 1996

Printed in Great Britain at the University Press, Cambridge

A catalogue record for this book is available from the British Library

Library of Congress cataloguing in publication data

Early German romanitic political writings / edited and translated by
Frederick C. Beiser.
p.   cm. – (Cambridge texts in the history of political thought)
Includes index.
ISBN 0 521 44501 9. ISBN 0 521 44951 0 (pbk.)
1. Political science – Germany – History. 2. Germany – Politics and goverment –
1740–1806. 3. Romanticism – Germany. I. Beiser, Frederick C., 1949–
II. Series
II. Title.   III. Series.
JA84.G3E25 1996
830.9'358'09034 – dc20   95-65120 CIP

ISBN 0 521 44501 9 hardback
ISBN 0 521 44951 0 paperback

Contents

Preface

The political thought of the German romantics covers a long period, beginning in the 1790s and extending into the 1830s. Since the most important and interesting texts from this period could not all be included in one volume, I have chosen material from a single phase of romantic thought. This is the period from 1797 to 1802, the most fertile and formative period of Romanticism, which is generally known as *Frühromantik*. Even within this period, it has been necessary to be selective because of the wealth of material. I have therefore concentrated upon the most important writings of three leading figures of the early romantic circle: Novalis, Schleiermacher and Friedrich Schlegel. Selecting texts from this period alone, and from these thinkers alone, provides a coherence and unity that would be impossible to achieve in a more comprehensive anthology.

Within my chosen parameters I have attempted to be as exhaustive and thorough as possible. I have included all kinds of writings relevant to the early political thought of Novalis, Schleiermacher and Schlegel: fragments, lectures, essays and treatises. No claim is made, however, to provide *all* the early political writings of the German romantics. I have had to exclude two major works from the early period: Schelling's *Deduktion des Naturrechts* (1796–7) and Schleiermacher's incomplete manuscript *Versuch einer Theorie des geselligen Betragens* (1799). Though these works are interesting and important, they are not suitable for an introductory edition. Schelling's *Deduktion* is comprehensible only to someone who has a good grasp of Fichte's early philosophy; and Schleiermacher's *Versuch* is best understood *after* reading the *Monologen*, which have been translated in part here.

Although Fichte was a crucial influence upon the early romantics, I have not included any of his writings in this volume. This is partly because they are available elsewhere in a very reliable recent edition, *Fichte: Early Philosophical Writings*, ed. Daniel Breazeale (Ithaca: New York: Cornell University Press, 1988). It is also a mistake to regard Fichte as a romantic in any strict sense of the term. He was not a regular participant in the meetings of the romantic circle; and some of the central ideas of the early romantics – the role of art in society, the organic concept of nature, the place of individuality in ethics – were formulated in reaction to him.

Since the young romantics stressed *the unity* of politics, aesthetics and religion, any edition of their political writings should not construe the term 'political' in a narrow sense. I have included, therefore, fragments on metaphysics, ethics and aesthetics when they are essential to understand the context of early romantic political thought. For this reason I have added the whole texts of Novalis' *Pollen* and Schlegel's *Ideas*.

The early German romantics never provided a systematic exposition of their political thought; it is is scattered throughout many fragments, aphorisms, essays and lectures. Its most condensed expression, and indeed its *locus classicus*, is Novalis' *Faith and Love* and *Political Aphorisms*. A reader who wants to proceed direct to the core of their thought is best advised to begin with these works.

Many of the texts have been translated for the first time. Those that have been translated before have been translated anew for this edition. Like most translations, mine have attempted to steer a middle path between the conflicting ideals of accuracy and readability. I have usually aimed at an accurate rather than a literary translation; but in many cases I have had to sacrifice accuracy for more readable English. I have often altered punctuation, divided lengthy paragraphs and eliminated redundancies. In the case of Novalis' and Schlegel's unpublished manuscripts I have sometimes deleted phrases or words when they were incidental to the main thought. In most cases, however, the original emphasis has been retained.

The translations are based upon the latest critical editions: the *Kritische Friedrich Schlegel Ausgabe* (Munich: Schöningh, 1966), ed.

Ernst Behler *et al.*; *Novalis Schriften. Die Werke von Friedrich von Hardenberg* (Stuttgart: Kohlhammer, 1960), ed. Richard Samuel *et al.*; *Monologen, Kritische Ausgabe*, ed. Friedrich Michael Schiele, Dritte Auflage (Hamburg: Felix Meiner Verlag, 1978) and the *Friedrich Schleiermacher Kritische Gesamtausgabe* (Berlin: de Gruyter, 1984), ed. Günter Meckenstock *et al.*

   The texts of the young romantics present formidable challenges to the commentator as well as translator. They rely much upon allusion and nuance, and they adopt the technical vocabulary of Kant, Fichte and Schiller while often altering its meaning. Even worse, they are sometimes deliberately obscure, ambiguous and mystifying. Schlegel and Novalis chose to write in a *Rätselsprache* or *Bildersprache*, whose meaning would be apparent only to the initiated. To make their texts more accessible to the modern reader, I have added many notes. In writing these, I have been especially indebted to three Novalis commentaries: that of Richard Samuel and Hans Joachim Mähl in the Hanser edition of the *Werke* (Munich, 1978); that of Gerhard Schulz in the *Studienausgabe* (Munich: Beck, 1969); and that of Hans Dietrich Dahnke and Rudolf Walbiner in *Novalis, Werke in Einem Band* (Berlin: Aufbau Verlag, 1983).

   In preparing this volume, I have been aided by several colleagues and friends. Christiane Goldmann, Michael Halberstam and Martin Schönfeld have advised me on questions of translation. Raymond Geuss, Quentin Skinner and two anonymous reviewers for Cambridge University Press gave me valuable comments on earlier drafts. The idea for a volume devoted entirely to the political writings of the early romantics came originally from Raymond Geuss.

Introduction

Romantic aesthetics and politics

Although it seems hopelessly abstract and vague, the term 'German Romanticism' has been given a definite historical meaning by generations of scholars. It denotes a loosely organized and vaguely self-conscious intellectual movement that began in Germany toward the close of the eighteenth century. It is even possible to identify specific times and places as the beginning of German Romanticism. The crucial period would be from 1797 to 1802, and the pivotal places would be Jena and Berlin. During this time, a group of writers met in the home of A. W. Schlegel in Jena, and in the literary salons of Henriette Herz and Rahel Levin in Berlin. There they held frank and free discussions about philosophy, poetry, politics and religion. The leading members of this circle were Ludwig Tieck (1773–1853), Wilhelm Heinrich Wackenroder (1773–1801), Friedrich Wilhelm Joseph Schelling (1775–1845), the brothers August Wilhelm (1767–1845) and Friedrich Schlegel (1772–1829), Ernst Daniel Schleiermacher (1767–1834), and Friedrich von Hardenberg (1772–1801), who was known by his pen name Novalis. The members of this group called themselves 'the new school', 'the new sect' and, later and more famously, 'the romantic school'. Though their meetings were charmed, they were also short lived. Their circle suffered some severe blows with the deaths of Novalis and Wackenroder in 1801; and it disbanded when the Schlegel brothers left Jena in 1802.

German Romanticism did not, of course, disappear with the demise of this early circle. Its legacy lived on, and it eventually became one of the most influential movements in modern intellectual history. German Romanticism proved to be very protean, evolving into distinct periods which are in some respects even contradictory to one another. Customarily, it is divided into three phases: early Romanticism or *Frühromantik* from 1797 to 1802, whose chief members have already been mentioned; high Romanticism or *Hochromantik* from 1803 to 1815, whose main representatives are Achim von Arnim, Joseph Görres, Adam Mueller, Caspar David Friedrich, Zacharais Werner, Clemens Brentano and Gotthilf Heinrich von Schubert; and finally late Romanticism or *Spätromantik* from 1816 to 1830, whose leading figures are Franz Baader, E. T. A. Hoffmann, Johann von Eichendorff and the elder Friedrich Schlegel and Schelling. Of course, there are continuities and family resemblances between these periods; but since they also have differing, even opposing, characteristics, it is important to distinguish between them. It is a common error to interpret early Romanticism in the light of later Romanticism, as if the later philosophy and politics of the movement are true without qualification for its earlier phase.

German Romanticism began as a literary movement. In its early period, its goals and interests were primarily aesthetic, preoccupied with the need to determine the standards of good taste and literature. The young romantics made art their highest value, their *raison d'être*, their be all and end all. They attributed great powers to art: it was the criterion of absolute knowledge, the means of unifying the personality, the mediator between man and nature, and the source of social harmony.

Although German Romanticism was essentially an aesthetic movement, it also deserves a prominent place in any history of modern political thought. In its formative period, it developed political ideas of the first historical importance. Novalis, Friedrich Schlegel and Schleiermacher developed a concept of community to counter the atomism and anomie of modern society; they formulated an ethic of love and self-realization in reaction to the formalism of Kant's ethics; they questioned some of the main presuppositions of the liberal tradition, especially its individualism; they criticized the inhumanity and 'philistinism' of civil society; and they championed many modern social values, such as the emancipation of women, sexual freedom and the right of divorce. The political thought of the young romantics remains of great interest today for its attempt to synthesize, and to avoid the troublesome extremes of, liberalism and conservatism. Their attempt to synthesize these traditions is apparent in several respects: although the young romantics stressed the value of community, they also insisted upon the need for individual liberty; while they emphasized the value of organic growth, continuity and tradition, they also championed progress, development and reform; and if they pointed out the dangers of a narrow rationalism, they also recognized the value of reason and defended the rights of free enquiry.

What is the connection between romantic aesthetics and politics? Prima facie there is none at all. It was a cardinal tenet of the young romantics that art is an end in itself, and that it should not be subordinated to social, moral and political goals. They reaffirmed the Kantian doctrine of the autonomy of art, the idea that art has its own *sui generis* rules and values, independent of science, religion and morality. For just this reason, they have often been accused of political indifference, of escaping the social and political world and taking refuge in the ideal world of art.

One cannot, however, take the romantics' aestheticism entirely at face value. We must place it in the context of their moral, social and political concerns. For, although they insisted upon the autonomy of art, the romantics also stressed that art should be subordinate to the interests of humanity. The value of beauty, Novalis and Schlegel sometimes said, is that it serves as a symbol of the good. Paradoxically, they emphasized the autonomy of art because this made art a symbol of freedom. Art represents freedom, they argued, only if it is completely autonomous, not subordinate to any social or political ends.

The more we examine the context of early German Romanticism the more it becomes clear that its aesthetics and politics are inseparable. If its politics conforms to aesthetic ideals, its aesthetics fits its political ends. This interconnection becomes especially apparent from one of the central themes of early romantic political thought: 'the poetic state'. Novalis and Schlegel held that the perfect state is created and organized according to the ideal of beauty. The ruler of the poetic state is 'the artist of artists', 'the poet of poets', the director of a vast public stage where all citizens are actors. Seen from a broader historical perspective, their poetic state is the very antithesis of Plato's republic. Here artists are not banished: they are enthroned. The romantics constantly invite us to reconsider Plato's famous question: what is the role of art in the state?

What drove the romantics to their poetic conception of the state? Why did they give such social and political importance to art? And what social and political purpose did their art serve? To answer these questions, we need to examine the romantics' reaction to two major developments of their time: the French Revolution, and the crisis of the German Enlightenment or *Aufklärung*.

The political ideals of the young romantics were formed in the 1790s, the decade in which all the problems and consequences of the Revolution became clear. Almost all of the romantics cheered the storming of the Bastille and celebrated the end of the *ancien régime*. They embraced the grand ideals of *liberté, egalité et fraternité*, defended the rights of man, and looked forward to the creation of a republic, 'the kingdom of God on earth'. Such enthusiasm was typical, of course, of most German intellectuals in the early 1790s. What is so striking about the romantics is the persistence of their optimism, which lasts into the late 1790s. Unlike so many of their contemporaries, they did not renounce the Revolution because of the September Massacres, the execution of Louis XVI, the invasion of the Rhineland or even the Terror. It is only around 1797 that they began to have deep reservations about the Revolution. Now they feared the social vacuum resulting from the wholesale destruction of traditional social institutions; they attacked the growing materialism and atheism in France; and they disapproved of the worst excesses of the mob. They started to recognize the need for some form of elite rule, and argued that the true republic should be a mixture of democracy, aristocracy and monarchy. Nevertheless, their increasing caution did not involve any abandonment of their basic political ideals. As late as 1800, Schlegel, Schleiermacher and Novalis continue to express republic sympathies. Indeed, their growing moderation was not especially conservative when measured by contemporary standards. Rather, it was typical of most German public opinion in the late 1790s; and it even mirrored the trend of opinion in France itself, where the most recent elections returned royalist majorities in the legislative councils.

Although the romantics approved of the principles of the Revolution, they disapproved of its practice. Like so many German intellectuals in the 1790s, they did not believe that fundamental social and political change could be achieved through violence or mass action from below. Rather, they stressed the need for gradual reform from above, reform led by a wise and responsible elite and adapted to the special conditions of a country. The continuing chaos and strife in France only strengthened their conviction that the French people, and *a fortiori* the German, were not ready for the high moral ideals of a republic. The main precondition for fundamental social and political change, they believed, is the education and enlightenment of the people.

As intellectuals in post-revolutionary Europe, the task of the young romantics was now cut out for them: to educate and enlighten the people, and so to prepare them for the grand moral ideals of a republic. Such was the aim of their common journal, the *Athenaeum*, which appeared from 1798 to 1800. The young romantics felt that, as intellectuals, they had moral and political responsibilities, and they had a deep faith in the power of ideas to effect social and political change. They were deeply influenced by Fichte's view, as set forth in his 1793 *Lectures on the Vocation of a Scholar*, that the role of the intellectual is to guide the progress of humanity. They endorsed Kant's famous adage that, if philosophers could not be kings, then at least kings should listen to philosophers; the only qualification they make to it is that philosophers should become artists.

We should place the romantics' aestheticism in the context of their reaction to the Revolution. Following Schiller's lead in his *Letters on the Aesthetic Education of Man* (1795), they gave primacy to art because it is the chief tool for the education and enlightenment of the public in the post-revolutionary age. They believed that art, and art alone, can inspire the people to act according to the principles of reason, the high moral ideals of a republic. Although they agreed with Kant and Fichte that reason has the power *to know* our moral principles, they insisted that it does not have the power to make us *act* by them. The main springs of human action are impulse, imagination and passion, which only art can arouse and direct. If the people only receive an aesthetic education, which paints the principles of reason in attractive colours, then they will feel motivated to act according to them. While reason is a harsh taskmaster, forcing us to repress our feelings and desires, art is an inspiring mistress, awakening our feelings and guiding them in a moral direction. If art only has its way, it will unify the two sides of our nature, reason and sensibility, so that we will then do our duty *from* and not *against* our inclinations. In sum, then, art became important for the young romantics because they saw it as the chief means of realizing their moral and political ideals: the liberty, equality and fraternity of a republic.

The romantics' aestheticism grew out of not only their reaction to the Revolution, but also their response to the crisis of the Enlightenment or *Aufklärung*. The *Aufklärung* had made reason its highest authority, its final court of appeal. Nothing could escape the scrutiny of reason: *all* moral, religious and political beliefs were subject to criticism, and abruptly dismissed if they lacked sufficient evidence. By the late 1790s, however, some of the critics of the *Aufklärung* – J. G. Hamann, F. H. Jacobi and Justus Möser – had made clear some of the disturbing consequences of such a ruthless rationalism. If reason had shown itself to be an omnipotent *negative* force, capable of destroying everything, it had also proved itself to be an impotent *positive* force, incapable of creating anything. Where the state, the church, nature and the community once stood, there was now only a vacuum. If modern individuals were rational and free, they were also rootless, attached to nothing, and without faith or allegiance. They had lost their bonds with the community, since reason condemned all its laws and customs as antiquated and oppressive. They also had lost their feeling for nature, because reason had deprived it of all mystery, magic and beauty. Finally, they had lost their religious faith, since reason had declared it to be nothing more than mythology. Sensing this condition of loss and rootlessness, Novalis stated that philosophy originates in 'homesickness' (*Heimweh*), the urge to feel at home again in a demystified world.

Though worried by the negative consequences of the *Aufklärung*, the young romantics resisted irrationalism. Unlike Burke or de Maistre, they did not defend the value of 'prejudice', nor did they advocate any return to 'the wisdom of our ancestors'. They valued the critical power of reason because it liberated the individual from all the fetters of custom and convention. Rather than laying down restraints on reason, they even advocated taking criticism to its limits, regardless of tender consciences and personal convictions. Nevertheless, their strong endorsement of reason was tempered by a clear recognition of its limits. Since the demand that we criticize *all* our beliefs is self-reflexive, applying to criticism itself, they stressed that a completely critical reason is self-conscious, aware of its limits. A fully self-conscious reason will acknowledge the vacuum it creates yet cannot fill.

The romantics' ambivalent reaction to the crisis of the *Aufklärung* – their recognition of reason's powers *and* limits – left them with a very disturbing dilemma. How is it possible to fill the vacuum left by reason without betraying reason? How is it possible to restore unity with nature and the community without forfeiting the freedom that comes with criticism? Their middle path between this dilemma was their aestheticism. They believed that art, and art alone, could fill the vacuum left by reason. If reason is essentially a negative power, art is basically a positive one. While reason can only criticize, art can create. For the instrument of art is the imagination, which has the power to produce an entire world. The romantics built upon one of Kant's and Fichte's fundamental insights: that we live in a world that we create; they add to it only that our creation should be a work of art. That is the sum and substance of their famous 'magical idealism'.

One reason the romantics were persuaded of the powers of art is that, unlike the old customs, laws and religion, it has the power to incorporate yet withstand criticism. Art stands on a higher plateau than reason because its products are the result of play, of self-conscious semblance, whereas reason takes every proposition literally and seriously, because it treats it as a claim to truth. Thanks to irony, the romantic artist can distance himself from his creations and free himself to create anew. Although any one of his creations is bound to be limited and flawed, none of them perfectly represents his powers and energy, which are unbounded and ready to create again. Thus the artist internalizes yet transcends rational criticism.

The task of romantic art, then, was *to create* on a sophisticated, self-conscious level that unity with nature and society that had once been *given* on a naive subconscious level to primitive man. If only we make nature, society and the state beautiful, magical and mysterious again, the young romantics believed, then we will restore our sense of belonging to them. Cured of our homesickness, we will finally feel at home again in our world.

Romantic religion and politics

By the early 1800s religion had replaced art at the pinnacle of the romantic hierarcy of values. Now it was religion that was the key to *Bildung*, the mainspring of cultural renewal, and the *raison d'être* of social and political life. In the spring of 1799 Schleiermacher, Friedrich Schlegel and Novalis all wrote of the need to create a new religion, or at least to go back to the roots of all religion. They demanded a new Bible, which would not give rise to the idolatry, prejudice and superstition of the past; and they called for a new church, whose sole foundation would be the brotherhood of the spirit rather than the coercion of the state. Such are the guiding ideals behind Schlegel's *Ideas*, Schleiermacher's *Monologues* and Novalis' *Christianity or Europe*.

However, religion did not completely eclipse art as the source of romantic inspiration. The romantics did not abandon their aestheticism but simply transformed it. They now cast art in a new role as the handmaiden to religion. If they once made a religion out of art, they now made religion into an art. They stressed that poetry is the 'organon' of religion, the means of its expression and criterion of its inspiration. So, if art must be sacred, religion must be beautiful. Nevertheless, despite their abiding aestheticism, the romantics now gave pride of place to religion, because they saw it as the *source* of artistic inspiration. It is as if they now recognize that, in making the world divine, mysterious and beautiful again, the artist is reviving the age-old function of the priest.

Liberal and socialist critics of Romanticism have often contended that its religious revival was the basis for its conservative or reactionary politics. In attempting to revive religion, the romantics, it seems, were reacting against the ideals of the Revolution and the progressive tendencies of the *Aufklärung*. As evidence for this point, these critics cite the notorious symapthies for, or even conversions to, the Roman Catholic church among some of the romantics.

There is indeed some element of truth in this criticism. In their later years, Friedrich Schlegel, Franz Baader and Adam Mueller appealed to religion to defend the monarchy, aristocracy and church. Nevertheless, we must be careful to avoid anachronism here. We must not judge the original inspiration and ideals of romantic religion in the light of the later beliefs of Schlegel, Baader and Mueller. That romantic religion, at least in the formative years of *Frühromantik*, was not reactionary can be seen from its origin and context.

The initial stimulus for the romantic religious revival came from one man and one book: Schleiermacher's *On Religion: Speeches to its Cultured Despisers*, which appeared in the autumn of 1799. In this famous work, Schleiermacher put foward the thesis that the essence of religion consists in the 'intuition of the universe' (*Anschauung des Universums*), the feeling of dependence upon the infinite. The enlightened critics of religion had failed to understand its essence, he argued, because they reduced it to a mere support for morality or to a primitive cosmology or metaphysics. Religion, however, should not be confused with morality or metaphysics. Its purpose is not to guide conduct, still less to explain nature. Rather, its main aim is to cultivate our 'spiritual sense', to foster our experience of the infinite, to nurture our feeling of dependence upon the universe as a whole. Unashamedly admitting his Spinozist sympathies, Schleiermacher avowed a form of pantheism, a belief in God's immanence and presence throughout nature. God is not a person existing in some supernatural heaven, he insisted, but the infinite whole of all nature. Such pantheism was attractive to Schleiermacher because it seemed to avoid the perennial conflict between religion and science. Since God exists within nature, and since nature consists in a system of laws, pantheism is the very faith of science itself. By thus defending religion against its enlightened detractors, Schleiermacher paved the way for a religious revival that would be intellectually respectable and not just a relapse into the discredited orthodox theism of the past.

But Schleiermacher's book was only the *immediate occasion* for the romantic religious revival, which had much deeper roots in one of the more radical currents of the Reformation. Ever since the dawn of the Reformation in Germany, a religious movement arose that had remarkably progressive social and political goals, such as liberty of conscience, toleration, ecumenism, egalitarianism and activism. Among the leading thinkers of this tradition were Kaspar Schwenkfeld (1498–1561), Sebastian Franck (1499–1542), Valentin

Weigel (1533–1588), Johann Arndt (1555–1621), Jakob Boehme (1675–1624), Conrad Dippel (1673–1734), Gottfried Arnold (1666–1714) and Johann Christian Edelmann (1698–1767). What these thinkers have in common is a loyalty to Luther's original ideals and a belief that he betrayed them. They embraced Luther's grand ideals of religious liberty and the priesthood of all believers; but they felt that Luther had compromised them, first by making the Bible the sole rule of faith, and second by giving the state authority over the church. If Luther's ideals were to be realized, these radicals argued, then it would be necessary to separate the church and state. Since all genuine faith comes from the inner heart of the believer, the true church is 'invisible', a purely voluntary association of kindred spirits. For the same reason, these thinkers held that the rule of faith cannot be the Bible, for it is only the record of *someone else's* beliefs and experience, and therefore should not be binding upon *my* belief and experience. Rather, the true rule of faith is inspiration, the possession of the spirit, which comes only from the depths of every individual soul.

One of the leitmotifs of this tradition, which reappears later in Romanticism, is its activism and chiliasm, the convictions that the responsible Christian should strive to realize 'the kingdom of God on earth'. The radicals believed that Luther's ideals should be practised not only in the church, but also in social and political life. In other words, they held that liberty and equality should be valid not only for 'the heavenly realm' of the Christian, but also for 'the earthly realm' of the citizen.

Another leitmotif of this tradition, which also resurfaces in Romanticism, is its pantheism, its belief in the immanence and omnipresence of God. This doctrine provided the radicals with the metaphysical underpinning for their social and political ideals. If God is immanent in his creation, present equally within everyone alike, then we all have equal access to him, and there is no need for a religious or political elite to establish and confirm our relationship with him.

The culmination and triumph of the radical Reformation came in the late eighteenth century with the Spinoza revival and the 'pantheism controversy' between Jacobi and Mendelssohn. For more than a century, Spinoza had been a much maligned figure in Germany among the orthodox Lutherans, who condemned him for his 'atheism and fatalism'. But he was also much admired among the later generation of radical reformers, who embraced the pantheism of the *Ethica* and the egalitarianism and Biblical criticism of the *Tractatus*. Indeed, so widespread was the sympathy for Spinoza among the heterodox that Heine called Spinozism 'the secret religion of Germany'. Among these admirers of Spinoza were no less than Johann Gottfried Herder (1744–1801) and Gotthold Ephraim Lessing (1729–1781), who supported many of the ideals of the radical reformers.

The radicals' hour of victory came in the spring of 1786 when Jacobi published his famous *Letters on Spinoza*, which revealed Lessing's confession of Spinozism. Since Lessing was such a revered thinker, his confession gave the stamp of legitimacy to this hitherto proscribed doctrine. After Lessing's confession was made public, other intellectuals came out of their closet to declare their Spinozism too. Among them were thinkers of the stature of Goethe and Herder. Growing up during the late 1780s and early 1790s, the young romantics soon added their names to the rolecall of Spinoza's admirers. The early letters and notebooks of Schelling, Schleiermacher, Novalis and Schlegel reveal their sympathy with Spinozism.

It is indeed the legacy of Spinoza and the radical Reformation – rather than Catholicism, orthodox Lutheranism or pietism – that emerges time and again in the religious writings of the young romantics. Schlegel, Novalis and Schleiermacher swear their allegiance to the same ideals as the radical reformers: the invisible church, the kingdom of God on earth, ecumenism and tolerance. They, too, sympathize with Spinoza's pantheism, biblical criticism and egalitarianism. Again like the radical reformers, they despise Luther's bibliolatry and stress the need for the contemplation of the inner spirit. It is indeed telling that the religious thinker the young romantics revere most is Lessing.

It should now be clear that, in its original form, romantic religion was anything but reactionary. Rather, it was the final flowering of all the progressive social and political ideals of the radical Reformation. Romantic religion was not, then, simply a reassertion of the authority of the traditional church, whether Protestant or Catholic. For, throughout the 1790s and even after 1800, Schlegel, Schleiermacher and Novalis continued to uphold the liberal ideals of the radical reformers, such as freedom of conscience, toleration, and the separation of church and state. Rather than breaking with the ideals of liberty, equality and fraternity because of religion, the romantics supported them by appealing to religion. After 1799 they saw religion, rather than art, as the chief instrument of *Bildung*, as the main means of educating the public to act according to the moral ideals of a republic. They were indeed fascinated by the various experiments with a civil religion in revolutionary France.

Whence, then, the sympathies for Catholicism among some of the romantics, sympathies that are apparent even in the late 1790s? Surely, there is a paradox here. If the romantics began as radical reformers, how did at least some of them end as Roman Catholics? Naturally, the answer to this question is involved and complicated, and so cannot be provided in the space available here. All that is at stake now, however, is simply the sympathy for Catholicism in *Frühromantik*. If we carefully examine the chief documents regarding the romantics' early flirtation with the medieval church – Novalis' *Christianity or Europe*, Schlegel's *Fragments* and Wackenroder's *Effusions of an Artloving Monk* – then we find many reasons for their sympathy for it. The medieval church gave people a sense of community; it represented the highest spiritual values; it taught, and to some extent even practised, an ethic of love, the noblest moral philosophy; and, above all, it inspired and gave pride of place to art. None of these reasons betray, however, the spirit of the radical Reformation. The early romantics' sympathy for the Catholic Church was primarily a love for the medieval *ideal*, not an approval of, still less a conversion to, the actual historical institution. What they especially admire is the ideal of a single universal church, a cosmopolitan church that transcends all sectarian differences and unites all people in brotherhood. Such a church is no more Catholic than Protestant but the ecumenical ideal of the radical Reformation.

Romanticism and the German political tradition

Although the young romantics did not write systematic treatises on political philosophy, they were anything but ignorant of, or unresponsive to, the latest thinking. A careful reading of Novalis' *Faith and Love*, or Schlegel's *Essay on Republicanism*, shows that they knew contemporary doctrine all too well. Indeed, we can understand early romantic political thought only by placing it in the context of the two rival traditions of political thought: enlightened absolutism and liberalism.

The theory of enlightened absolutism had held sway in Germany ever since the beginning of the seventeenth century, and it continued to show signs of life even after the French Revolution. Among its chief advocates were V. L. Seckendorff, Samuel Pufendorf, Christian Wolff, Christian Garve, C. G. Svarez and J. A. Eberhard. According to enlightened absolutism, the purpose of the state is to ensure the happiness, morality and piety of its subjects through wise legislation and administration. Although the welfare of the people is the main rationale of the government, the people themselves are not the best judge of their interests, and so should not participate in the business of government. 'All government *for* the people, but none *by* the people', as Friedrich II of Prussia, the greatest practitioner of this theory, summarized it.

The liberal tradition was not so well established in Germany, and during the 1790s it was barely self-conscious. Indeed, the term 'liberal' would not come into common use until the 1830s. Nevertheless, many later liberal ideals were clearly anticipated by thinkers in the 1790s. Among the early defenders of liberal ideals in Germany were Kant, Schiller, Jacobi, Wilhelm von Humboldt, Christian Dohm and Georg Forster. Early liberal doctrine was a reaction against absolutism. According to the liberals, the purpose of the state is simply to protect the rights of its citizens, who should be left to pursue their own happiness as they see fit. The government should never interfere in the private life of its citizens, for liberty is the precondition not only of a prosperous economy, but also true morality and religion. All citizens should be given the maximum of liberty, the right to do anything as long as it does not interfere with a similar right of others. Unlike later liberal doctrine, which championed democracy, early liberalism usually kept a discreet silence about the best form of government; it could be a monarchy, aristocracy or democracy, provided that it had a constitution ensuring the maximal freedom for all.

By the late 1790s, when the romantics came of age, both these traditions seemed antiquated. They could not do justice to two recent developments: the Revolution and the growth of civil society.

While enlightened absolutism clung to the last remnants of the *ancien régime*, liberalism turned a blind eye to all the problems arising from the growth of free trade, rural manufacturing and urbanization. Although Germany would not have an industrial economy until the late nineteenth century, many of the basic problems of civil society were already plain by the end of the eighteenth century: poverty, homelessness, unemployment and dehumanizing methods of production. The romantics were among the first to recognize these problems.

Spending some of their early days in Berlin, when memories of the reign of Friedrich II were still strong, Schlegel, Schleiermacher and Novalis grew to despise absolutism, which they associated with 'the machine state' of that monarch. They condemned absolutism first and foremost because its centralized administration and bureaucracy regulated and controlled every aspect of life, permitting no local self-government or initiative. All the power was in the hands of the central government, while the people were simply the passive recepients of any welfare that the ruler condescended to give them. The chief problem with absolutism, in the view of the young romantics, was that it failed to acknowledge the growing demands for more popular participation in government, which had become so vocal, urgent and widespread since the Revolution. Hence Novalis in his *Fragments*, and Schlegel in his *Essay on Republicanism*, would defend the demand for more popular government against the absolutist tradition.

Another serious problem with absolutism, according to the romantics, was that it did not provide any guarantee for individual liberty. In their early years, the romantics passionately declared the right of the individual to develop his or her personality, to realize all his or her capacities, free from the constraints of custom, convention and law. The young romantics revelled in the moral autonomy discovered by Kant, and they were determined to extend it to all aspects of social, political and cultural life. The 'divine egoism' proclaimed by Schlegel in the *Athenaeum Fragments* was the slogan for their campaign to liberate the individual from all the stifling conventions and repressive laws of the day.

In the eyes of the young romantics, the liberal tradition was guilty of the opposite failing from absolutism. While the absolutists underrated the demand for liberty, the liberals exaggerated it, pushing it to extremes. The liberals made the pursuit of individual happiness and self-realization the sole purpose of life, so that there was no value in living for the sake of the community as a whole. Hence they severed all the individual's ties to the community, leaving him or her bereft of any sense of allegiance or belonging. Against this growing social dislocation, the romantics would stress the need for, and value of, community. 'Flight from the communal spirit is death', as Novalis so dramatically put it in his *Pollen*.

The romantics maintained that there was a deeper reason for the liberals' failure to stress the importance of community. This was their conception of an *a-social* human nature, according to which the individual is complete in all needs and desires apart from society, and self-interest is the basis for all social action. The romantics are among the first to question these endemic assumptions of the liberal tradition. From such premises, Novalis argues in his *Political Fragments*, it is impossible to derive any kind of social order. We cannot justify the state through the idea of a social contract between self-interested individuals – a true squaring of the circle – because the individual will then be able to quit the contract whenever it suits him. Hence, in the romantic view, liberalism is ultimately anarchic.

Although liberalism and absolutism have opposing problems, the romantics also argued that they have a common shortcoming: both reduce the state down to a *direct* relationship between the central government and people, whether that government consists in a representative assembly or the bureaucracy of the prince. In any case, neither give any place for *intermediate groups* between the government and people, for the various guilds, councils and corporations that had been the traditional source of self-government and personal affiliation in medieval society. The absolute princes of Germany, and the representative assemblies of France, were both eager to sweep away these institutions in their drive toward greater centralization and modernization. They both abolished the old guilds, estates and corporations on the grounds that they limited the sovereignty of the prince or the liberty of the citizen. But, to the romantics, the destruction of these traditional organizations posed a double danger: tyranny from the central government and anomie for the individual. With no centres of self-government to oppose them, the prince or assembly could do whatever it wished; and with no guilds to protect their employment or to represent their interests, the individual would be cut loose without any social mooring, left to compete against others in the fray of civil society. Hence, despite all their points of conflict, absolutism and liberalism were strange bedfellows in one dangerous respect: both undermined a differentiated society for the sake of centralized authority.

The romantic critique of the liberal and absolutist traditions then left them with an apparently irresolvable problem. If the absolutist underestimated the value of liberty, and if the liberal underrated the need for community, then it was necessary to reconcile two seemingly irreconcilable ideals: individual liberty and community. This was indeed the central political problem for the entire post-revolutionary generation, which could not approve of the anomie, atomism and alienation of civil society, but which also could not abandon the principles of liberty, equality and fraternity of the Revolution.

The romantic solution to this problem was their concept of the organic state, which was sketched as early as 1800 by Novalis in *Faith and Love*, by Schlegel in his *Lectures on Transcendental Philosophy*, and by Schleiermacher in the third of his *Monologues*. The purpose of this model of the state was to ensure community *and* liberty, freedom and equality *within* a framework of continuity and tradition. There are two essential components to this model. First, like the complex, differentiated structure of a living being, the organic state will consist in many intermediate groups, such as guilds, councils and corporations. These groups will be a source of local self-government and popular representation. So rather than consisting of only a central government and a mass of isolated individuals, like the machine states of Prussia and France, the organic state will also comprise many autonomous groups. On the one hand, these will ensure the liberty of the people because they represent their interests and are independent of central control; on the other hand, they will provide for community because they will permit individuals to participate in, and belong to, them. Second, unlike the machine states, the organic state will not be designed according to some abstract plan or blueprint imposed from above, whether that is by a monarch or a revolutionary committee. Rather, like a living being, the organic state will adapt slowly to its local environment, evolving gradually from below according to the local traditions, needs and beliefs of the people. Since it develops slowly by degrees, the organic state will preserve continuity and tradition, and so provide for an element of community, which had been lost by all the revolutionary upheaval and dislocation in France; but since it develops from below rather than above, according to the will of the people rather than some prince or directorate, it will also provide for an element of liberty.

The romantic emphasis upon gradual organic change is reminiscent of Burke, who was indeed an important influence upon Schlegel and Novalis. But the romantics' organicism was much more progressive and populist than Burke's. They defended organic growth not because it would preserve the old corporate order, but because it was much more democratic, responsive to the local needs and traditions of the people. This organic growth also had to be progressive, evolving towards the grand ideals of liberty, equality and fraternity promised by the Revolution. There was always an element of utopian republicanism in early romantic political thought, which is due to the influence of the early radical writings of Fichte.

The foundation of the concept of the organic state is the romantics' philosophical anthropology, which Schlegel outlines in his *Lectures*, Schleiermacher in his *Monologues*, and Novalis in his *Faith and Love*. Contrary to the liberal tradition, this philosophical anthropology stresses the *social* nature of human beings: that values, needs and beliefs do not depend upon any fixed essence or universal nature, but a specific place in society and history. Armed with this social conception of human nature, the romantics think that they can reconcile the demands of liberty and community. They do not see any contradiction in affirming *both* the need for community *and* the right of the individual to develop his or her personality to the fullest. There is no contradiction, in their view, because people can discover and develop their individuality only through interaction with others. We realize our unique individuality, the romantics argue, only through mutual effort, through sharing ourselves with others and by participating in group life. To live in a group is perfectly natural for us, the romantics believe, because it springs from the deepest and most powerful impulse of our nature: the need for love, the desire to give and receive affection. Love is a much more powerful drive than self-interest, they argue, because the lover will gladly renounce all his interests for the sake of the beloved.

This concept of love plays a pivotal role in romantic political thought. It is indeed the leitmotif of Schlegel's *Lectures*, Novalis' *Faith and Love* and Schleiermacher's *Monologues*. What self-interest is to the liberal tradition love is to the romantic tradition. The romantics believed that the foundation of all true community is an ethic of love, and that love should replace law as the chief bond of social life. It is a fundamental mistake of both the liberal and absolutist traditions, the romantics contended, that they see only the law as the basis of social and political life. That simply follows from their mistaken philosophical anthropology: if people are inherently self-interested, then only the force of law will make them social. Although the romantics sometimes took their ethic of love to its final anarchist conclusion, demanding the abolition of the state, they usually admitted that this was a utopian goal, a regulative ideal that could be approached though never attained.

This ethic of love with all its Christian connotations, and the organic state with all its guilds, corporations and estates, are both strongly reminiscent of the Middle Ages. For this reason too, as well as their revival of religion, the romantics have been dismissed by their liberal and socialist opponents as reactionaries, as defenders of the *ancien régime* and the *Restauration*. Here again, though, it would be anachronistic to extend these criticisms to the romantics in their earlier years. Although the romantics admired the Middle Ages even in their formative period, it would be wrong to interpret this as reactionary. Why? There are several reasons.

First, the young romantics admired the Middle Ages not because they were the antithesis of the ideals of the Revolution but because they were an illustration of them. As Schlegel put the point in his *Apprenticeship*: 'there was never more liberty, equality and fraternity than in the Middle Ages'. To defend this view, the romantics pointed to the more popular institutions of the Middle Ages, such as the free cities, the assemblies, the local councils, guilds and corporations. If these could only be reformed and purged of their privileges, they argued, then they could also provide a source of popular representation in the modern state, and serve as a bulwark against the dangers of despotism and bureaucratization.

Second, such a reassessment of the Middle Ages was not characteristic of the romantics but the culmination of a long trend in
historiography, which began in the *Aufklärung* itself. The reevalu-
ation of the Middle Ages began in earnest in Germany since the
1770s with works like Herder's *Auch eine Philosophie der Geschichte
der Menschheit* (1774), Johannes Müller's *Geschichte schweizerischer
Eidgenossenschaft* (1780), Ludwig Spittler's *Grundriß der christlichen
Kirche* (1782) and Justus Möser's *Osnabrückische Geschichte* (1768).
By the 1790s and early 1800s it was virtually a commonplace for
German intellectuals to look back upon the Middle Ages as a refuge
against all the absolutist tendencies of modern politics. This theme
can be found in thinkers like Möser, Müller and Hegel, who had
little sympathy with the romantics. We tend to forget that medievalism was not a romantic invention but a commonplace of the *Aufklärung* itself. Originally, it was not a cult of the *Restauration*, but a
protest against absolutism and centralization.

Third, the communitarian ideals of the romantics were antitheti-
cal to those of the German conservatives of the 1790s, to thinkers
like Justus Möser and the Hanoverian school. While these writers
also defended traditional pluralistic society against the dangers of
centralized government, they were much more sceptical of the ideals
of the Revolution. Unlike the romantics, their hope was more to
limit than to realize popular participation in government. They have
indeed no sympathy for the romantics' idealism, utopianism and
belief in progress, which distinguishes them from the German conservatives of the 1790s.

If the romantics' medievalism is not reactionary, it does seem
antiquated, even quaint. But to focus upon the historical *illustration*
of their beliefs is to miss the point. Ultimately, romantic medievalism was an expression of much deeper poltical ideals, ideals that
are all too contemporary: the demand for community, the need for
social belonging, the insufficiency of civil society and 'market forces'. When current political thought gives voice to these themes, it
returns to forms of experience and expression typical of the early
romantic generation. Perhaps, then, we have more to learn from
the romantics than we thought. In any case, the time for a reexamination of romantic political thought is long overdue.

Chronology of early Romanticism

Publication of Gentz's translation of Burke's *Reflections on the Revolution in France*.

Publication of Kant's *Essay on Theory and Practice*, and the beginning of his dispute with Gentz, Rehberg and Möser in the *Berlinische Monatsschrift*

1794   Fichte gives lectures *On the Vocation of the Scholar*
Festival of the Supreme Being (8 June)
Fall of Robespierre (28–29 July)
Jacobin Club closed (12 November)
Publication of Fichte's *Wissenschaftslehre*

1795   Publication of Schiller's *Aesthetic Letters* and *On Naive and Sentimental Poetry*
Publication of Fichte's *Foundations of Natural Right*
Publication of Kant's *Perpetual Peace*

1796   Publication of Schelling's *New Deduction of Natural Right*
Publication of Goethe's *Wilhelm Meister* (October)

1797   First meeting of the Berlin circle: F. Schlegel meets Schleiermacher and Tieck at the salons of Henriette Herz and Rahel Levin
Publication of Schlegel's *Essay on the Concept of Republicanism*
Publication of Schelling's *Ideas for a Philosophy of Nature*
Peace of Campo Formio (18 October)
Publication of Wackenroder's *Effusions of an Art-loving Monk*

1798   Death of Wackenroder (February)
Publication of first issue of *Athenæum* (May)
Publication of Novalis' *Faith and Love* and *Pollen*
The Schlegel brothers, Novalis, Fichte meet in Dresden (summer)
Accession of Friedrich Wilhelm III as King of Prussia

1799   Publication of Schleiermacher's *On Religion* (October)
Publication of Schlegel's *Lucinde*
Schelling, the Schlegel brothers, Novalis and Tieck meet in Jena (September)

	Novalis reads the manuscript of *Christianity or Europe* to the Jena circle
	Pope Pius VI dies in French captivity (August)
1800	F. Schlegel gives his lectures *On Transcendental Philosophy* at the University of Jena (winter semester)
	Appearance of the last issue of the *Athenæum* (August)
	Publication of Schleiermacher's *Monologues*
	Bonaparte overthrows the Directory (November 9–10)
	Publication of Schelling's *System of Transcendental Idealism*
1801	Death of Novalis (March 25)
	Friedrich Schlegel moves to Berlin
1802	Friedrich Schlegel in Paris (July)
	Publication of Schelling's *Philosophy of Art*

Bibliographical note

Because the political thought of the German romantics has been so controversial and influential, there is a large literature surrounding it. Only the most important works can be reviewed here. I limit myself to literature that deals with the philosophical and political aspects of *Frühromantik*.

General surveys

There are many general surveys of German Romanticism that treat not only its literary but also its philosophical and political aspects. The first was Heinrich Heine's *Die romantische Schule*, which was published in 1833 (*Kritische Ausgabe*, Stuttgart: Reclam, 1976, ed. Helga Weidmann). Filled with strong opinions and witty caricatures, Heine's book is still provocative and fun. The classic scholarly account is Rudolf Haym's *Die romantische Schule* (Berlin: Gaertner, 1870; reprinted Darmstadt: Wissenschaftliche Buchgesellschaft, 1977). This is a detailed study of the context and early works of the young romantics. No serious student should ignore it. The study of the romantics was revived around the turn of the century by Ricarda Huch in her *Blüthezeit der Romantik* (Leipzig: Haessel, 1899) and *Ausbreitung und Verfall der Romantik* (Leipzig: Haessel, 1902). These were combined into one volume as *Die Romantik* (Leipzig: Haessel, 1924). This is the work of a writer rather than scholar, but for just that reason often very perceptive.

The study of the origins of German Romanticism blossomed in Germany in the early twentieth century. One of the better products of this renaissance was Oskar Walzel's brief but incisive *Deutsche Romantik* (Leipzig: Tuebner, 1908; translated by A. E. Lussky as *German Romanticism*, New York: Putnam, 1932). Other useful studies from this period are Erwin Kirchner, *Philosophie der Romantik* (Jena: Eugen Diedrichs, 1906) and Georg Stefansky *Das Wesen der deutschen Romantik* (Stuttgart: Metzler, 1922). There are two works in English on German Romanticism that also appeared in the early twentieth century. One of these is Walter Silz's *Early German Romanticism* (Cambridge: Harvard, 1929), which provides a clear interpretation of *Frühromantik* that exposes many of the anachronistic interpretations. The other is Wernaer's *Romanticism and the Romantic School in Germany* (Cambridge, Mass: Harvard, 1909), which provides an introduction to many of the philosophical aspects of German Romanticism. One of the most useful short surveys is Paul Kluckhohn's *Das Ideengut der deutschen Romantik* (Tubingen: Niemeyer, 1966, fourth edition). Kluckhohn has several informative chapters on the social, political and anthropological aspects of Romanticism. The most extensive and detailed general survey of early Romanticism is Roger Ayrault's *La Genèse du romantisme allemand* (Paris: Aubier, 1961). Volume I, pp. 61–173, treats the political context.

Studies of political thought

There are many good studies devoted to various aspects of romantic political thought. A general survey of romantic political philosophy is given by Jakob Baxa, *Einführung in die romantische Staatswissenschaft* (Jena: Fischer, 1923). Another general study is Paul Kluckhohn, *Persönlichkeit und Gemeinschaft. Studien zur Staatsauffassung der deutschen Romantik* (Halle: Max Niemeyer, 1925). Kluckhohn investigated in detail the theme of love in German Romanticism in his *Die Auffassung der Liebe in der Literatur des 18. Jahrhunderts und in der deutschen Romantik* (Tubingen: Max Niemeyer, 1966, third edition). An important general interpretation of romantic political thought is given by Jacques Droz in his *Le Romantisme allemand et l'état* (Paris: Payot, 1966).

From the 1920s to the end of the 1930s in Germany, the political philosophy of the German romantics became a subject of intense debate. One of the most influential studies from this period is Carl

Schmitt's *Politische Romantik* (Munich: Duncker and Humblot, 1925), which argues that the romantics were indifferent to politics. An opposing standpoint, appropriating the romantics for Nazi ends, is given by Walter Linden, 'Umwertung der deutschen Romantik', *Zeitschrift für Deutschkunde*, 47 (1933), 65–91 (reprinted in *Begriffsbestimmung der Romantik*, ed. Helmut Prang, Darmstadt: Wissenschaftliche Buchgesellschaft, 1968, pp. 243–75). Linden argues that Romanticism was essentially a German movement and a reaction against the rationalism, cosmopolitanism and egalitarianism of the Enlightenment. There have been more careful recent studies of the relationship between Romanticism and Enlightenment. See, for example, Helmut Schanze, *Romantik und Aufklärung. Untersuchungen zu Friedrich Schlegel und Novalis* (Nuremberg: Carl Verlag, 1966), and Wolfgang Mederer, *Romantik als Aufklärung der Aufklärung?* (Frankfurt: Peter Lang, 1987).

There are several works devoted to the relationship of the romantics to the French Revolution. An early, but still useful study is Andreas Müller, *Die Auseinandersetzung der Romantik mit den Ideen der Revolution* (Halle: Max Niemeyer, 1929). Several chapters deal with this subject in detail in Jacques Droz's classic study *L'Allemagne et la revolution française* (Paris: Presses Universitaires de France, 1949), pp. 395–490. A very useful anthology on the issue is *Les Romantiques allemands et la révolution française* ed. Gonthier-Louis Fink (Strasbourg: Université des Sciences Humaines, 1989).

The relationship of the young romantics to nationalism has also been the subject of several studies. See especially Friedrich Meinecke, *Weltbürgertum und Nationalstaat* (Munich: Oldenbourg, 1908). An opposing perspective is given by A. D. Verschoor, *Die ältere deutsche Romantik und die Nationalidee* (Amsterdam: Paris, 1928).

Unfortunately, there is very little in English on the political thought of the German romantics. The standard work has been Reinhold Aris, *A History of Political Thought in Germany, 1789–1815* (London: Cass, 1936), pp. 207–340. In reaction to Aris, Droz and Schmitt, I have attempted a reexamination of the early political thought of the German romantics in three chapters of my *Enlightenment, Revolution, and Romanticism: The Genesis of Modern German Political Thought* 1790–1800 (Cambridge, Mass.: Harvard University Press, 1992), pp. 222–78.

Special studies

The most influential study of Novalis' political thought is Richard Samuel, *Die poetische Staats und Geschichtsauffassung von Friedrich von Hardenberg* (*Novalis*) (Frankfurt: Moritz Diesterweg, 1925) (reprint ed: Hildesheim: Gerstenberg, 1975). An important reexamination of Novalis' political thought is Hermann Kurzke's *Romantik und Konservatismus: Das politische Werk Friedrich von Hardenbergs im Horizont seiner Wirkungsgeschichte* (Munich: Wilhelm Fink, 1987). An incisive historical treatment of the development of Novalis' political views is that of Hans Wolfgang Kuhn, *Der Apokalyptiker und die Politik. Studien zur Staatsphilosophie des Novalis* (Freiburg: Rombach, 1961). A thorough examination of the utopian aspects of Novalis' political thought is provided by Hans-Joachim Mähl, *Die Idee des goldenen Zeitalters im Werk des Novalis* (Heidelberg: Winter, 1965). For a detailed interpretation of Novalis' *Christianity or Europe*, see Wilfried Malsch, *Europa. Poetische Rede des Novalis* (Stuttgart: Metzler, 1955).

There are few good studies of Schlegel's political thought. The development of his political philosophy has been the subject of several works: Benno von Wiese, *Friedrich von Schlegel. Ein Beitrag zur Geschichte der romantische Konversionen* (Berlin: Springer, 1927); Fanny Imle, *Friedrich von Schlegels Entwicklung von Kant zum Katholicismus* (Paderborn: Schoningh, 1927); and Gerd Hendrix, *Das politische Weltbild Friedrich Schlegels* (Bonn: Bouvier, 1962). Schlegel's early political ideals are treated by Klaus Peter, *Idealismus als Kritik. Friedrich Schlegels Philosophie der unvollendeten Welt* (Stuttgart: Kohlhammer, 1973). The connection between Schlegel's politics and aesthetics is the subject of Werner Weiland's *Der junge Friedrich Schlegel oder die Revolution in der Frühromantik* (Stuttgart: Kohlhammer, 1968).

There is even less on the political thought of Schleiermacher. The standard work is G. Holstein, *Die Staatsphilosophie Schleiermachers* (Bonn, 1923). For the evolution of Schleiermacher's political thought, see Jerry Dawson, *Friedrich Schleiermacher: The Evolution of a Nationalist* (Austin: University of Texas Press, 1966).

Translations

Another edition and translation of the political writings of the German romantics is that of Hans Reiss, *The Political Thought of the German Romantics* (Oxford: Blackwell, 1955). In a very short compass Reiss collects writings from all phases of Romanticism, including selections from Fichte, Novalis, Savigny and Mueller.

There is a good translation of all of Schlegel's early published fragments by Peter Firchow: *Philosophical Fragments* (Minneapolis: University of Minnesota Press, 1991). The unpublished notebooks have been translated and edited by Hans Eichner, *Literary Notebooks, 1797–1801* (Toronto: University of Toronto Press, 1957).

There is an old but complete translation of Schleiermacher's *Monologen*: *Soliloquies*, edited and translated by H. L. Friess (Chicago: Open Court, 1926). There is also a new excellent translation of Schleiermacher's *Ueber die Religion*: *On Religion. Speeches to its Cultured Despisers*, edited and translated by Richard Crouter (Cambridge: Cambridge University Press, 1988).

Editions cited and abbreviations

Fichte, J. G.
Sämmtliche Werke, ed. I. H. Fichte (Berlin: Veit, 1845–6).
Early Philosophical Writings, ed. Daniel Breazeale (Ithaca, New York: Cornell University Press, 1988), abbreviated as *EPW*.

Goethe, J. W.
Werke, Hamburger Ausgabe (Hamburg: Christian Wegner Verlag, 1959).

Hardenberg, Friedrich von (Novalis)
Novalis Schriften, Die Werke von Friedrich von Hardenberg, ed. Richard Samuel *et al*. (Stuttgart: Kohlhammer, 1960).

Hölderlin, Friedrich
Sämtliche Werke, Grosse Stuttgarter Ausgabe, ed. Friedrich Beissner (Stuttgart: Kohlhammer, 1961).

Humboldt, Wilhelm von
Werke in Fünf Bänden, ed. Andreas Flitner and Klaus Giel (Darmstadt: Wissenschaftliche Buchgesellschaft, 1960).

Kant, Immanuel
Schriften, Preussischen Akademie der Wissenschaften, ed. Wilhelm Dilthey *et al*. (Berlin: de Gruyter, 1902f), abbreviated as *Ak*.
Political Writings, ed. Hans Reiss (Cambridge: Cambridge University Press, 1970) abbreviated as *PW*.
Religion with the Limits of Reason Alone, translated by Theodore Greene and Hoyt Hudson (New York, Harper and Row, 1960), abbreviated as *RR*.

Critique of Pure Reason, translated by Norman Kemp Smith (New York: St Martin's Press, 1965), abbreviated as *CPR* and cited according to the first (A) and second (B) edition.

Critique of Practical Reason, translated by Lewis White Beck (New York: Bobbs Merrill, 1956).

Lessing, G. E.

Sämmtliche Schriften, ed. K. Lachmann (Stuttgart: Göschen, 1886–1924).

Schelling, F. W. J.

Werke, ed. Manfred Schröter (Munich: Beck, 1927).

Schiller, Friedrich

Werke, Nationalausgabe, ed. L. Blumenthal and Benno von Wiese (Weimar: Böhlaus Nachfolger, 1943–67).

Schlegel, Friedrich

Kritische Friedrich Schlegel Ausgabe, ed. Ernst Behler *et al.*, abbreviated as *KA*.

Schleiermacher, Friedrich Daniel

Friedrich Schleiermacher Kritische Gesamtausgabe, ed. Günter Meckenstock *et al.* (Berlin: de Gruyter, 1984f), abbreviated as *KGA*.

On Religion: Speeches to its Cultured Despisers, translated by Richard Crouter (Cambridge: Cambridge University Press, 1989).

The Oldest Systematic Programme of
German Idealism
[Anon]

An *ethics*. Since in the future the whole of metaphysics will collapse into morals – of which Kant, with his two practical postulates,[1] has given only an example and *exhausted* nothing – all ethics will be nothing more than a complete system of all ideas, or, what amounts to the same, of all practical postulates. Naturally, the first idea is the representation of *myself* as an absolute free being. With the free self-conscious being a whole world comes forth from nothing – the only true and thinkable *creation from nothing*. At this point I will descend to the realm of physics. The question is this: how must a world be constituted for a moral being?[2] I would like to give wings again to our physics, which progresses laboriously with experiments.

So, if philosophy gives the ideas and experience the data, we can finally have the essentials of the physics that I expect of future epochs. It seems that the present physics cannot satisfy the creative spirit as ours is or should be.

From nature I come to the *works of man*. First of all the *idea* of humanity. I want to show that there is no more an idea of the *state* than there is an idea of the machine, because the state is something

The *Oldest Systematic Programme* was probably written in the summer of 1796, at the latest in early 1797. The author is not known and has been the subject of much dispute. The manuscript is in Hegel's handwriting. Since, however, the ideas seemed very unHegelian, Franz Rosenzweig, who first discovered and published the manuscript in 1917, assumed that Hegel simply copied a manuscript of Schelling, who was the real author (see his *Kleinere Schriften*, Berlin, 1937, pp. 230–77). More recently, however, it has been argued on both philological and thematic grounds that the author could very well be Hegel. See Otto Pöggeler. 'Hegel, der Verfasser des ältesten Systemprogramms des deutschen Idealismus', *Hegel-Studien*, 4 (1969), 17–32; and H. S. Harris, *Hegel's Development: Toward the Sunlight 1770–1801* (Oxford: Oxford University Press, 1972), pp. 249–57.

Whoever the author was, the *Programme* clearly and succinctly presents some of the fundamental themes of the early romantic movement: beauty as the highest idea, the educational role of art, a mythology of reason, a critique of the mechanical state and a utopian anarchism. All these ideas are developed in various ways by Schlegel, Schelling, Novalis, Schleiermacher and Hölderlin in the late 1790s. The translation follows the text of *Hölderlin, Sämtliche Werke*, IV/1, pp. 297–9.

[1] Kant says that there are *three* practical postulates: the existence of God, immortality and freedom. See *Critique of Practical Reason*, Ak. V, p. 133. These ideas are 'postulates' in the sense that, although reason cannot demonstrate them to be true, it can justify belief in them for the purposes of moral conduct.

[2] The author develops a Fichtean theme: that the existence of the external world is a necessary condition of moral action. Although Fichte argued this point in his 1794 *Wissenschaftslehre*, it is expressed most clearly in his later *Vocation of Man*, *Werke*, II, pp. 261.

mechanical. Only that which is an object of freedom can be called an *idea*.[3] We must therefore go beyond the state! For every state must treat free human beings as if they were cogs in a machine; but that it should not do; therefore it should *cease* to exist. You can see for yourself that here all ideas, for example that of eternal peace, are only *subordinate* ideas of a higher idea. At the same time I want to lay down here the principles for a *history of humanity*, and to expose down to the bone the whole miserable apparatus of state, constitution, government and legislation. Finally come the ideas of a moral world, divinity, immortality – through reason itself the overthrow of all superstition, and the persecution of the priesthood, which recently pretends to reason. Then comes absolute freedom of all spirits, which carry the intellectual world in themselves, and which may not seek God or immortality *outside themselves.*

Finally, the idea that unites all others, the idea of *beauty*, taking the word in a higher Platonic sense. I am now convinced that the highest act of reason is an aesthetic act since it comprises all ideas, and that *truth* and *goodness* are fraternally united only in beauty. The philosopher must possess as much aesthetic power as the poet. People without an aesthetic sense are only philosophers of the letter.[4] The philosophy of the spirit is an aesthetic philosophy. One cannot have spirit in anything,[5] one cannot even reason in an inspired way about history, without aesthetic sense. Here it should become obvious what people are lacking who cannot understand ideas, and who frankly enough confess that everything is obscure to them as soon as it goes beyond charts and indices.

In this manner poetry will gain a higher dignity, and it will again become at the end what it was at the beginning – the *teacher of humanity*. For there is no more philosophy, no more history; poetry alone will outlive all other sciences and arts.

---

[3] Here the term 'idea' (*Idee*) is used in the technical Kantian sense. According to Kant, an idea prescribes an ideal or goal for human conduct or enquiry. This idea can be approached, but never attained. An example of an idea is the republican constitution, a constitution ensuring the greatest possible freedom. See *CPR*, B, pp. 373–4; *PW*, p. 191.

[4] Philosophers of the letter: *Buchstabenphilosophen*. Here a philosopher of the letter, as opposed to one of the spirit, is someone who believes in only what he can perceive or precisely formulate in words.

[5] 'Have spirit': *geistreich seyn*. Literally, *geistreich* means to be rich in spirit or inspired; less literally, it means ingenious or clever.

At the same time we are so often told that the great multitude should have a *religion of the senses*.[6] But not only the great multitude needs one, the philosopher does so too. Monotheism of reason and the heart, polytheism of imagination and art – this is what we need!

First I will speak of an idea here that, as far as I know, has still not occurred to anyone else. We must have a new mythology, but this mythology must be in service of the ideas; it must be a mythology of *reason*.

Before we make ideas aesthetic, i.e. mythological, they will have no interest for the people. Conversely, before mythology is rational, the philosopher must be ashamed of it. Hence finally the enlightened and unenlightened must shake hands: mythology must become philosophical to make people rational, and philosophy must become mythological to make philosophers sensuous. Then eternal unity will reign among us. No more will there be the contemptuous glance, never more the blind trembling of the people before its wise men and priests. Only then can we expect equal development of *all* powers, of each individual as well as all individuals. No longer will any power be repressed, and then will rule the universal freedom and equality of the spirits! A higher spirit sent from heaven must establish this new religion among us. It will be the last and greatest work of humanity.

---

[6] 'Religion of the senses': *sinnliche Religion*. This is a religion that appeals to the heart and imagination, not one the promises or provides sensual gratification.

Novalis
Pollen

Friends, the earth is barren, we must strew ample seeds that only a modest harvest prospers for us.

1 We seek everywhere the unconditioned, and always find only the conditioned.[1]

2 To signify through sounds and tones is a remarkable abstraction. With three letters I signify God; and with a few strokes a million things. How easy is the manipulation of the universe, how vivid the concentration of the spiritual world! The theory of language is the dynamics of the spiritual world. A word of command moves armies, the word 'freedom' nations.

3 The world state is the body that the beautiful world, the social world, animates.[2] It is the necessary organ of that world.

4 An apprenticeship is for the poetical youth, a university education is for the philosophical. Universities should be completely philosophical institutions. There should be only one faculty, the whole establishment organized for the awakening and effective practice of the power to think.

5 An apprenticeship in the proper sense is an apprenticeship in the art of living. Through planned, ordered experiments one learns its principles and acquires the capacity to act on them as one wishes.

Pollen (*Blüthenstaub*) was first published in May 1798 in the first issue of the *Athenæum*, the chief journal of the early romantic movement, edited by Friedrich and August Wilhelm Schlegel. Novalis probably wrote the first draft of these fragments in late 1797; he sent the final draft to A. W. Schlegel in February 1798.

Unfortunately, the Schlegels took a free hand in editing the manuscript. Friedrich added four fragments of his own, deleted thirteen, divided others, and altered the grammar of many. See Friedrich to August Wilhelm Schlegel, mid-March 1798, *KA* XXIV, p. 103. Since the original manuscript has been lost, it is not possible to determine the full extent of the Schlegels' editing.

In the spirit of romantic 'symphilosophy', Friedrich Schlegel added some aphorisms of his own to Novalis' collection. These are indicated by brackets after the aphorism.

The paragraph numbers, which do not appear in the first edition, have been added by later editors and have now become conventional.

[1] The point of this aphorism rests upon an untranslatable German pun. The German term *das Unbedingte* means both what is not a thing and what is not conditioned. The aphorism could also be translated as 'We seek everywhere what is not a thing and always find only things.' In playing upon this double meaning Novalis follows Schelling, *On the Ego as the Principle of Philosophy* (1795), nos. 2–3, *Werke*, I, pp. 87–94.

[2] On the concept of a world state (*Weltstaat*), see Kant's essay 'Idea for a Universal History', *Ak.* VIII, pp. 24–5; *PW*, pp. 47–8.

6 We will never completely explain ourselves; but we will and can do more than explain ourselves.[3]

7 Certain restraints are like the touch of a flute-player, who, to produce various tones, closes now this, now that opening, and who appears to make arbitrary chains of silent and sounding openings.

8 The difference between illusion and truth lies in the difference of their life-functions. Illusion lives from truth; truth has its life in itself. One destroys an illusion as one destroys an illness; and illusion is therefore nothing more than a logical inflammation or expiration, enthusiasm or philistinism. The former usually leaves behind an apparent deficiency in the power to think, which can be relieved only by a decreasing series of stimuli or coercive measures. The latter often appears as a deceptive liveliness, whose dangerous revolutionary symptoms can be driven off only by an increasing series of violent measures. Both dispositions can be altered only through constant and strict treatment.[4]

9 Our total perceptual apparatus is like the eye. Objects must pass through opposed media to appear correctly to the pupil.

10 Experience is the test of the rational, and conversely. The insufficiency of mere theory in its application, about which the pragmatist frequently complains, has its counterpart in the rational application of mere experience. This point has been observed clearly enough by genuine philosophers, though they are modest about the necessity of their success. The pragmatist rejects mere theory entirely without suspecting how problematic the answer will be to the question: 'Is theory for the sake of its application, or the application for the sake of the theory?'[5]

[3] Novalis alludes to Fichte's doctrine of intellectual intuition. According to this doctrine, we have a direct intuition of ourselves as active intellectual beings; as a form of non-discursive knowledge, it is inexplicable.

[4] Novalis applies the physiological doctrine of the Scottish doctor John Brown (1735–1788), whose ideas became popular in Germany in the late 1790s. According to Brown, the essential characteristic of life resides in excitability, the power to react to stimuli. Health depends upon having the proper amount of stimulation. There are two kinds of diseases, one resulting from too much stimulation (sthenic) and the other from too little (asthenic). A cure would then consist in applying or removing stimulation to provide a proper balance.

[5] Novalis attempts to find a middle path in the debate concerning the role of theory or moral principle in politics, which began in 1793 in the wake of the French Revolution. While conservatives such as Justus Möser and A. W. Rehberg held the empiricist doctrine that theory had to be tested in terms of its applicability to existing circumstances and institutions, radicals or more progressive thinkers

11 The highest is the most comprehensible, the nearest is the most indispensable.[6]

12 Miracles alternate with natural effects; they limit one another reciprocally, and together form a whole. They are united in that they cancel one another. No miracle without a natural event, and conversely.

13 Nature is the enemy of eternal possessions. According to iron laws she destroys all signs of property, and erases all traces of permanency. The earth belongs to all kinds; everyone has a claim to everything. The firstborn are not entitled to any privilege of primogeniture simply because of an accident of birth.[7] The right to property disappears at certain times. Its improvement and deterioration is subject to unalterable conditions. If, however, my body is property, whereby I acquire the rights of an active citizen of the earth, then I cannot alienate myself through the loss of this property. I lose nothing more than my position in this school for princes and enter a higher organization where my classmates follow me.

14 Life is the beginning of death. Life is for the sake of death. Death is at the same time an ending and beginning, a parting and closer reunion with the self. Through death reduction is completed.[8]

15 Philosophy too has its blossoms. They are thoughts that one never knows whether to call beautiful or witty. [Friedrich Schlegel]

16 Fantasy puts the future world either in the heights or in the depths or in a metapsychosis to us. We dream of a journey through the universe. But is the universe then not in us? We do not know the depths of our spirit. Inward goes the secret path. Eternity with its worlds, the past and future, is in us or nowhere. The external world is the shadow world, casting its shadows into the world of light. Now it seems to us so dark within, so lonely and chaotic. But how different it will seem to us when this eclipse is past and the shadow is removed. We will enjoy ourselves more than ever, for our spirit has suffered such deprivation.

such as Kant and Fichte defended the rationalist doctrine that theory provided a moral standard to which these circumstances and institutions should conform.
[6] Nearest: *das Nächste*. The German is ambiguous. Literally, *das Nächste* is the nearest in a physical sense; but it can also be the nearest in an emotional or spiritual sense.
[7] On Novalis' views on property, cf. *Faith and Love*, no. 10.
[8] 'Reduction' (*Redukzion*): the processing of metal from ore, purification.

17 Darwin makes the observation that, if we have dreamed of visible objects, we are less blinded by light upon awakening.[9] Happy then are those that have already dreamed of seeing! They will bear sooner the glory of that world.

18 How can a person have the sense for something for which he does not have the germ in himself? What I should understand I should develop organically in myself; and what I appear to learn is only nourishment, incitement of the organism.[10]

19 The seat of the soul is where the inner and outer world touch. Where they interpenetrate it is at every point of the interpenetration.

20 If, in the communication of a thought, one alternates between absolute understanding and not understanding, then that might be called even a philosophical friendship. But are not things better with ourselves? And is the life of a thinking person any thing more than a steady inner symphilosophy?[11] [Friedrich Schlegel]

21 Genius is the capacity to describe imaginary objects as if they were real, and to act upon them as if they were real.[12] The talent to depict, to observe exactly, and to describe effectively is therefore distinct from genius. Without this talent one sees only half, and is only a half-genius; one can have the disposition to genius, which never comes to fruition if it lacks that talent.

22 The most arbitrary prejudice of them all is that man is denied the capacity to get outside himself and to have consciousness beyond the realm of the senses. At any moment man can become a supersensible being. Without this capacity he would not be a cosmopolitan but an animal. To be sure, in our present condition reflection and self-discovery are difficult, because it is incessantly and necessarily bound up with the change of our other circumstances. But the more we are capable of becoming conscious of this condition, the more lively, powerful and satisfying is the conviction

[9] Erasmus Darwin (1731–1802), English natural scientist, grandfather of Charles Darwin. The work in question is *Zoonomia or the Laws of Organic Life* (London, 1794). Novalis refers to the German translation by J. D. Brandais, *Zoonomie oder Gesetze des organischen Lebens* (Hanover, 1795), I, pp. 377–8.

[10] 'Incitement' (*Inzitament*): application of a stimulus, a technical term in Brown's physiology.

[11] 'Symphilosophy': a neologism of Friedrich Schlegel meaning to philosophize together.

[12] Cf. no. 31.

that stems from it: the belief in the true revelations of the spirit. It is not [just] a seeing, hearing or feeling; it is composed of all three, and is more than all three: a sensation of immediate certainty, a view of my truest and deepest life. Thoughts are transformed into laws, wishes into their fulfilment.[13] For the weaker, the reality of this moment is an article of faith. The revelation is especially apparent by the consideration of many human forms and faces, particularly by the observation of many eyes, many gestures, many movements, by listening to certain words, by reading many passages, by many views of life, of the world and fate. Many accidents, some natural events, especially times of the day and year, give us such experiences. Certain moods are especially favourable to such revelations. Most of them are momentary, a few of them lingering and the rarest enduring. In this respect there is much diversity among people. One has more capacity for revelation than another. One has more sensibility, another more understanding for it. The latter will always have his in a soft light, whereas the former will have alternating illuminations, though more luminous and various. This capacity is also capable of illness, which signifies either a surplus of sensibility and lack of understanding or surplus of understanding and lack of sensibility.

23 Shame is a feeling of profanation. Friendship, love and piety should be dealt with secretly. One should speak of them only in rare, confidential moments, and come to an understanding about them only tacitly. Many things are too delicate to think of, still less to speak about.

24 Self-denial is the source of all humiliation, but also the source of all genuine exaltation. The first step is the view within, the detached contemplation of the self. Who goes no further from here only half succeeds. The second step is the effective view without, the spontaneous, steady observation of the external world.

25 He will never achieve much as a writer who can portray nothing more than his experiences, his favourite objects, who can never bring himself to study diligently and to describe lovingly a completely alien, completely uninteresting object. The writer must be able and willing to describe everything. In this way arises the

---

[13] A fundamental proposition of Novalis' 'magical idealism', which is based upon two principles: that we know only what we create; and that our creative powers are directed by the will. Cf. *Sketches*, nos. 105, 381.

grand style of portrayal that one rightfully so much admires in Goethe.[14]

26 If one acquires the taste for the absolute and cannot refrain from it, then one has no other recourse than always to contradict oneself and to unite opposed extremes. Yet, inevitably, the principle of contradiction is overthrown, so that one has only one choice: either to accept this necessity passively or to ennoble it to a free action by recognizing it. [Friedrich Schlegel]

27 It is a remarkable peculiarity of Goethe to connect small, insignificant incidents with important events.[15] He seems to have no other purpose in mind than to busy the imagination in a poetic manner with a mysterious game. Even here the extraordinary genius follows the trail of nature and notes a clever trick of hers. Everyday life is filled with similar incidents. Like all games, they make a game that boils down to surprise and delusion.

Many popular sayings rest upon the observation of this perverse connection. So, for example, bad dreams mean luck; a rumour of death, a long life; a rabbit that crosses one's path, unhappiness. Almost all the superstition of common people rests upon interpretations of this game.

28 The highest goal of education is to grasp one's transcendental self, to be the self of one's self.[16] All the less strange, then, is the lack of complete feeling and understanding of others. Without perfect self-understanding one will never learn truly to understand others.

29 Humour is a whimsically adopted style. Whimsy provides its piquancy. Humour is the result of a free mixture of the conditioned and unconditioned. Through humour the peculiarly conditioned becomes generally interesting and receives an objective worth. Where fantasy and judgement meet arises wit; where reason and whimsy join there is humour. Persiflage belongs to humour, but it is of a lower degree: it is no longer purely artistic and much more limited. What Friedrich Schlegel characterizes as irony is, in my

---

[14] Novalis was probably thinking of Goethe's *Wilhelm Meister*, which he read in early summer 1797.

[15] A reference to the style of Goethe's *Wilhelm Meister*. Novalis shares the opinion of Friedrich Schlegel in his review of Goethe's work, 'Ueber Goethes Wilhelm Meister', *KA* II, pp. 126–46, esp. 133.

[16] Novalis alludes to a fundamental theme of Fichte's early philosophy, self-realization as a purely rational being, self-consciousness of the transcendental self. See Fichte, *Lectures on the Vocation of a Scholar, Werke*, VI, pp. 293–301; *EPW*, pp. 145–53.

view, the consequence, the character of reflection, of true presence of mind. Schlegel's irony seems to me to be genuine humour.[17] Several names are useful for one idea.

30 The insignificant, common, crude, ugly and rude becomes sociable only through wit. It is as if it were only for the sake of wit; the purpose of its existence is wit.[18]

31 If one is not common oneself, to treat the commonplace with such energy and lightness that grace springs from it, one must find nothing more extraordinary than the commonplace, and have a sense for the strange, seeking and sensing it in the commonplace. In this manner someone who lives in completely different spheres can so please more common people that they take no offence in him and take him for nothing more than what they regard as charming among themselves. [Friedrich Schlegel]

32 We are on a mission. We have been called to educate the earth.[19]

33 If a spirit were to appear to us, we would at the same time grasp our own spirituality. We would be inspired by ourselves and that spirit at the same time. Without inspiration there is no appearance of spirit. Inspiration is at once appearance and counter-appearance, appropriation and communication.

34 Man lives, and continues to live, only through the idea, through the memory of his existence.[20] For the time being there is no other means of spiritual activity in this world. Hence it is a duty

[17] Novalis refers to Schlegel's *Critical Fragments*, no. 108: 'Socratic irony is the only completely involuntary yet completely deliberate dissimulation . . . In it everything should be a joke and serious, everything should be open and disguised. It derives from the unification of a *savoir vivre* and scientific spirit, from the coincidence of a perfect philosophy of nature and a perfect philosophy of art. It contains and arouses a feeling for the irresolvable conflict of the unconditioned and conditioned, the impossibility and necessity of complete communication. It is the freest of all licences, for through it one stands above even oneself; but it is also the most bound to law, for it is unconditionally necessary' (*KA* II, p. 160).

[18] 'Wit': the contemporary meaning was explained by Kant, *Anthropology from a Pragmatic Point of View*, no. 44 (*Ak.* VII, p. 201): 'Just as the capacity to find the particular for the universal is judgement, so the capacity to find the universal for the particular is wit. The first attempts to observe the differences under a manifold of partly identical things; the second attempts to find the identity of a manifold of partly distinct things.' Cf. nos. 54–5, *Ak.* VII, pp. 220–3.

[19] An allusion to the purpose of the *Athenæum* and the romantic circle in general, the education of the public.

[20] An allusion to the Platonic doctrines of the Dutch philosopher Franz Hemsterhuis, an important influence upon Novalis, whom he studied intensively in the autumn of 1797.

to think of the dead. It is the only way to remain in communion with them. In no other way is God himself present for us through faith.

35 Interest is participation in the suffering and activity of another being. Something interests me when it knows how to stimulate me to participate in it. No interest is more interesting than that one takes in oneself, just as the basis for a remarkable friendship and love is the sympathy which someone excites in me who is preoccupied with himself, and who by communicating with me invites me to participate in his affairs.

36 Who may have discovered wit? Every quality brought to mind, every activity of our spirit, is in the proper sense of the word a newly discovered world.

37 The spirit always appears in an alien, vaporous form.

38 Now the spirit stirs only here and there. When will the spirit stir everywhere? When will humanity begin to reflect on itself *en masse*?

39 Man lives only through the truth. He who surrenders the truth surrenders himself. He who betrays the truth betrays himself. One speaks here not of lies, but of actions against conscience.

40 In serene souls there is no wit. Wit reveals a disturbed balance.[21] It is the consequence of such disturbance and the means to restore it. The strongest wit is possessed by passion. The state of complete collapse, despair or spiritual death is the most terribly witty.

41 Of a lovable object we cannot hear, we cannot speak, enough. We are pleased over every new, accurate laudatory word. It is not our fault if it is not the object of all objects.

42 We grasp lifeless matter through its relations, its forms. We love matter in so far as it belongs to some loved being, or shows traces of such a being or some similarity to it.

43 A genuine club is a mixture of an institute and society.[22] It has a purpose, like the institute; not a determinate one, but one *in*determinate and free: humanity in general. All purposes are serious; but a society is completely joyful.

[21] A term from Brown's physiology. See note 4 above.
[22] Novalis had plans to establish a masonic order, 'a literary republican order ... a genuine cosmopolitan lodge'. See to Friedrich Schlegel, 10 December 1798, *Schriften*, IV, pp. 268–9.

44 The objects of social conversation are nothing more than means of stimulation. This determines the choice, change and treatment of them. Society is nothing more than communal life: an indivisible thinking and feeling person. Each person is a small society.[23]

45 For us, to go into oneself means to abstract from the outer world. Similarly, for spirits, earthly life means an inner reflection, a turning into oneself, an immanent activity. Thus earthly life springs from an original reflection, a primitive going into oneself, a collection of oneself, that is as free as our reflection. Conversely, spiritual life in this world springs from breaking through such primitive reflection. Spirit unfolds itself, goes outside itself again, cancels this reflection again, and in this moment it says for the first time 'I'.[24] One can see from this how relative the activities of going outside oneself and returning to oneself are. What we call going into ourselves is really going outside ourselves, a reacceptance of the original form.

46 Is it not possible to say something in favour of the recently so abused common man? Does not persistent mediocrity require the greatest exertion? And should man be anything more than one of the *Popolo*?[25]

47 Where a genuine disposition to thought, and not merely thinking this or that thought, is predominant, there is progressivity. Very many scholars do not have this disposition. They have learned to derive and deduce, like a shoemaker learns his trade, without ever having the idea, or making the effort, to find the foundation of the thought. Nevertheless, salvation lies along no other path. For many this disposition lasts only a short time. It increases and decreases, often with the years, and often with the discovery of a system they sought only to be spared the effort of further reflection.

48 Error and prejudice are burdens, an indirect stimulus for the independent, for those grown used to every burden. For the weaker they are a positive weakening agent.

---

[23] The germ of the organic conception of society. Cf. nos. 49, 59, 65, 81; *Universal Brouillon*, no. 261.
[24] Novalis develops a Kantian and Fichtean theme: that self-consciousness requires consciousness of an external world.
[25] *Popolo*: people (Italian).

49 A nation is an idea. We should become a nation.[26] A perfect person is a small nation. True popularity is the highest goal of humanity.[27]

50 Each stage of education begins with childhood. Hence the most educated, worldly person is so akin to the child.

51 Every loved object is the centre of a paradise.

52 The interesting is what sets me in motion, not for my own sake but as a means or member. The classical does not disturb me; it affects me only indirectly through myself.[28] It is not classical for me, unless I posit it as something that does not affect me, unless I arouse myself to produce the classical in me, unless I tear away a piece from myself and let this germ develop before me in its own characteristic manner. Such a development often takes only a moment and coincides with the sensible perception of an object, so that I see an object before me in which the common object and ideal interpenetrate one another, forming one wonderful individual.

53 To find formulae for art objects, through which alone they can be understood in the proper sense, is the business of the artistic critic, whose work prepares the history of art.

54 Although confused people are often called fools, the more confused a person is the more that can come out of him through diligent self-study. On the other hand, ordered minds must aspire to become genuine scholars, thorough encyclopaedists. In the beginning the confused have to struggle with mighty obstacles; they progress only slowly and learn to work with difficulty; but then they are lords and masters forever. The ordered mind gets quickly into something, but also quickly out of it. He soon reaches the second stage; but there he also usually remains. The last steps are difficult for him; and seldom can he bring himself, even after a certain degree of mastery, to put himself again in the position of the beginner. Confusion indicates superfluity of power and ability, but

---

[26] On Novalis' idea of a nation, see nos. 61 and 64, and *Christianity or Europe*, p. 73.

[27] 'Popularity' (*Popularität*): the universal characteristics of humanity. Cf. *Athenæum Fragments* no. 291.

[28] Novalis applies Friedrich Schlegel's early distinction between classical and modern art. In his *On the Study of the Greeks and Romans* (1795), Schlegel argued that while classical art attempts to imitate some objective norm of beauty in nature, modern art attempts to be merely 'interesting', to create striking and novel effects to catch the reader's interest. See *KA* I, pp. 217–22, 253–5.

deficient circumstances; clarity indicates adequate circumstances but modest power and ability. Hence the confused is so progressive, so perfectible, whereas the ordered mind ends so early as a philistine. Order and precision alone is not clarity. Through self-exertion the confused comes to that divine transparency, to that self-illumination, that the ordered mind seldom achieves. The true genius unites these extremes. He shares the speed of the second with the richness of the first.

55 The individual only interests me; hence everything classical is not individual.

56 A true letter is by its very nature poetic.

57 Wit, as the principle of affinity, is at the same time the *menstruum universale.*[29] Witty combinations are, for example, the Jew and cosmopolitan, childhood and wisdom, robbery and generosity, virtue and prostitution, superfluity and deficiency in judgement, in naivety, and so on *ad infinitum.*

58 Man appears his most dignified if the first impression he makes is the impression of an absolutely witty idea: namely, to be, at one and the same time, a spirit and determinate individual. A spirit must appear to shine through every superior person, a spirit that as an ideal parodies its visible appearance. With many people it is as if this spirit of the visible appearance pulls a face.

59 The drive toward society is the drive toward organization. Through this spiritual assimilation there often arises from the most common ingredients a good society centred around one spiritual individual.

60 The interesting is the material that revolves around beauty. Where there is spirit and beauty the best of every nature gathers in concentric vibrations.

61 The German has long been the fool. But he may indeed soon become the fool to end all fools. Things are for him as they are for many stupid children: he will prosper and become clever, when his more prodigal siblings have long since grown tired,[30] and he alone is lord of the manor.

---

[29] *Menstruum universale*: the universal solvent or dissolving agent of alchemy, which creates all kinds of new combinations of elements.

[30] On Novalis' attitude toward the Germans, see below nos. 49, 64 and 107, and *Christianity or Europe*, p. 73.

62 Like the life in an organic body, the best in the sciences is their philosophical ingredients. If one dephilosophizes the sciences, what remains? Earth, air and water.

63 Humanity is a humorous role.

64 Our old nationality was, it seems to me, genuinely Roman. Naturally, this is because we originated in the same manner as the Romans; hence the name 'Roman Empire' was a nice, clever piece of luck.[31] Germany is Rome, as a country. A country is a big place with its gardens. Perhaps the capital can be determined by the crying of the geese before the Gauls.[32] The instinctive universal politics and tendency of the Romans also lay in the German nation. The best that the French have gained from their Revolution is a portion of Germanness.[33]

65 Tribunals, theatres, courts, churches, governments, public meetings, colleges and so on, are, as it were, the special, inner organs of the mystical state-individual.

66 All the accidents of life are materials from which we can fashion whatever we want. Whoever has much spirit makes a lot out of his life. Every acquaintance, every incident, is for the spirited person the first link of an infinite chain, the beginning of an infinite novel.

67 The true commercial spirit, genuine wholesale trade, blossomed only in the Middle Ages, especially at the time of the German Hansa.[34] The Medicis and Fuggers were merchants as they should be. Our merchants are on the whole, the largest not excepted, nothing more than shopkeepers.

68 A translation is either grammatical, modifying or mythical. Mythical translations are translations in the highest style. They portray the pure, perfect character of the individual work of art. They give us not the existing work of art but the ideal of it. I

[31] Roman Empire (*römisches Reich*): a reference to the official name of Germany before 1806, 'Holy Roman Empire of the German Nation' (*Heiliges Römisches Reich Deutscher Nation*).

[32] According to legend, when the Gauls attempted to storm Rome in 390 BC, the sentries were awakened by the crying of geese. Novalis alludes to the political situation in Germany, the onslaught of the French revolutionary army.

[33] Cf. note 26 above.

[34] German Hansa: a confederation of German cities, established in 1161, to form a trading zone in the Baltic. The Hansaeatic cities were Hamburg, Lübeck, Riga, Rostock and Danzig. The Hansa cities flourished chiefly during the late Middle Ages.

believe there still does not exist a whole model for them. But one sees clear traces of them in the spirit of many criticisms and descriptions of works of art. To produce such a translation one must have a talent in which the poetical and philosophical spirit have interpenetrated in all their richness. Greek mythology is, in part, such a translation of a national religion. The modern madonna is such a myth.

Grammatical translations are translations in the usual sense. They require much scholarship, but only discursive abilities.

Modifying translations require, if they are to be genuine, the highest poetic spirit. They easily degenerate into travesties, such as Bürger's iambic Homer, Pope's Homer or French translations in general.[35] The true translator of this genre must be in fact an artist and be able to give the idea of the whole in any particular way. He must be the poet of poets, and be able to allow the poet to speak according to his and the poet's own voice. The genius of humanity stands to each individual in a similar relation.

Not only books but everything can be translated in these three ways.

69 The greatest pain at times gives rise to a paralysis of sensibility. The soul dissects itself. Hence the deadly frost, the free power of thought, the crushing, relentless wit of this kind of despair. A person loses all desire and stands alone feeling his mortality. Disconnected with the rest of the world he gradually consumes himself and becomes in principle a misanthrope and mistheologue.[36]

70 Our language is either mechanical, atomistic or dynamic. A genuine poetic language should be, however, organic, lively. How often we feel the poverty of words, because we cannot grasp several ideas with one stroke.

71 In the beginning poets and priests were one, and only later times have separated them. The genuine poet, however, is always a priest, just as the genuine priest has always been a poet. And

---

[35] Gottfried August Bürger (1747–1794) translated books 1–6 of the *Iliad* into iambic pentameters; he published it in 1771 in the *Deutschen Bibliothek der schönen Wissenschaften*, vol. VI, part 21. Alexander Pope (1688–1744) translated both Homer's epics into heroic couplets; his *Iliad* appeared in six volumes in 1715–20, his *Odyssey* in five volumes in 1725–6.

[36] 'Mistheologue' (*Misotheos*): an enemy of God, Novalis' neologism.

should not the future again re-establish the old state of things?[37]

72 Writings are the thoughts of the state, the archives of its memory.

73 The more we refine our senses the more we become capable of discriminating between individuals. The most developed sense would have the greatest sensitivity for something's characteristic nature. Corresponding to this sense is the talent for focusing upon an individual, a talent whose facility and energy is relative. If the will expresses itself in relation to this sense, there arise the passions for or against individuals: love and hate. By directing this sense toward oneself with a controlling reason, one can acquire mastery in the role of playing oneself.

74 Nothing is more indispensable to true religiosity than a mediator that binds us to the divine.[38] In no respect can man stand in an immediate relation to the divine. The individual must remain completely free in the choice of this mediator. The least coercion damages his religion.[39] The choice will depend upon a person's character. Educated people will choose rather similar mediators, whereas uneducated people will be usually determined through accident. But since so few people are capable of making a free choice, many mediators will become more common, whether through accident, association, or special talent. In this manner national religions arise. The more independent a person becomes, the more the quantity of mediators diminishes and the quality becomes refined, and the more the person's relations to his mediators become more diverse and cultivated (fetishes, stars, animals, heros, idols, gods, a divine person). One quickly sees how relative these choices are; and without noticing it one is driven to the idea that the essence of religion depends not so much on the quality of the mediator but purely on the attitude toward it, in one's relation to it.

It is idolatry in a broader sense should I regard this mediator as truly God himself. It is irreligion if I accept no mediator; and to that extent superstition and idolatry, unbelief or theism, which can

---

[37] Cf. Schlegel, *Ideen* nos. 8, 34, 46, 85 and 149; and Schleiermacher, *Reden über die Religion, KGA* 1/2, pp. 262–3.

[38] On the application of this doctrine of mediation to politics, see *Universal Brouillon*, nos. 398, 781.

[39] Here Novalis clearly separates church and state, much in contrast to later romantic thought. Cf. *Christianity or Europe*, p. 79.

also be called older Judaism, are both irreligion. On the other hand, atheism is only the negation of all religion in general, and therefore has nothing at all to do with religion. True religion is what regards a mediator as a mediator, what sees it as the organ of divinity, as its sensible appearance. In this regard the Jews at the time of the Babylonian captivity maintained a genuine religious tendency, a religious hope, a belief in a future religion, which transformed them fundamentally in a miraculous manner, and which has preserved them with remarkable persistence to the present.

By closer reflection, however, true religion appears again to be divided into the antinomy of pantheism and monotheism. I avail myself here of the liberty of using 'pantheism' in an unconventional sense. By it I mean the idea that everything can be the organ of the divine, a mediator, in so far as I elevate it to such status. On the other hand, 'monotheism' designates the belief that there is only one such organ in the world for us, that it alone is adequate to the idea of a mediator, and through it alone can God make himself heard. I am compelled through myself to choose this organ, for without it monotheism would not be true religion.

As incompatible as both appear, their reconciliation can still be effected if one makes the monotheistic mediator the mediator of the mediating world of pantheism, centring this world on him so that both are necessary for one another, though each in a different way.

Prayer, or religious thought, therefore consists in a threefold ascending, indivisible abstraction or positing. To the religious person every object can be a temple in the sense of the auguries.[40] The spirit of this temple is the omnipresent high priest, the mono-theistic mediator, who alone stands in an immediate relation to God.

75 The basis of all eternal union is an absolute tendency in all directions. Upon this rests the power of the hierarchy, genuine masonry and the invisible bond of all true thinkers. Here lies the possibility of a universal republic, which the Romans began to real-ize until the advent of the emperors. First Augustus departed from its true basis, and then Hadrian totally destroyed it.[41]

---

[40] 'Auguries' (*Auguren*): Roman priests who attempted to divine the will of the gods through thunder and lightning, the behaviour of animals and the flight of birds. They indicated the place from which they wished to prophesy by etching a square in the earth. The inscribed area was called a *templum*.

[41] Augustus: Gaius Julius Caesar Octavius (63–114 BC), nephew of Julius Caesar, gained complete sovereignty around 27 BC and founded the Roman empire.

76 Almost always one has conflated the leader or first official of the state with the representative of the spirit of humanity, who belongs to the unity of society or the nation. In the state everything is a spectacle, the life of the people is theatre; hence the spirit of the people should be visible. This visible spirit comes either, like the thousand-year kingdom,[42] without our effort, or it is elected through our implicit or explicit consent.

It is an indisputable fact that most princes are not true princes, but usually more or less representative of the spirit of their times. For the most part their government was in the hands of subordinates.

A perfect representative of this spirit of humanity could easily be a genuine priest and a poet *kat exochin*.[43]

77 Our daily life consists in merely preservative, forever recurrent tasks. This circle of habits is only a means to another chief means, our earthly existence in general, which is mixed with various ways of existing.

Philistines lead only a daily life.[44] The chief means appears to be their only end. They do everything for the sake of their earthly life, as it seems and must seem from their behaviour. They mingle poetry with their lives only according to need because they have grown used to a little distraction from their daily routine. Usually this diversion happens every seven days and could be called a poetic weekly fever. On Sundays work ceases; they live a little better than usual and this festivity ends with a deeper sleep; but only so that on Monday everything can resume a brisker pace. Their *parties de*

Hadrian: Publius Aelius Hadrianus (76–138), Roman emperor from 117, who centralized and bureaucratized the administration of the empire.

[42] 'Thousand-year kingdom' (*tausendjährigen Reich*): the chiliastic belief that, at the end of history, Christ will return to earth with his disciples and establish a reign of peace lasting 1000 years. The doctrine was defended from a philosophical perspective by both Lessing and Kant. See Lessing, *Education of the Human Race* nos. 85–90 (*Sämtliche Schriften*, XIII, pp. 433–4) and Kant, *Religion within the Limits of Reason Alone*, (*Ak.* VI, p. 34).

[43] *Kat exochin*: absolutely, in the proper sense (Greek).

[44] 'Philistines' (*Philister*): the term for the enemies of Israel in Luther's translation of the Bible. The word was frequently used in theological controversies in the sixteenth and seventeenth centuries for any opponent of one's own viewpoint. In the seventeenth century it was frequently used by students to refer to town-dwellers. Goethe used the term in his *Leiden des jungen Werther* for those who lead a comfortable bourgeois life as opposed to a life of passion and personal commitment. See *Werke*, VI, pp. 15–16.

plaisir must be conventional, habitual and fashionable; but even their pleasures are worked through like everything else, laboriously and formally.

The philistine reaches the highest degree of his poetic existence during a journey, wedding, baptism and in the church. Here his boldest wishes are satisfied, and often surpassed.

Their so-called religion serves merely as an opiate: stimulative yet numbing, deadening pain from weakness. Their morning and evening prayers, just like breakfast and supper, are necessary to them. They cannot bring themselves to renounce it. The vulgar philistine imagines the joys of heaven according to the image of a parish fair, a wedding, a journey or a ball. The more refined see heaven as a splendid cathedral with beautiful music, much pomp, with chairs for the *parterre* or the common folk, a choir and balcony for the more distinguished.

The worst among them are the revolutionary philistines, to which belongs the dregs of the progressive minds, the greedy ilk.[45]

Gross self-interest is the miserable result of a pathetic narrowness. For a wretch the present passing sensation is the most lively, the highest. He knows nothing higher than this. It is no wonder that the intellect, trained *par force* by external circumstances, is only the clever slave of such an obtuse master, plotting and catering for only his whims.

78 In the age when judgement was first discovered every new judgement was a find. The worth of this find increased the more applicable and fruitful this judgement proved to be. Maxims, which now seem very commonplace to us, then required an uncommon degree of intellectual vitality. One had to muster genius and acumen to find novel relationships with this new tool. Its application to the most characteristic, interesting and general sides of humanity must have excited special admiration and attracted the attention of all good minds. Hence arose the multitude of gnomes,[46] which one has so highly prized at all times and among all peoples. It is easily possible that our present ingenious discoveries meet with a similar fate in the course of time. The time might well come when it all becomes as commonplace as moral maxims are nowadays, and when new sublime discoveries preoccupy the restless spirit of man.

[45] Cf. *Faith and Love* no. 23.
[46] 'Multitude of gnomes' (*gnomische Massen*): short didactic poems.

79 By its very concept a law is active. An inactive law is no law. A law is a causal concept, a mixture of power and thought. Hence one is never conscious of a law as such. In so far as one thinks of a law it is only a proposition, i.e. a thought united with a capacity. A resilient, persistent thought is a striving thought, mediating law and mere thoughts.

80 A too great facility with one's capacities would be dangerous for one's earthly existence. In its present condition the spirit will make a destructive application of them. A certain degree of ponderousness prevents it from a too capricious activity and wakens it to a more regular participation in life, which is more suitable for this earthly existence. It is in virtue of the imperfect condition of its powers that such participation binds the spirit so exclusively to the earth. For this reason, such participation is in principle limited.

81 The philosophy of law corresponds to physiology, morals to psychology. The rational laws of legal and moral philosophy transformed into laws of nature yield the principles of physiology and psychology.

82 Flight from the communal spirit is death.

83 In most religious systems we are regarded as members of the divine. Should these members not follow the impetus of the whole – should they merely want to go their own way and not be members without intentionally acting against its laws – they are still treated medically by the divinity. They are either painfully cured or completely cut off.

84 Every specific incitement reveals a specific sense. The more new it is, the more clumsy, but also the stronger. The more specific, developed and complex the weaker it becomes. Hence the first thought of God arouses a mighty emotion in the whole individual; the same for the first idea of philosophy, humanity, the cosmos, etc.

85 The most intimate communion of all knowledge, the scientific republic, is the lofty goal of intellectuals.

86 Should not the distance of a special science from the whole, and so the rank of the sciences under one another, be reckoned according to the number of their principles? The fewer the principles the higher the science.

87 One usually understands the artificial better than the natural. The simple requires more spirit than the complex but less talent.

88 Tools arm the human race. One can well say that man understands how to produce a world; he lacks only the appropriate instruments, the required armament for his sense organs. A beginning has been made. Hence the principle of a warship is in the idea of the shipbuilder, who knows how to realize this plan through a mass of workers, and appropriate tools and instruments, by turning them all into one gigantic machine. Thus the idea of a moment often demands immense tools, immense masses of materials. Man is therefore the creator, if not *en actu* at least *potentia*.

89 Through every contact a substance arises, whose effect lasts as long as the contact. This is the [reason] for all synthetic modification of the individual. There are, however, one-sided and reciprocal contacts. The former provide the basis for the latter.

90 The more ignorant one is of nature the greater one's capacity for knowledge. Every new piece of knowledge makes a much deeper, more lively impression. One observes this clearly with one's entrance into a science. Hence through too much study one loses capacity. It is an ignorance opposed to our first ignorance. One is ignorant from a lack of knowledge, the other from a superfluity. The latter cultivates the symptons of scepticism. But it is an ungenuine scepticism arising from the indirect weakness of our faculty of knowledge. One is not in a position to penetrate the mass of material and to bring it completely to life in some determinate form. Our plastic powers are not sufficient for that. Hence the inventiveness of young minds and the enthusiast, as well as the lucky stroke of talented beginners or laymen, is easily explicable.

91 To build worlds satisfies not the deep, delving mind; but a loving heart sates the striving spirit.

92 We stand in relation to all parts of the universe, just as to the future and past. It depends only on the direction and duration of our attention which relation we especially want to develop, or which should be especially important and effective for us. A genuine method for this activity may be nothing less than a long sought method of invention; but it may still be more than this. With each hour man acts according to these laws, and the possibility of finding them through ingenious self-observation is undeniable.

93 The historian organizes historical material. The data of history are the mass to which the historian gives a form by bestowing life upon it. Thus history stands under the laws of animation and

organization in general. Before [the application of] these principles there is no genuine historical work of art, but nothing more than chance traces of animation where an unimaginative genius has held sway.

94 Hitherto almost all genius has been one-sided, the result of a morbid constitution. One class has too much outer, the other too much inner sense. Rarely did nature achieve a balance between the two, the perfect constitution of genius. By accident there often arose a perfect constitution, but this could not be of any duration because it was not comprehended and fixed by the spirit; it remained only for fortunate moments. The first genius, who saw through himself, discovered the germ of an immeasurable world; he made a discovery, the most remarkable in world history, for it begins a completely new epoch of humanity, and only on this level did true history of every kind become possible. For the way that had been travelled hitherto now became a unique, completely explicable whole. That point outside the world has been given, and Archimedes can now fulfil his promise.

95 Prior to abstraction everything is one, but it is the unity of chaos. After abstraction it is again unified, but unification is a free combination of independent, self-determining beings. A mere aggregate has become a society, the chaos has been transformed into a diverse world.

96 If the world is, as it were, the precipitate of human nature, so heaven is its sublimation. Both happen *uno actu*. No precipitation without sublimation. What gets lost in one is gained in the other.

97 Where there are children there is a golden age.

98 Hitherto the foundation of all ecclesiastical states has been security for oneself and all invisible powers.

99 The course of approximation is composed of increasing progressions and regressions. Both retard, both accelerate, and both lead to the same goal. Hence in a novel the poet appears now to approach, now to distance himself from, the game; and it is closest when it appears furthest away.

100 A criminal cannot complain of injustice if one treats him severely and inhumanely. His crime was an entrance into the world of force, of tyranny. There is no measure and proportion in this world, so that the disproportion of the counter-measure should not surprise him.

101 Mythology contains the history of the archetypal world, grasping past, present and future.

102 If the spirit sanctifies, then every genuine book is a Bible. But a book is seldom written for its own sake; and if the spirit is like a noble metal, most books are ephraimites.[47] Of course, every useful book must be at least heavily alloyed. In trade and life the noble metals are not to be used in their purity. Many true books are like the clumps of gold in Ireland: for many years they serve only as weights.

103 Many books are longer than they seem. In fact, they have no end. The boredom they generate is absolute and infinite. Excellent examples of this kind have been set by Messrs. Heydenreich, Jacob, Abicht and Pölitz. This is a pot into which everyone can throw their own example.

104 Many anti-revolutionary books have been written for the Revolution. But Burke has written a revolutionary book against the Revolution.[48]

105 Most observers of the Revolution, especially the clever and reputable, have declared it to be a dangerous and contagious disease. They have not gone beyond the symptoms, which have been confused and construed in many ways. Many have held it to be a merely local evil. The most ingenious opponents insist upon castration. They have rightly observed that this supposed disease is nothing but a crisis of emerging puberty.[49]

106 How desirable it is to be the contemporary of a truly great man! The present majority of cultivated Germans are not of this opinion. They are sufficiently refined to deny everything great and to follow the planned system. If the Copernican system were not so well established, they would be quite content to make the sun and stars will-of-the-wisps and the earth the centre of the universe. Hence Goethe, who is now the true governer of poetry on earth, is treated as rudely as possible and regarded with contempt when he does not satisfy the expectations of conventional entertainment

---

[47] 'Ephraimites' (*Ephraimiten*): worthless Prussian coins from the time of the Seven Years' War, named after the treasurer Veitel Ephraim.

[48] Novalis refers to Burke's *Reflections on the Revolution in France* (London, 1790), which appeared in a German translation by Friedrich Gentz in 1793 as *Betrachtungen über die französische Revolution*.

[49] On Novalis' reaction to the French Revolution, cf. *Faith and Love* nos. 11–14, 21, 23.

and embarrasses them for a moment. An interesting symptom of this direct weakness of the soul is the reception of *Hermann and Dorothea*.[50]

107 The geologists believe that the physical centre of gravity lies underneath Fez and Morocco. Goethe, the anthropologist, maintains in his *Meister* that the intellectual centre of gravity lies under the German nation.[51]

108 Until now it has been impossible to describe people because one does not know what man is. If we first know what man is then we will be able to describe individuals truly genetically.

109 Nothing is more poetic than memory and the intuition or presentiment of the future. The representation of the past draws us to death, to dissolution. The representations of the future drive us to living, to shortening, to assimilative activity. Hence all memory is melancholy, all presentiment joyful. The former contains a too great liveliness, the latter elevates a too weak life. The usual present binds past and future through limitation. Contiguity arises, and through rigidity crystallization. But there is also a spiritual presence, which unites both through dissolution. Such a mixture is the element, the atmosphere of the poet.

110 The human world is the communal organ of the gods. Poetry unites them, just like us.

111 Something appears absolutely at rest that, with respect to the outer world, is absolutely immovable. However much it changes itself, it still remains at rest in relation to the outer world. This proposition holds for all changes of self. Hence the beautiful appears so peaceful. Everything beautiful is a self-illuminating, complete individual.

112 Every human form enlivens an individual core in the observer. Hence this intuition becomes infinite; it is bound with the feeling of an inexhaustible power; and it is therefore absolutely enlivening. As we observe ourselves so we enliven ourselves.

Without this visible and tangible form of immortality we would not be able to think truly.

[50] *Hermann and Dorothea*: an epic by Goethe, which first appeared in 1797 to mixed reviews.
[51] *Wilhelm Meisters Lehrjahre*, book IV, chapter 20: 'It is the character of the Germans that they complain so much about everything that it becomes difficult for them.' (*Werke*, VII, p. 278). Novalis makes a pun on the German: the word for gravity, *die Schwere*, also means seriousness and difficulty.

This perceptible inadequacy of the earthly physical form for the expression and organ of the inner spirit is that vague, compelling thought that is the basis of all genuine thoughts, the occasion for the evolution of the intelligence. It is what forces us to assume an intelligible world, and an infinite series of expressions and organs of every spirit, whose exponent or root is its individuality.

113 The more narrow a system the more it pleases the worldly wise. Thus the system of the materialists, the doctrine of Helvetius and Locke, have received most praise from this group. So too Kant will find more disciples than Fichte.

114 The art of writing books is still to be discovered. But it is on the verge of being discovered. Fragments of this kind are like a literary sowing of the fields. Of course, there may be many sterile seeds in them. Nevertheless, if only a few of them blossom!

Novalis
Faith and Love

Preface

1

If one wishes to say something secret to a few in a large, mixed company, and when one is not sitting close to another, one must speak in a special language. This special language can be foreign either in its *tone* or in its *images*. The latter will be a metaphoric and cryptic language.

2

Many have thought that one should use a learned language to speak of delicate, abusable things, for example, that one should write in Latin about such matters. But the attempt should be made to see if one cannot speak in the customary language of the land, so that only those can understand who should understand. Every true mystery excludes the profane by itself. Whoever understands it is of his own accord, and with good reason, an *initiate*.

3

A mystical expression is one more stimulus for thought. All truth is ancient. The attraction of novelty resides only in the variation of expression. The more contrasting the appearance, the greater the joy of recognition.

4

What one loves one finds everywhere and sees similarities to it

---

Faith and Love (*Glauben und Liebe*) first appeared in the July 1798 edition of the *Jahrbücher der Preussischen Monarchie*, vol. II, pp. 269–86. It was probably written in early 1797.

Faith and Love was a *pièce d'occasion*. It was written for the coronation of Friedrich Wilhelm III and his wife Luise to the Prussian throne, which took place on 16 November 1797. The article reflects the popular hopes for reform after the reactionary and incompetent reign of Friedrich Wilhelm II (1767–1797), who had reversed his father's (Friedrich II) programme of enlightenment, reinstated censorship and emptied the public purse. Life at the court of Friedrich II was notoriously corrupt and decadent – the king had many mistresses and committed bigamy twice – and was mirrored by the low level of public morality in Berlin. In reaction to his predecessor, Friedrich Wilhelm III planned to introduce wide-ranging reforms. He intended to approve the long-planned constitution, to abolish serfdom, and to set an example for public morality through his domestic life. By timely reform from above it was hoped to counteract the influence of the French Revolution in Prussia.

The numbering of the preface is Novalis' own. All other numbers are editorial and conventional.

everywhere. The greater the love the wider and more varied the resembling world. My beloved is the abbreviation of the universe, the universe the elongation of my beloved. To its friend the sciences offer everything, flowers and mementoes for his beloved.

5

But whence the serious mystical-political philosophy? The inspired expresses his higher life in all his functions; hence he philosophizes too, and indeed in a more lively manner than usual, in a more *poetic* vein. This deep tone too belongs to the symphony of his powers and organs. But does not the universal gain from individual, the individual from universal, relations?

6

Let the dragonflies[1] loose; innocent *strangers*[2] they are,
Following the double star[3] gladly, bearing gifts, hither.

7 A flourishing land is a more royal work of art than a park.[4] An elegant park is an English invention. A country that satisfies heart and spirit might become a German invention; and its inventor would be the king of all inventors.

8 The best of the previous French monarchs had intended to make each of his subjects so well off that they could all put a chicken with rice on the table every Sunday.[5] But would not that government be preferable for which a peasant ate mouldy bread rather than a roast, and for which he thanked God for the good fortune of being born in its land?

---

[1] *Libellen*. The literal meaning of the German term is dragonflies. Novalis is also playing on the Latin analogue, *libellus*, little book. The little book would be the author's own.
[2] *Fremdling*. For Novalis, the stranger is someone who carries the memory of a past golden age and who believes in its return. See his poem *Der Fremdling*, *Schriften*, I, p. 399.
[3] The king and queen.
[4] An implicit critique of the English form of government, and probably Burke's flattering portrait of it.
[5] Henry IV, king of France from 1589 to 1610. Allegedly, he told the duke of Savoy: 'If God only grants me further life, then I vow that there will be no peasant in my kingdom who cannot put a chicken in his pot.'

9 If I became prince tomorrow, I would ask the king for a eudi-ometer[6] like his own. No instrument is more necessary for a prince. I would also, like the king, seek to draw the vital air for my state more from blossoming plantlings than saltpetre.[7]

10 Gold and silver are the blood of the state. An accumulation of blood in either head or heart reveals frailty in both. The stronger the heart the more lively and generously it drives the blood to the extremities. Each limb is warmed and invigorated, and swift and mighty the blood surges back toward the heart.[8]

11 A collapsing throne is like a falling mountain that shatters the plain. It leaves behind a dead sea where there was once a fertile earth and happy dwellings.

12 Make all the mountains the same height and the sea will be grateful to you. The sea is the element of freedom and equality. Nevertheless, we should be warned against stepping on sulphuric gravel;[9] otherwise, there will be a volcano there and with it the germ of a new continent.

13 The mephitic vapours[10] of the moral world behave differently than their namesakes in nature. The former gladly climb to the heights, whereas the latter cling to the earth. For those who dwell in the heights there is no better remedy against them than flowers and sunshine. Both are rarely found together in the heights. But

---

[6] 'Eudiometer': a device for measuring the oxygen content of the air. Novalis plays on the Greek root *eudai*, which literally means fair weather, but which also occurs in *eudamonia*, happiness. Hence the eudiometer would measure the happiness of the state.

[7] Novalis is alluding to two recently discovered scientific facts: Priestly's discovery that plants produce oxygen in sunlight; and that oxygen can also be produced from burning saltpetre, potassium nitrate. The contrast is between a natural and artificial means of creating unity in a state. Since saltpetre is also used in gunpowder, Novalis could also mean that forming the vital air of the state from it is not the best means to ensure peace.

[8] Here Novalis is probably criticizing not only economic inequality in general, but also the economic policies of absolutism in particular, which aimed chiefly at increasing the prince's revenues.

[9] Sulphuric gravel, *Schwefelkies*, played an important role in the explanation of volcanic activity in the eighteenth century. It was thought to be so volatile that merely stepping on it would ignite it. In a famous experiment, first performed in 1700, a mixture of sulphuric gravel and iron were buried under the earth; in a few days the earth exploded in flames.

[10] Mephitic vapours are harmful, foul-smelling vapours from decomposing organic matter. Mephitic air is a non-inhalable gas that arises from combustion; because it is heavier than air it clings to the ground.

on one of the highest moral heights one can now enjoy the purest air and see a lily[11] in the sun.

14 It was no wonder when the mountain peaks thundered down mostly only into the valleys and devastated the fields. Evil clouds gathered around them,[12] concealing their descent from the land. The plain then appeared to them like a dark abyss, above which they seemed to carry the clouds; or it seemed like an angry sea, though nothing was enraged against them. They were gradually worn down and washed away, like the apparently loyal clouds.

15 What a true royal couple is for the whole man that a constitution is for the mere understanding. One can interest oneself in a constitution only as a dead letter. If a sign is not a beautiful image, or a song, then attachment to signs is the most perverse of all inclinations.

What is a law if it is not the expression of the will of a loved and respected person? Does not the mystical sovereign, like every idea, need a symbol? And what symbol is more worthy and fitting than a lovable and excellent human being? The brevity of a symbol is surely worth something, and is not one person a shorter, more beautiful symbol of the spirit than an assembly? Whoever has very much spirit is not hemmed by restrictions and distinctions; rather, they only excite him. Only the spiritless feel a burden and an imposition. Moreoever, a born king is better than a created one. The best man will not be able to suffer such elevation without agitation. Whoever is born to it is not made dizzy or overexcited by such a position. And, in the end, is not birth a primitive form of choice? Those who doubt the freedom of this choice, the unanimity of it, must not have felt very deeply within themselves.

Whoever approaches this with his historical experience knows not at all what I am talking about and from what standpoint I am speaking; to him I might as well speak Arabic and he would do best to go his own way and not mix among listeners whose customs and manners of speaking are utterly alien to him.

16 So far as I am concerned the time is now over for the letter. It is no great praise for the present that it is so far removed from nature, so insensitive toward family life, so disinclined toward the

---

[11] Allusion to the queen. The lily is a traditional symbol of purity and, as in the House of Bourbon, of royalty.

[12] An allusion to the French court.

more beautiful poetic forms of society. How would our cosmopolitans be amazed if the time of eternal peace dawned upon them and they saw the highest and most developed humanity in its monarchic form?[13] Then the stale paste that now sticks humanity together will dissolve into dust, and the spirit will scare off all the ghosts that now appear in dead letters and go forth dismembered from pens and presses. All humanity will melt together like a pair of lovers.

17 The king is the pure life principle of the state, just like the sun in the planetary system. Consequently, immediately surrounding this principle, the highest life in the state, the atmosphere of light,[14] generates itself. It is more or less emblazoned on every citizen. Hence the discourse of the citizen in the proximity of the king will be brilliant, and as poetic as possible, the expression of the highest animation. Since the spirit is its most effective in its highest animation, since its effects are reflections, and since reflection is in its very essence formative – so that the highest animation will be then connected with beautiful or perfect reflection – the expression of the citizen in the proximity of the king will be the expression of the highest and most restrained exuberance, the expression of the most lively impulses as they are ruled by the most worthy restraint, a conduct to be brought under rules. No court can exist without etiquette. But just as there is a natural etiquette, the beautiful form, so there is an artificial one, the ugly form. The creation of the former will not be an unimportant concern for the thoughtful king, as it has a significant influence on taste and the love for monarchy.

18 Every citizen is a state official. He has his income only as such. One goes astray in calling the king the first official of the state.[15] The king is not a citizen, and hence also not an official. It is precisely the distinctive feature of monarchy that it rests in the belief in the higher born, in the voluntary acceptance of an ideal

---

[13] Novalis is taking issue with Kant's argument in *Perpetual Peace* that the form of government most likely to ensure peace is republican. See *Ak.* VIII, p. 351; *PW*, 100.

[14] *Lichtatmosphäre.* An allusion to the eighteenth-century discussion whether the sun has an atmosphere in which light originates. The question was answered in the affirmative by Schelling in his *Ideas toward a Philosophy of Nature*, book I, chapter 2, *Werke* 1/2, pp. 92–118.

[15] Novalis refers to the famous dictum of Friedrich II: 'Un prince est le premier serviteur et le premier magistrate de l'État.' Kant endorsed the maxim in his *Perpetual Peace*. See *Ak.* VIII, pp. 352–3; *PW*, p. 101.

human being. Among equals I cannot choose a superior; and to someone who is involved in the same questions as me I cannot entrust anything. Hence monarchy is a genuine system, because it is connected to a middle point, to something that belongs to humanity but not the state. The king is a person ordained to his earthly fate. Such a fiction forces itself upon people. It satisfies all the higher impulses of their nature. Every one should be able to ascend the throne. The means of education for this distant goal is a king. He gradually assimilates the mass of his subjects. Each has sprouted from an ancient royal stem. Yet how few show the signs of such descent?

19 It is a great mistake of our states that one sees so little of the state. The state should be visible everywhere, and every person should be marked as its citizen. Can not badges and uniforms be introduced everywhere? Whoever regards these matters as trivial does not know the essential characteristics of our nature.

20 In the present times a ruler can do nothing more useful for the preservation of his state than attempting to individualize it as much as possible.

21 The old hypothesis that comets are the omens of revolution in the physical cosmos also holds for the other kind of comets that periodically revolutionize and rejuvenate the spiritual cosmos. The spiritual astronomer has recognized long ago the influence of such a comet on a considerable part of the spiritual planets that we call humanity. Mighty floods, changes in climate, swervings from the centre of gravity, a universal tendency toward chaos, strange meteors – these are the symptons of this violent incitation,[16] whose consequences will make up the content of a new age. Just as it is perhaps necessary that at certain intervals everything be brought into flux to create new necessary mixtures and new purer crystallizations, so it is also indispensable to alleviate a crisis and to prevent total dissolution, so that a branch, a seed, remains from which a new plant can grow and form beautiful branches. What is firm should pull itself together even more firmly, so that superfluous warming matter[17] is reduced; one should spare no means to prevent a softening of the bones, a dissolution of the central fibres.

[16] 'Incitation': cf. *Pollen*, notes 4, 10.

[17] *Wärmestoff*. A reference to the eighteenth-century doctrine of the *Fluida imponderable*. Its main assumption is that light, warmth, magnetism and electricity each inhere in their own kind of substance, which is imponderable, imperceptible and

Would it not be nonsense to make a crisis permanent, and to believe that a state of fever is the true healthy state, for which people should sacrifice everything? Who would also like to doubt its necessity, its beneficial effect?

22 A time will come, and that will be soon, when everyone will be convinced that no king can exist without a republic and no republic without a king, that both king and republic are indivisible, just like the body and soul, and that a king without a republic and a republic without a king are words without meaning. Hence with a true republic a king arises at the same time, and with a true king a republic at the same time. The true king becomes a republic, the true republic becomes a king.

23 Those who nowadays declaim against princes as such, who affirm salvation only in the new French manner, who recognize even a republic only under a representative form, and who dogmatically maintain that there is a republic only where there are primary and elective assemblies, directories and committees, municipalities and liberty trees[18] – they are miserable philistines, empty in spirit and poor in heart, and mere pedants who attempt to conceal their shallowness and inner weakness behind the colourful banner of the latest pompous fashion and under the imposing mask of cosmopolitanism. They deserve an enemy as much as the obscurantists,[19] so that their frog and mouse war[20] becomes perfectly visualized.

---

elastic. The famous phlogiston theory was only one version of this doctrine: phlogiston was the special substance behind combustion. Although Priestly and Lavoisier had done much to discredit phlogiston theory by the end of the eighteenth century, the general theory of imponderable fluids remained. The belief in warming material was held well into the nineteenth century. It was advanced by the romantic *Naturphilosoph* Franz Baader, who was much admired by Novalis and Schlegel. See his *Vom Wärmestoff* (1786) in *Sämtliche Werke*, ed. Franz Hoffmann (Leipzig, 1852), III, pp. 1–180.

[18] Directories ... liberty trees. The Directory became the executive power in France in 1795 after the dissolution of the committee of public safety, which reigned during the Terror. Municipalities were magistrates for city districts during the Revolution. Liberty trees were planted in honour of liberty, usually decorated with a tricolour and crowned with a Jacobin cap.

[19] 'Obscurantists' (*Obscuranten*): literally, a person who obscures the light. A term applied by the *Aufklärer*, the German champions of enlightenment, to their reactionary enemies.

[20] 'Frog and mouse war' (*Frosch und Mäusekrieg*): a ridiculous struggle between unheroic parties. An allusion to the Greek satiric epic *Betrachtomachie* (*The Frog and mouse war*), written in the third century BC, which portrays the heroic conflicts in Homer's *Iliad* as a battle between mice and frogs.

24 Is the king not a king simply through the inner feeling of *her*[21] worth?

25 What is the coronation with other princes should be here only a day in the life of the king. For most kings the government lasts only as long as the first day. The first day is the life of these ephemera. Then they die, and much abuse is wreaked with their relics. Hence most so-called governments are only interregnums; the princes are only the red, sacred wax that sanctions the decrees.

26 What are decorations? Will-of-the-wisps or shooting stars? The decorations of an order should be a milky way, though it is usually only a rainbow, the edge of a storm. A letter, a portrait of the queen – these are decorations, distinctions of the highest kind, distinctions that inspire to the most distinguished deeds. Even deserving housewives should receive titles of honour.

27 The queen has indeed no political sphere of influence, but she does have a domestic one. To her duties belongs, by right, especially the education of her sex, the supervision of children in their early years and of morals at home, the care for the sick and poor, particularly those of her sex, the tasteful decoration of the home, the organization of family celebrations, and the arrangements of court life. She should have her own chancellery, and her husband should be her first minister, with whom she deliberates on everything. Part of the education of her sex would be the abolition of all houses of corruption.[22] Should the queen not shudder by her entry into a city where the deepest degradation of her sex is a public trade? The harshest punishment would not be too harsh for these veritable sellers of souls. A murder is much more innocent. The much vaunted public safety, which is intended by it, is only an extraordinary concession to brutality. As little as the government should interfere in the private sphere, it should strenuously investigate every complaint, every public scandal, every piece of information or accusation concerning a violated woman. Who has more a duty to protect her sex than the queen? She must blush to stay in a city that offers refuge and training schools for depravity.

Moreover, her example will work wonders. Happy marriages will become more frequent, and domesticity more than a fashion. She

---

[21] *Ihre*: that is, the worth of the queen.
[22] Houses of corruption (*Anstalten seiner Corruption*): a reference to the notorious Berlin brothels.

will become at the same time a true model for feminine dress. Costume is surely a very proper ethometer.[23] Unfortunately, the ethometer has always stood at a very low point in Berlin, often below zero. What could the company of the queen not do for young girls in Berlin? It would be by itself a sign of honoured distinction and would make public opinion moral again; and, in the end, public opinion is indeed the most powerful means for the restoration and development of morals.

28 The conduct of the state depends upon the public ethos. The ennoblement of this ethos is the only basis for the genuine reform of the state. The king and queen as such can and must be the principle of the public ethos. There is no longer a monarchy where the king and the intelligence of the state are not identical. Hence the king of France was dethroned long before the Revolution, and the same was the case for most of the princes of Europe. It would be a very dangerous sympton for the New Prussian state if one were too obtuse to the beneficial influence of the king and queen, and if there were missing a sense for this classical couple. This will soon be made clear. If these geniuses do not work, then the complete dissolution of the modern world is certain, and the heavenly appearance is nothing more than the flash of a fading vitality, the music of the spheres of one dying, and the visible intuition of a better world that stands before more noble generations.

29 The court is the true model for a household. The higher households of the state are modelled after it, and the lower households after these higher ones, and so on down the scale. What a powerful influence a reform of the court can have! The king should not be frugal, like a farmer, or even a wealthy private individual. Yet there is such a thing as royal frugality, and this the king seems to know. The court should set an example for private life. The housewife is the mainspring of the home, and so the queen is the mainspring of the court. The husband earns, the wife orders and manages. A frivolous household is usually the fault of the wife. That the queen is the very antipode of frivolity is known by everyone. Hence I cannot conceive how she can bear life at court as it is. Her taste, which is so at one with her heart, must find the dull monotony unbearable.

---

[23] 'Ethometer': a device for measuring morals.

Apart from the drama and concerts, and now and then some interior decorations, one hardly finds even a trace of taste in the usual court life in Europe; and even these exceptions are sometimes tasteless, or at least frequently appreciated in a tasteless way. But how extremely diverting things could be? A spirited *Maître des Plaisirs*,[24] guided by the queen's taste, could make an earthly paradise out of the court; she could put the simple theme of life's pleasures through inexhaustible variations and so let us see the objects of public reverence in a constantly new and stimulating environment. What feeling could be more heavenly than to see one's beloved enjoying life's truest delights?

30 Every educated woman and every conscientious mother should have the portrait of the queen in her living room. What a beautiful, potent reminder of the model that everyone should emulate. Imitation of the queen should be the distinctive character of the new Prussian woman, her national characteristic. One charming being under a thousandfold forms. A ceremony for a royal blessing could be introduced for every wedding; and by such means one could ennoble daily life through the king and queen as the ancients once did with their gods. Then there was a genuine religiosity through the constant mixture of the divine in daily life. Now a genuine patriotism can emerge through the constant interweaving of the royal couple in domestic and public life.

31 Respectable society in Berlin should attempt to preserve the sculpture of von Schadow.[25] It should establish a lodge devoted to moral grace and place it in the exhibition room. This lodge can provide a school for the young feminine world of the cultivated classes; a royal ceremony would then be analogous to what a religious ceremony should be: the decoration and reward of the most excellent of their sex.

32 In the past one had to flee from the courts as one did with wife and child from a pestilence. Now a court is like an enchanted island that allows one to withdraw from the universal moral corruption. To find an innocent woman, a prudent young man once had to go to the more distant provinces, at least to those families

---

[24] *Maître des Plaisirs*: person responsible for the entertainments at court.
[25] A marble sculpture of Queen Luise and her sister Frederike by the sculptor Johann Gottfried Schadow (1764–1850). The sculpture was completed in 1797 and exhibited in the *Parole-Saal* of the Berliner Schloss.

removed from city and court; in the future, though, as it should be by nature, one will go to the court as the meeting place of the best and beautiful, and one will count oneself lucky to receive a lady from the hand of the queen.

33 This king is the first king of Prussia. Every day he places the crown on his head by himself, and recognition of him requires no negotiations.

34 The king and queen protect the monarchy more than 200,000 troops.

35 Nothing is more refreshing than to speak of our wishes as they are already being fulfilled.

36 No state has been run more like a factory than Prussia since the death of Friedrich I.[26] As necessary as such a mechanical administration may be for physical health, strength, and efficiency in a state, a state goes to ruin when it is governed only in this manner. The principle of the old famous system is to bind everyone to the state by self-interest.[27] The clever politician had the ideal of the state where the interests of the state were as self-centred as those of its subjects, yet where the interests of both are so artificially connected that they reciprocally promoted one another.

Much effort has been spent on this political squaring of the circle. Yet raw self-interest seems to be immeasurable, anti-systematic. It has not allowed itself to be limited at all, though the nature of every political organization demands this. Nevertheless, this formal acceptance of common egoism as a principle has done untold damage. The germ of the revolution of our day rests nowhere but here.

With growing civilization our needs must multiply, and the more the value of the means of their satisfaction increases, the more our moral sensibility lags behind all of these new inventions of luxury,

---

[26] Friedrich Wilhelm I (1688–1740), 'the soldier king', who ruled Prussia from 1713. He began the administrative reforms that made Prussia into an efficient bureaucratic and military state.

[27] A critique of contract theory in general and of the philosophy of enlightened absolutism in particular. According to Wolff and Pufendorf, two chief defenders of enlightened absolutism, the citizen was obliged to obey the sovereign because he guaranteed their safety, comfort and property. See Christian Wolff, *Vernünftige Gedanken von dem gemeine Wesen* (Halle, 1756), nos. 42–4, pp. 3–7; and Samuel Pufendorf, *De jure naturae et gentium* (New York, 1934), book 7, chapter 1, section 7, and chapter 2, sections 1–8.

and all the refinements in comfort and the enjoyment of life. Our sensuality has too quickly won enormous ground. To just the degree that people cultivate this side of their nature and lose themselves in the most varied distractions and the most comfortable complacency, so the other side of themselves must appear invisible, confining and distant. With sensuality they thought that they had found their proper vocation as human beings, and that they must exert all their powers in this direction. Hence crude self-interest became a passion, and at the same time its maxims became the result of the highest understanding; it was this that made the passion so dangerous, so insurmountable. How splendid it would be were the present king to become convinced that, in this way, one can achieve only the fleeting happiness of a gambler, a happiness which depends upon such fickle factors as the stupidity and the lack of practice and finesse of the other players. By being deceived one learns how to deceive; the tables are soon turned and the teacher becomes the student of his students. Enduring happiness comes from only the just man and the just state. What good do all riches do me when they stay only so long as to take fresh horses and more quickly complete their journey around the world? Selfless love in the heart and its maxims in the head – that is the eternal basis of all true, indissoluble union. What is political union but a marriage?

37 A king, like a father, must not show partiality. He should not have only military companions and subordinates. Why not also civilian ones? When he makes able generals of his military adjutants, why should he not make able presidents and ministers from their civilian counterparts? All strands of government run together in him. Only from his vantage point can all the wheels of the state be overseen. Only from there can one view the state as a whole and in detail. Nowhere can one be better trained for a directorial post than from the cabinet, where the political wisdom of the land is concentrated, where every matter is thoroughly considered, and where one can follow the course of business down to its smallest details. From here alone would that narrow mindedness disappear, that pedantry of businessmen, whereby they give an infallible and singular importance to their own projects and activities, whereby they judge everything according to their own sphere of action, and whereby they often lead even higher tribunals astray by unfair, impartial measures. This provincial mentality is visible everywhere

and prevents true republicanism, general participation in the state, the inner contact and harmony of all its members. The king should have still more military and civilian adjutants. As the former make up the highest military school in the state, so the latter do the same for its practical-political academy. A position in either would be distinction and incentive enough. For the king this alternating company of the best young men of his country would be most pleasant and advantageous. But for these young men such an apprenticeship would be the most splendid celebration of their lives, the occasion for a life-long enthusiasm. Personal affection would bond them to their sovereign; and the king would have the most beautiful opportunity to know his staff well, to select from among them, and to love and respect them personally. The noble simplicity of royal private life, the image of the happy, intimate couple, would have the most beneficial influence on the moral education of the core of Prussian youth; and thus the king would have secured in the most easy manner the innate wish of his heart: to become the true reformer and restorer of his nation and age.

38 A king should have nothing more at heart than to be as many sided, well instructed, well informed and impartial as possible – in short, to be and remain a perfect human being. No other person than a king has as much at his disposal to become in such an easy manner this highest form of humanity. By social intercourse and constant learning he can always keep himself young. An old king can make a state as gloomy as himself. How easily the king could acquaint himself with the scientific progress of humanity. He already has learned academies. When, if necessary, he organizes interchanges between them, and demands from them complete, detailed and precise reports on the past and present state of literature, regular reports on the most notable events in everything that interests humanity as such – excerpts from the best books and comments upon them, instruction about those products of the fine arts that deserve his own consideration and enjoyment, and finally suggestions for the promotion of the scientific culture of his subjects, for the endorsement and support of propitious and significant projects and poor promising scholars, for the filling in of gaps in our knowledge, and for the development of new literary seeds – then this will put him in a position to see himself in a larger perspective, to see how his state relates to others and his nation to

humanity, and indeed to make himself into a truly regal human being. Saved from the labour of an enormous amount of reading, he can enjoy in extract the fruits of European learning; and from diligent reflection on this concentrated and simplified material new mighty powers of mind will emerge, so that he can see things in a purer element and from the apex of his age. How perceptive his vision, how sharp his judgement, and how noble his disposition will become!

39 A true prince is the artist of artists, that is, the director of artists. Every person should be an artist. Everything can become a fine art. The material of the prince is his artists; his will is his chisel: he educates, employs and directs his artists, because only he oversees the whole from the correct standpoint, and because only he has completely in mind the idea that is to be executed through the united powers of all. The ruler creates an infinitely diverse theatre, where the stage and parterre, the actors and spectators, are one, and where he is at once poet, director and hero of the piece. How charming when, as is the case with the king, the directress is at once the beloved of the hero, the heroine of the play, and when one sees in her the muse that fills the poet with a pure ardour, making him tune his harp in a gentle, heavenly manner.

40 In our day true wonders of transubstantiation[28] have taken place. Does not a court transform itself into a family, a throne into a shrine, a royal wedding into an eternal bond of love?

41 When the dove becomes the companion and favourite of the eagle, the golden age is dawning or already arrived, even if it is not publicly recognized and universally promulgated

42 Whoever wants to see and grow fond of eternal peace should travel to Berlin and see the queen. There everyone can clearly convince themselves that eternal peace loves sincere justice above all, and that it can be possessed eternally only by this alone.[29]

43 What do I wish for more than anything else? Let me tell you: an inspired account of the childhood and youth of the queen.

---

[28] The doctrine of the Roman Catholic church (since 1215) that the wine and bread of the communion are transformed into the blood and body of Christ upon the consecration of a priest.

[29] An allusion to Kant's *Perpetual Peace*. Novalis takes issue with Kant's argument that even a nation of devils could establish a republican constitution, and that the mechanism of selfish inclination is sufficient to ensure eternal peace. See *Ak.* VIII, pp. 365–8; *PW*, pp. 112–14.

Certainly, in the most proper sense of the word, an account of her education as a woman. This would be perhaps nothing else than Natalie's apprenticeship. Natalie is to me like the portrait of the queen.[30] Ideals should resemble one another.

Novalis

---

[30] Natalie: a figure in Goethe's *Wilhelm Meisters Lehrjahre*.

Novalis
Political Aphorisms

44 The basis of all perversity in opinions and attitudes is confusing the ends with the means.

45 Certainly, most revolutionaries have not known exactly what they wanted: order or disorder.

46 Revolutions are more a proof against the true energy of a nation. There is an energy from sickness and weakness that is more violent than true energy; unfortunately, it ceases with even greater weakness.

47 When one judges a whole nation one usually judges the especially conspicuous, striking part of it.

48 No argument is stronger against the old system of government than what one can make against the disproportionate strength of the various parts of the state, which especially comes to the fore in a revolution. Its administration must have been gravely faulty that many parts could become deficient and such deep-seated weakness took root everywhere.

49 The weaker the part the more it inclines to disorder and infection.

50 What are slaves? Completely weakened, compromised human beings. What are sultans? Slaves aroused through strong stimuli. How do sultans and slaves end? Violently. The former easily as slaves, the latter easily as sultans, that is, frenetic and insane. How can we cure slaves? Through very cautious emancipation and enlightenment. We must treat them like those suffering from frostbite. And sultans? In the manner that Dionysus and Croesus were cured.[1] One began with shock, fasting, and monastic discipline and gradually increased restoratives [and tonics]. Sultans and slaves were extremes. There are many classes in between from the king

Novalis wrote the *Political Aphorisms* (*Politische Aphorismen*) in early 1798. They were probably originally conceived as a continuation of his reflections in *Faith and Love* (hence the numbering). In any case, Novalis hoped to publish them along with *Faith and Love* in the *Jahrbücher der Preussischen Monarchie*. However, because of the negative reaction to *Faith and Love* in the Prussian court, publication of any further work under the name of 'Novalis' was prohibited by the Prussian censor. The *Aphorisms* were first published by Ludwig Tieck and Eduard von Bülow in their edition of Novalis' works, *Novalis Schriften* (Berlin, 1846) III, pp. 212–15.

[1] Dionysus II of Syracuse (396–337 BC), whose reign was characterized by brutality and dissipation. After his defeat by Timoleon he spent his final years in Corinth undergoing re-education. Croesus, legendary king of Lydia (560–546 BC), was also famous for his cruelty and decadence.

to the genuine cynic[2] – the classes of the most complete health. Terrorists and sycophants belong in the next class after sultans and slaves – and exchange places with one another just as these do. Both represent the forms of disease of a very weak constitution.

51 The king represents the most healthy constitution under a maximum of stimuli. The cynic represents the same under a minimum of stimuli. The more they are alike, and the more they can exchange roles unaltered, the more their constitution approximates to the ideal constitution.[3] Hence the more the king lives independently from the throne the more he is a king.

52 All stimuli are relative; they are quantities, except for one, which is absolute and more than a quantity.

53 A perfect constitution arises from incitement and an absolute connection with this stimulus. With it the constitution can dispense with all other stimuli, for it works more the less the relative stimuli do, and conversely. If this stimulus penetrates the constitution, then people will be indifferent to the relative ones. This stimulus is *absolute love*.

54 Without love a cynic and a king are only figureheads.

55 Every improvement of an imperfect constitution comes down to making it more capable of love.

56 The best state consists in indifferentists of this kind.[4]

57 In imperfect states they are the best citizens. They participate in everything good, laugh in silence over the buffoonery of their contemporaries, and refrain from all evil. They do not change anything because they know that every change of such a kind and under these circumstances would be a mistake, and that the best cannot come from outside. They leave everything in its dignity; and just as

---

[2] A reference to the ancient philosophical sect founded by Socrates' pupil Antisthenes around 400 BC. According to the cynics, the final end for all human beings is a life of virtue, which should be prized above all social conventions and worldly possessions. Novalis probably borrowed the idea from Friedrich Schlegel, who gave the term 'cynicism' a positive meaning. See the *Athenæum Fragments* nos. 16 and 35 and *Lyceumsfragment* no. 111, *KA* II, pp. 167, 171, 161.

[3] Another analogy from Brown's physiology, according to which health resides in a balance between overstimulation and lack of stimulation. See *Novalis Vorarbeiten*, no. 235, *Schriften*, II, p. 577: 'Highest receptivity and highest energy united would be the most perfect constitution.'

[4] The indifferentists are those indifferent to relative stimuli, as in no. 53; that is, those stimulated by absolute love.

they trouble no one, so no one troubles them and they are welcome everywhere.

58 The present debate concerning the forms of government is a debate concerning the superiority of mature age or blossoming youth.

59 A republic is the *Fluidum deferens* of youth.[5] Where there is youth there is a republic.

60 With marriage the whole system of thought changes. The married man demands order, security and peace; he wants, as a family, to live within a family, in an orderly household; he seeks genuine monarchy.

61 A prince who does not have the family spirit is no monarch.

62 Yet whence a single, absolute head of a family? What arbitrariness is one then not exposed to?

63 In all relative situations the individual is once and for all exposed to arbitrariness. Even if I go into a desert, is not my essential interest still exposed to the arbitrariness of my individuality? The individual, as such, is by nature subject to *chance*. In a perfect democracy I stand under the arbitrary fate of many; in a representative democracy under a few; and in a monarchy under one.[6]

64 But does not reason demand that every one should be his own lawgiver?[7] Man should obey only his own laws.

65 When Solon and Lycurgus gave humanity laws, true and universal laws, where did they get them? It is to be hoped, from their feeling for humanity and their observation of it. If I am human like them, where do I get my laws? Probably still from the same source. And am I, if I then live according to Solon's and Lycurgus' laws, disloyal to reason? Every true law is my law, whoever proclaims and establishes it. Yet to proclaim and establish such laws, or to

---

[5] *Fluidum deferens*: a fluid capable of conducting electricity.
[6] Here Novalis considers Rousseau's question of which form of government departs least from the general will. He takes issue with Rousseau, who had argued that monarchy is most removed from this ideal because it exposes the public to the arbitrariness of a single individual. See *Contrat social*, III, no. 6. He also takes issue with Friedrich Schlegel, who also argues that democracy is the closest approximation to the general will. See below, p. 102.
[7] A reference to Kant's doctrine of autonomy, and in particular to the third formulation of the categorical imperative, according to which a rational agent should obey only the laws of his own making. See Kant, *Ak.* IV, pp. 432, 440.

observe and describe our original feelings, must not be that easy; otherwise, would we need any special written laws? Must it not therefore be an art? Indeed, even to apply laws presupposes a lengthy training and sharpening of judgement. Why do estates and guilds arise? From the lack of time and energy of the individual. Hitherto not every person could learn, and at the same time practise, all arts and sciences; he could not do everything at once. Labour and the arts became divided. But should that not also be the case with the art of government? According to the general demand of reason, all people should become doctors, poets and so on. With the other arts it is already for the most part customary that people accept them as they are. But with the art of government and philosophy everyone thinks that it is only a matter of boldness; everyone presumes to speak as an expert and has pretensions to practising and becoming masters in them.

66 But the superiority of representative democracy is still undeniable. A natural, perfect human being is a poetic fiction. So what else can we do? Create an artificial one. The most perfect people of a nation complement one another. In such a society the pure spirit of society is awakened. Its decrees are the emanations of such a spirit – and the ideal ruler is realized.

67 First I cast doubt on the most perfect people of the nation and the awakening of the pure spirit.[8] I do not want to appeal even once to a very contradictory experience. It is obvious that one cannot compose from dead matter any living body; and that from the unjust, selfish and partisan nothing just, unselfish and liberal can be fashioned. Of course, that is an error of a partisan majority, and a long time will elapse before one becomes convinced of this simple truth. A majority so composed will elect not the best, but on average only the most narrow-minded and worldly-wise. By the 'narrow-minded' I mean those whose mediocrity has become second nature, the classical model of the great masses. By the 'worldly-wise' I mean the slickest panderers to the great masses. Here no spirit will awaken, least of all a pure one. A great machine will be formed, whose inefficiency is occasionally interrupted only by intrigues. The reins of government will swerve back and forth between the empty

---

[8] Here Novalis questions another aspect of Rousseau's defence of democracy: that the people will be more likely to elect the most deserving and able to high office. See *Contrat social*, III, no. 6.

constitutional plans and their many partisans. The despotism of a single individual is superior to this despotism in that at least one saves time and effort when one has to deal with the government. The former plays with an open deck, while with the latter one does not know who exactly is the government and in which way the most advantageous policy is to be pursued.

If the representative is made more mature and pure when he is raised up to only his level, how much more should this be the case with the individual ruler? If people were that which they should be and can become, then all forms of government would be the same; humanity would be governed in one manner, everywhere according to the original laws of humanity. Then one would choose the most *beautiful, poetic,* and natural form, the form of the family, monarchy. Several masters – several families; one master – one family!

68 Now the perfect democracy and monarchy appear caught in an irresolvable antinomy; the advantage of one is balanced by the opposing advantage of the other. Young people stand on the side of the first, while the more established father of a household stands on the side of the second. Complete divergence in inclination seems to have occasioned this split. One loves change, but not the other. Perhaps in certain years we all love revolutions, free competition, elections and similar democratic phenomena. But for most those years soon pass, and we feel ourselves drawn by a more peaceful world where a central sun leads the dance, and where one prefers to be a planet rather than to fight a destructive battle for the first dance. At the very least, therefore, one should be politically, as well as religiously, tolerant. One should accept the possibility that another rational being could incline differently from ourselves. Such tolerance gradually leads, I fancy, to the sublime conviction of the relativity of every positive form – and of the genuine independence of a mature spirit from every individual form, which to him is nothing but a necessary tool. The time must come when political entheism and pantheism are most intimately united as necessary counterparts.[9]

---

[9] Cf. *Pollen*, no. 74.

Novalis
Christianity or Europe
A Fragment

Those were beautiful, magnificent times, when Europe was a Christian land, when *one* Christianity dwelled on this civilized continent, and when *one* common interest joined the most distant provinces of this vast spiritual empire. Without great worldly possessions *one* sovereign governed and unified the great political forces. Immediately under him stood one enormous guild,[1] open to all, executing his every wish and zealously striving to consolidate his beneficent power. Every member of this society was honoured everywhere. If the common people sought from their clergyman comfort or help, protection or advice, gladly caring for his various needs in return, he also gained protection, respect and audience from his superiors. Everyone saw these elect men, armed with miraculous powers, as the children of heaven, whose mere presence and affection dispensed all kinds of blessings. Childlike faith bound the people to their teachings. How happily everyone could complete their earthly labours, since these holy men had safeguarded them a future life, forgave every sin, explained and erased every blackspot in this life. They were the experienced pilots on the great uncharted seas, in whose shelter one could scorn all storms, and whom one could trust to reach and land safely on the shores of the real paternal world. The wildest and most voracious appetites had to yield with honour and obedience to their words. Peace emanated from them.

Novalis wrote *Christianity or Europe* (*Christenheit oder Europa*) some time between early October and early November 1799. He read it before the romantic circle in Jena on 13 or 14 November of that year.

Novalis' essay is a response to recent historical events. In the summer and autumn of 1799 the future of Europe seemed very bleak. After nearly a decade of war there appeared to be no prospect for peace. In the summer the Grand Alliance formed again to do battle against Napoleon, who toppled the Directory and established a virtual dictatorship in October. The Roman Catholic church was also on the verge of collapse. On 29 August Pope Pius VI died in prison and the French forbade the election of a new pope. These events explain Novalis' fervent messianic hopes, and desperate pleas for peace, at the close of the essay.

The essay was not published in Novalis' lifetime. The first edition of Novalis' *Schriften*, edited by Tieck and Friedrich Schlegel, omitted the essay entirely for fear that it would be misunderstood. The second and third editions (1805, 1815) printed only excerpts. The essay was published in its entirety for the first time in the fourth edition of 1826.

Since the original manuscript has been lost, it is unclear whether the subtitle 'Ein Fragment' is from Novalis' hand or is an addition of his editors or publishers.

[1] 'Guild' (*Zunft*): here Novalis uses the word in an extended sense to refer to the clergy.

They preached nothing but love for the holy, beautiful lady of Christianity[2] who, endowed with divine power, was ready to rescue every believer from the most terrible dangers. They told of saintly men of long ago who had achieved divine honour by withstanding earthly temptations through their devotion to the blessed mother and her heavenly sweet child. These men had become for their living brothers protective beneficent powers, willing helpers in need, intercessors for human frailties, and the powerful friends of humanity, before the heavenly throne. With what serenity people left the beautiful congregations in mysterious churches, adorned with inspiring pictures, filled with sweet fragrances, and animated with heavenly music! In them the consecrated remains of former god-fearing souls were gratefully preserved in precious shrines.

Through glorious miracles and signs the divine goodness and omnipotence, the powerful beneficence of these blessed pious souls, were revealed in relics. In the same way lovers keep a lock of hair or letters of their departed sweethearts, so that they can nurture their sweet ardour until death reunites them. With inner devotion one collected everything that belonged to these cherished souls; everyone regarded themselves as fortunate if they received, or only touched, one of these consoling relics. Now and then divine grace seemed to have favoured some strange image or tomb. From all parts people flocked to it, and they returned with heavenly gifts: peace of soul and health of body.

This mighty peace loving society ardently sought to make all men share its beautiful faith, and sent its disciples to all parts of the globe to preach the gospel and to make the heavenly kingdom the only kingdom on earth. With justice, the wise head of the church resisted impudent developments of the human powers, and untimely discoveries in the realm of knowledge, that were at the expense of the sense for the divine.[3] Thus he prevented the bold thinkers from maintaining publicly that the earth is an insignificant planet,[4] for he knew all too well that, if people lost respect for their

[2] 'Lady of Christianity' (*Frau der Christenheit*): the Virgin Mary, an allusion to the cult of the virgin.
[3] Here Novalis explains rather than justifies the inquisition. As he makes clear toward the close of the essay, the true church consists in genuine freedom. Cf. *Pollen*, no. 74.
[4] 'Bold thinkers': an allusion to Galileo and Copernicus.

earthly residence and home, they would also lose their respect for their heavenly home and race, that they would prefer finite knowledge to an infinite faith, and that they would grow accustomed to despising everything great and miraculous and regard it as the dead effect of natural laws.

All the wise and respected men of Europe assembled at his court. All treasures flowed there; destroyed Jerusalem was avenged and Rome itself had become Jerusalem,[5] the holy residence of divine government on earth. Princes submitted their disputes before the father of Christendom and willingly laid down their crowns and splendour at his feet; indeed, they saw it as their glory to be members of this holy guild and to close the evening of their lives in divine meditation within lonely cloistered walls.[6] The mighty aspirations of all human powers, the harmonious development of all abilities, the immeasurable heights reached by all individuals in all fields of knowledge and the arts, and the flourishing trade in spiritual and earthly wares within all of Europe and as far as the distant Indies – all these show how beneficial, how suitable to the inner nature of man, this government and organization were.

Such were the beautiful chief characteristics of these truly catholic and truly Christian times. But for this splendid realm mankind was not mature or educated enough. It was a first love, which died under the pressure of commercial life, whose devotion was repressed by selfish concerns, and whose bond was later denounced as deceit and delusion and then judged according to later experience. Thus it was for ever destroyed by a large number of Europeans. Accompanied by destructive wars, this great inner schism was a remarkable sign of how harmful culture – or at least how temporarily harmful culture of a certain level – can be for the spiritual sense. That immortal sense can never be destroyed; but it can be dimmed, paralysed, or repressed by other senses.

A longer association of men diminishes their inclinations toward, their faith in their race; and it accustoms them to applying their thought and effort to acquiring the means of material comfort.

---

[5] 'Jerusalem': after the destruction of Jerusalem by the Romans in AD 70, Jewish and Christian eschatology expressed the hope for a second Jerusalem, which would be the holy city for the kingdom of God on earth.

[6] A reference to Charles V, German emperor from 1519 to 1556, who lived after his abdication until his death (1558) in the Spanish cloister San Yuste.

Needs, and the arts of satisfying them, grow more complicated;
greedy man then requires so much time to know and acquire skill
in these arts, that he no longer has time for the quiet collection of
mind for the attentive consideration of the inner world. Should a
conflict arise, his present interest seems to mean more to him; and
so withers the beautiful blossoms of his youth, faith and love,[7]
giving way to the bitter fruits of knowledge and possession. In late
Autumn one looks back upon spring as a childish dream with its
childish hope that the filled granaries will last forever. Some degree
of solitude seems necessary for the growth of the higher sense, and
so too extensive association of people with one another will suffocate
the sacred germs within them and frighten away the gods, who flee
the tumult of social distractions and the business of petty concerns.
Moreover, here we have to deal with times and periods, and is not
oscillation, an alternation of opposed tendencies, essential to them?
Is not a limited duration proper to them, a growth and decay part
of their nature? And is not resurrection, a rejuvenation in new vital
form, to be expected with certainty of them? Progressive, constantly
expanding evolution is the very stuff of history.

What does not now reach perfection will do in a future attempt,
or in another later one. Nothing in the grasp of history is transient;
from innumerable transformations it always proceeds anew to ever
richer forms. Christianity once appeared with full power and splendour; its ruins, and the mere letter of its law, ruled with ever
increasing impotence and mockery until a new world inspiration.
Infinite inertia lay heavily on the complacent guild of the clergy.
They stagnated in the feeling for their authority and material comfort, while the laity snatched from them the torch of experience
and learning, surpassing them with great strides on the path of
education. Forgetting their proper mission to be the first among
men in spirit, knowledge and education, their lower desires went
to their heads. The banality and baseness of their attitude became
all the more offensive because of their clothing and calling. Thus
respect and trust, the basis of this and any empire, gradually col-
lapsed, destroying this guild and silently undermining the real authority of Rome long before the powerful insurrection. Only prudent,
and therefore merely expedient, measures held the corpse of the old

---

[7] 'Faith and love': cf. *Faith and Love* no. 36, and *Mixed Remarks*, no. 122.

constitution together and preserved it from a too hasty dissolution. Among such measures was, for example, the abolition of the right of priests to marry.[8] Such a measure, had it been applied to the similar profession of soldiers,[9] could have given it a formidable coherence and prolonged its life. What was more natural than that a fiery agitator should preach open rebellion against the despotic letter of the previous constitution, and with such great success because he was a member of that guild.[10]

The insurgents rightly called themselves Protestants, for they solemnly protested against any pretension to rule over conscience by an apparently tyrannical and unjust force. For a while they reclaimed their once tacitly surrendered right to investigate, determine and choose their religion. They also established a number of correct principles, introduced a number of laudable things, and abolished a number of corrupt statutes. But they forgot the necessary consequences of their actions: they separated the inseparable, divided the indivisible church, and impiously divorced themselves from the universal Christian union, through and in which alone genuine lasting rebirth was possible. A condition of religious anarchy should be no more than transitional, for the basic need for a number of people to devote themselves to this high vocation, and to make themselves independent of secular power in regard to these concerns, remains pressing and valid.

Establishing consistories and retaining a kind of clergy did not satisfy this need and was not a sufficient substitute.[11] Unfortunately, the princes intervened in this split, and many used the dispute to consolidate and expand their sovereign power and revenue. They were happy to rid themselves of that higher influence and took the new consistories under their paternal

---

[8] The abolition was advocated by the popes since the ninth century but never fully enforced. Celibacy was finally decreed by the Tridentine Council only in 1563.

[9] Whether the military should marry was a much discussed question in Germany in the second half of the eighteenth century. See, for example, J. M. R. Lenz, *Ueber die Soldatenehen* (1776).

[10] An allusion to Luther.

[11] Consistories. Since the Peace of Augsburg (1555), all Protestant lands had consistories, partially autonomous ecclesiastical authorities responsible for the government of the church. They had jurisdiction over the clergy, liturgy and doctrine, and were also responsible for education and matrimonial affairs. The civil sovereign still had important powers over the church, however, especially the right to appoint people to office.

protection and direction. They were zealously concerned to prevent the complete reunion of Protestant churches. With religion sacrilegiously enclosed within the boundaries of the state, the foundation was laid for the gradual undermining of the religious cosmopolitan interest. Religion thus lost its great political influence as a peacemaker, its proper role as the unifying, characteristic principle of Christianity. The religious peace was concluded according to completely mistaken and sacrilegious principles[12] and, through the continuation of so-called Protestantism, something completely contradictory was declared – namely, a permanent revolutionary government.[13]

However, Protestantism is by no means based solely on this pure concept.[14] Luther generally treated Christianity in an arbitrary manner, misunderstood its spirit, and introduced another law and another religion, namely the universal authority of the Bible. In this manner another alien, earthly science – philology – interfered with religious concerns, and its corrosive influence has been unmistakable ever since. From the dark feeling of his error, a large part of the Protestants elevated Luther to the rank of an evangelist and canonized his translation.

This decision was fatal for the religious sense, since nothing destroys its sensibility as much as the dead letter. Previously, this could never have been so harmful, because of the broadness, flexibility and richness of the catholic faith, because of the esoteric stature of the Bible, and because of the holy might of the councils and pope. But now that these antidotes were destroyed, and the absolute popularity of the Bible maintained, the meagre content of the Bible, and its crude abstract scheme of religion, became even more obviously oppressive. It made the revival, penetration and revelation of the holy spirit infinitely more difficult.

---

[12] Novalis alludes to the peace concluded at the Augsburger Reichstag, 25 September 1555, between Ferdinand I and the territorial princes. This gave equal rights to the Protestant and Catholic churches, and held that princes should have the right to determine the religion of their subjects according to the principle *cuius regio, eius religio* (whose government, his religion).

[13] An allusion to the French National Convention of 1793, which declared the Revolution permanent.

[14] 'Pure concept' (*reiner Begriff*): that is, the ideal of liberty of conscience, of protest against all established authority.

Hence the history of Protestantism shows us no more splendid revelations of the heavenly realm. Only its beginning glowed from a passing fire from heaven; but shortly afterwards a withering of the holy sense is apparent. The worldly had now won the upper hand, and the feeling for art suffered in sympathy with religion. Only rarely does a pure, eternal spark of life emerge and a small community form. The spark dies and the community dissipates, swimming along with the stream. Thus it was with Zinzendorf, Jakob Boehme and several others.[15] The moderates got the upper hand, and the time approached for a total atony of the higher organs, the period of practical unbelief. With the Reformation Christianity was done for. From hence forth it existed no more. Catholics and Protestants or Reformers stood further apart from one another in their sectarian conflict than from Moslems and pagans. The remaining Catholic states continued to vegetate, not without vaguely feeling the corrupting influence of the neighbouring Protestant states. The new politics arose during this time: individual powerful states sought to take possession of the vacant universal see, now transformed into a throne.

It seemed humiliating to most princes to trouble themselves with an impotent clergy. They felt for the first time the weight of their physical power on earth; they saw that the heavenly powers were passive when their representatives were abused; and they gradually sought, without their still zealously papist subjects noticing it, to throw off the Roman yoke and to make themselves sovereign on earth. Their uneasy conscience was consoled by clever pastors, who lost nothing by their spiritual children laying claim to the disposition of the church's wealth.

Fortunately for the old order, a new society arose,[16] upon which the dying spirit of the hierarchy seemed to have poured its last

---

[15] Nikolaus Ludwig Graf von Zinzendorf (1700–1760), founder of the Moravian brotherhood, a religious community emphasizing mystical experience and a personal relation to God. Jakob Boehme (1575–1624), a mystical philosopher of nature, much read and admired in romantic circles. Both Zinzendorf and Boehme criticized Protestant orthodoxy for re-establishing the church as an authority between man and God.

[16] 'A new society': an allusion to the Society of Jesus. Founded by Ignaz von Loyola in 1534, this order served the cause of the Counter-Reformation and quickly spread over wide parts of Europe. It also established missions in every continent.

gifts. Arming the old order with new energy, it espoused the cause, more cleverly than before, of the papal realm and its mightier regeneration with remarkable insight and persistence. No such society had been seen before in world history. The old Roman Senate did not conceive its plans of world domination with greater certainty of success. Never before was greater intellect used in the execution of a greater idea. This society will be forever a model for all societies that have an organic longing for infinite expansion and eternal permanence. But it will also be proof that the unguarded moment alone spoils the cleverest undertakings, and that the natural growth of the whole race necessarily represses the artificial growth of one part. Everything individual has its own measure for its abilities; only the capacity of the race as a whole is immeasurable. All plans must fail that do not completely take into account all powers of the race. This society is all the more remarkable as the mother of so-called secret societies – a still immature but certainly important seed of historical growth.[17] The new Lutheranism, not Protestantism, could not have a more dangerous rival. All the magic of the Catholic faith became more powerful in its hands, the treasures of the sciences flowed back into its cell. What was lost in Europe they attempted to regain in other parts of the world – in the most distant west and east – and they sought to appropriate and legitimate the apostolic dignity and vocation. They too did not shirk from the attempt to be popular, knowing well how much Luther owed to his demagogic arts, to his study of the common man. Everywhere they founded schools, infiltrated confessionals, mounted the rostrums, busied the presses; they became poets and philosophers, ministers and martyrs, and remained in the most wonderful unanimity about doctrine and action throughout the vast expanse from America to Europe and to China. With wise selectivity they recruited their future order from their schools. They preached against the Lutherans with destructive zeal, and sought to make the most urgent duty of Catholic Christendom the cruellest persecution of these heretics as the devil's very

In the late eighteenth century it was banished in many European countries, which finally led to its formal dissolution by Pope Clemens XIV in 1773. The order was reinstated in 1814 in the wake of the *Restauration*.

[17] During the late eighteenth century, the Jesuit order was thought to have secret rites. Novalis assumes, incorrectly, that they were the model for such secret societies as the Rosicrucians, Free Masons and *Illuminati*.

companions. It was thanks to them alone that the Catholic states, and especially the papal see, survived the Reformation for so long. If it were not for weak superiors, for the jealousy of princes and other ecclesiastical orders, and for court intrigues and other unusual circumstances, which interrupted their bold course and destroyed this last bulwark of the Catholic establishment, who knows how old the world would still seem? Now this formidable order sleeps in miserable shape at the edges of Europe,[18] perhaps so that from there, under a new name, it will one day spread with new force over its old home, much like the people that protects it.

The Reformation had been a sign of the times. It was significant for all Europe, even if it had broken out publicly only in free Germany. The better minds of all nations had secretly grown mature,[19] and in the delusive self-confidence of their mission they rebelled all the more boldly against obsolete constraint. In the old order the intellectual was instinctively an enemy of the clergy. The intellectual and clerical estate, once they were divided, had to fight a war of extermination, for they were fighting for one position. This division became increasingly prominent, and the intellectuals won more ground the more the history of Europe approached the age of triumphant learning, and the more faith and knowledge came into a more decisive opposition. One saw in faith the source of universal stagnation; and through a more penetrating knowledge one hoped to destroy it. Everywhere the sense for the sacred suffered from various persecutions of its past nature, its temporal personality.

The result of the modern manner of thinking one called 'philosophy',[20] and regarded it as anything opposed to the old order, especially therefore as any whim contrary to religion. The original personal hatred against the Catholic faith gradually became a hatred of the Bible, of Christian belief, and finally of all religion. Furthermore, the hatred of religion extended very naturally and consistently

---

[18] After its official dissolution in 1773, the Jesuit order persisted only in parts of Russia and in Prussia under Friedrich II.

[19] 'Grown mature' (*mündig geworden*): an ironic allusion to Kant's conception of Enlightenment. See Kant's essay 'What is Enlightenment?', *Ak.* VIII, p. 35; *PW*, p. 54.

[20] Philosophy: Jean Baptiste D'Alembert (1717–1783), one of the leading *philosophes* of the French Enlightenment, describes his age as *le siècle de la philosophie*. See his *Essai sur les éléments de Philosophie, Œuvres philosophiques, historiques et littéraires* (Paris, 1805), II, p. 9.

to all objects of enthusiasm, disparaging fantasy and feeling, morality and the love of art, the future and past. This new philosophy placed man of necessity at the top of the series of natural beings, and made the infinite creative music of the cosmos into the uniform clattering of a gigantic mill – a mill in itself driven by and swimming in the stream of chance, without architect or miller, a genuine *Perpetuum mobile*, a self-grinding mill.[21]

One enthusiasm was generously left to the poor human race, and made indispensable for everyone concerned, as a touchstone of the highest education: the enthusiasm for this splendid, magnificent philosophy, and especially for its priests and mystagogues. France was especially fortunate to be the nursery and home of this new faith, which was stuck together out of pieces of mere knowledge. However disreputable poetry was in this new church, there were still a few poets in it, who for the sake of effect, used the old ornaments and lights; in doing so, however, they were in danger of igniting the new world system with old fire. More clever members knew how to throw cold water on their inspired audience. The members were constantly preoccupied with purging poetry from nature, the earth, the human soul and the sciences. Every trace of the sacred was to be destroyed, all memory of noble events and people was to be spoiled by satire, and the world stripped of colourful ornament. Their favourite theme, on account of its mathematical obedience and impudence,[22] was light. They were pleased that it refracted rather than played with its colours, and so they called their great enterprise 'Enlightenment'. One was more thorough with this business in Germany: education was reformed,[23] the old religion was given a new, rational and common sense meaning by carefully cleansing it of everything miraculous and mysterious; all

---

[21] An allusion to the materialism of the French *philosophes*, especially that of Denis Diderot (1713–1784), Claude-Adrian Helvétius (1715–1771), and Paul Heinrich von Holbach (1723–1789). Cf. *Pollen*, no. 113.

[22] 'Impudence' (*Frechheit*): the French *philosophes* called their age, the eighteenth century, the age of Enlightenment, '*siècle des lumières*'. Isaac Newton's analysis of light was often seen as a triumph of the new scientific methodology, which the *philosophes* championed. The source of light was, of course, reason. Novalis speaks of the 'impudence' of light probably because reason was given the right to examine anything, no matter how sacred.

[23] An allusion to the educational reforms of Johann Bernhard Basedow (1724–1790), whose schools emphasized the natural development of the child and useful learning.

scholarship was summoned to cut off taking any refuge in history, which they struggled to ennoble by making it into a domestic and civil portrait of family and morals. God was made into the idle spectator of the great moving drama, performed by intellectuals,[24] whom the poets and actors should entertain and admire at the end.

Rightly, the common people were enlightened with pleasure and educated to an enthusiasm for culture. Hence arose that new European guild: the philanthropists and enlighteners. It is a pity that nature remained so wonderful and incomprehensible, so poetic and infinite, defying all attempts to modernize it. If anywhere there still crept the old superstition of a higher world and the like, alarm was immediately raised from all sides, and wherever possible the dangerous spark would be extinguished by philosophy and wit. Nevertheless, the watchword of the educated was 'tolerance', and especially in France it was synonomous with philosophy.

The history of modern unbelief is extremely remarkable, and the key to all the monstrous phenomena of the modern age. Only in this century, and especially in the latter half, has it begun and grown in little time to an immense size and variety. A second Reformation,[25] a more comprehensive and proper one, was unavoidable. It would have to affect that country that was most modernized and that had laid in an asthenic state longest because of a lack of freedom. Long ago the supernatural fire would have been released and would have foiled the clever schemes of enlightenment if worldly pressure and influence had not come to their rescue. But at the very moment when a dispute arose between the intellectuals and government, and among the enemies of religion and their whole confederacy, religion had to step forward again as a third leading, mediating party. Every one of its friends should now recognize and proclaim this role, if it is not already clear enough. That the time of the resurrection has come, and that precisely the events that seemed to be directed against its revival and to complete its demise have become the propitious signs of its regeneration – this cannot be denied by the historical mind.

[24] A reference to deism, a prevalent doctrine in the late eighteenth century, especially popular among free thinkers, *philosophes* and *Aufklärer*. According to deism, God does not interfere with the operations of nature after its creation.
[25] A second Reformation: the French Revolution.

True anarchy is the creative element of religion. From the destruction of everything positive it lifts up its glorious head as the creator of a new world.[26] If nothing more binds him, man climbs to heaven by his own powers. The higher faculties, the original germ for the transformation of the earth, free themselves from the uniform mediocre mixture, from the complete dissolution of all human talents and powers. The spirit of god hovers over the waters,[27] and a heavenly island becomes visible over the receding waves as the dwelling place of the new man, as the birthplace of eternal life.

Calmly and impartially, the genuine observor considers the new revolutionary times. Does not the revolutionary seem like Sisyphus to him? Now he has reached the summit only for his mighty burden to roll down again. It will never stay on top unless an attraction toward heaven keeps it balanced there. All of your pillars are too weak if your state retains its tendency toward earth. But link it through a higher longing to the heights of heaven and give it a connection to the cosmos, then you will have a never tiring spring in it and all your efforts will be richly rewarded. I refer you to history. Search in its instructive continuum for similar times and learn to use the magic wand of analogy.[28]

France defends a worldly Protestantism. Should now worldly Jesuits arise and renew the history of the last centuries? Should the Revolution remain French, as the Reformation was Lutheran? Should Protestantism again be established – contrary to nature – as a revolutionary government? Should the dead letter be replaced only by another dead letter? Do you seek the seed of corruption also in the old constitution, the old spirit? And do you think you know a better constitution, a better spirit? Oh! that the spirit of spirits fill you and lead you away from this foolish attempt to mould and direct history and humanity. Is history not independent, autonomous, virtually infinitely lovable and prophetic? To study it, to follow it, to learn from it, to keep step with it, faithfully to follow its promises and suggestions – this no one has thought of.

---

[26] 'Destruction of everything positive' (*Vernichtung alles Positiven*): here used in the sense of the destruction of everything established or laid down by authority.

[27] An intentional Biblical allusion: Moses 1: 2.

[28] 'Magic wand of analogy' (*Zauberstab der Analogie*): for Novalis, as for all the romantics, analogy was regarded as crucial for the study of nature and history. Only analogy could grasp the unity of these realms.

In France much has been done for religion, in not only one of its forms but in all its countless forms, by depriving it of its civil rights and by granting it merely the right of asylum. As an insignificant alien orphan it must first win back hearts and be loved everywhere before it is publicly worshipped and combined with worldly things to give friendly advice and heart to the spirit. The attempt of that great iron mask, which went by the name of Robespierre,[29] to make religion the middle point and heart of the republic remains historically remarkable. Equally remarkable is the coldness with which theophilanthropy,[30] the mysticism of the new Enlightenment, has been received, not to mention the conquests of the Jesuits,[31] and the closer relation to the Orient with the new politics.[32]

Concerning the other European countries, except Germany, one can only prophesy that *peace* will bring a new higher religious life and will soon consume all other worldly interests. In Germany, though, one can point out with complete certainity the traces of a new world. In its slow but sure way Germany advances before the other European countries. While the other countries are preoccupied with war, speculation and partisanship, the German diligently educates himself to be the witness of a higher epoch of culture; and such progress must give him a great superiority over other countries in the course of time. In the sciences and arts one perceives a powerful ferment. An infinite amount of spirit is developed. New fresh mines are being tapped. Never were the sciences in better hands, and never have they aroused greater expectations. The most various aspects of things are traced; nothing is left untouched, unjudged or unexamined. No stone is left unturned. Writers

[29] An allusion to Robespierre's cult of the supreme being, which was inaugurated in Paris in June 1794. The purpose of the cult was to give a religious sanction to the fundamental values of the Revolution. The iron mask is an allusion to the famous mysterious prisoner of the Bastille during the reign of Louis XIV, who wore a mask to conceal his identity. According to Voltaire in his *Siècle de Louis XIV*, he was regarded as the brother of the French king.

[30] 'Theophilanthropy' (*Theophilantropie*): a religious society under this name was formed in Paris in 1796 with the purpose of maintaining religion. It emphasized the rational aspects of Christianity.

[31] 'New conquests of the Jesuits': it is unclear what specific events are intended, especially because the order had been disbanded. In 1794, however, some ex-Jesuits attempted to resurrect their order as the *Société du Sacré Coeur*.

[32] 'Closer relations to the Orient': probably an allusion to Napoleon's campaign in Egypt, which took place in 1798–9.

become more original and powerful; every monument of history, every art, every science finds new friends and is embraced and made more fruitful. A diversity without parallel, a wonderful depth, a brilliant polish, extensive knowledge and a rich powerful fantasy can be found everywhere and are often boldly joined together. A powerful intuition of creative wilfulness, of boundlessness, of infinite diversity, of sacred originality and the omnipotence of inner humanity appears to stir everywhere. Woken from the morning dream of helpless childhood, one part of the human race exercises its powers on the vipers that encircle its cradle and attempt to deprive it of the use of its limbs.[33] These are still intimations, unconnected and crude, but they betray to the historical eye a universal individuality, a new history, a new humanity, the sweetest embrace of a young surprised church and a loving god, not to mention the inner reception of a new messiah in all his thousand forms. Who does not feel hope with sweet shame? The new born will be the image of its father, a new golden age with dark infinite eyes, a prophetic, miraculous, healing, consoling time that generates eternal life. It will be a great age of reconciliation, of a redeemer who, like a true genius, will be at home with men, believed but not seen. He will be visible to the believer in countless forms: consumed as bread and wine, embraced as a lover, breathed as air, heard as word and song, and as death received into the heart of the departing body with heavenly joy and the highest pains of love.

Now we stand high enough to smile back amiably upon those former times and to recognize in those strange follies remarkable crystallizations of historical matter. Thankfully we should shake hands with those intellectuals and philosophers; for this delusion had to be exhausted for the sake of posterity and the scientific view of things had to be legitimated. More charming and colourful, poetry stands like an ornate India in contrast to the cold, dead pointed arches of an academic reason.[34] So that India might be

---

[33] According to the classical myth, Hercules, son of Zeus and Alkeme, killed snakes in his cradle, which had been sent by Hera to strangle him. The myth was popular among the romantic circle, who used it to express their longing for social, political and cultural reform. Thus Friedrich Schlegel wanted to call their journal *Herkules* rather than *Athenæum*. See Friedrich to August Wilhelm and Caroline Schlegel, 28 November, 1797, *KA* XXIII, p. 43.

[34] 'An ornate India': Novalis held the popular romantic view that India is the birthplace of poetry. The chief instigator of this doctrine was Georg Forster, whose translation of Kalidasas' *Sakontala* appeared in 1790.

warm and magnificent in the centre of our planet, a cold, frozen sea, desolate cliffs and fog, rather than the starry sky and a long night, had to make both poles inhospitable. The deeper meaning of mechanics troubled these hermits in the desert of the understanding. The excitement of their first discovery overwhelmed them, the old order revenged itself on them. With wonderful self-denial they sacrificed the most holy and beautiful things in the world to their first self-awareness. They were the first to recognize and proclaim again the sanctity of nature, the infinitude of art, the necessity of knowledge, the respect for the secular, and the omnipresence of the truly historical. They put an end to a higher, more widespread and horrible reign of phantoms than they themselves believed.

Only through a more exact knowledge of religion will one be able to judge the dreadful products of a religious sleep, those dreams and deliria of the sacred organ. Only then will one be able to assess properly the importance of such a gift. Where there are no gods, phantoms rule. The period of the genesis of European phantoms, which also rather completely explains their form, is the period of transition from Greek mythology to Christianity. So come then, you philanthropists and encyclopædists, into the peace making lodge and receive the kiss of brotherhood! Strip off your grey veil and look with young love at the miraculous magnificence of nature, history and humanity. I want to lead you to a brother who shall speak to you,[35] so that your hearts will open again, and so that your dormant intuition,[36] now clothed with a new body, will again embrace and recognize what you feel and what your ponderous earthly intellect cannot grasp.

This brother is the pulse of the new age. Who has felt him does not doubt its coming, and with a sweet pride in his generation steps forward from the mass into the new band of disciples. He has made a new veil for the saints,[37] which betrays their heavenly figure by fitting so close and yet which conceals them more chastely than before. The veil is for the virgin what the spirit is for the body:

---

[35] 'A brother': a reference to Schleiermacher, whose *Speeches on Religion* was a decisive influence on Novalis during the composition of his essay. See Schlegel to Schleiermacher, end of October, 1799, *Novalis Schriften* IV, p. 641.

[36] Dormant intuition (*abgestorbene Ahndung*): a reference to Schleiermacher's doctrine that the divine is known only through intuition, *eine Anschauung des Unisums*.

[37] 'A new veil for the saints' (*neuen Schleier für die Heiligen*): a play on Schleiermacher's name, which literally means 'veilmaker'.

its indispensable organ, whose folds are the letters of her sweet annunciation. The infinite play of these folds is a secret music, for language is too wooden and impudent for the virgin, whose lips open only for song. To me it is nothing more than the solemn call to a new assembly, the powerful beating of wings of a passing angelic herald. They are the first labour pains; let everyone prepare himself for the birth.

Physics has now reached its heights, and we can now more easily survey the scientific guild. In recent times the poverty of the external sciences has become more apparent the more we have known about them. Nature began to look more barren; and, accustomed to the splendour of our discoveries, we saw more clearly that it was only a borrowed light, and that with our known tools and methods we would not find or construct the essential, or that which we were looking for. Every enquirer must admit that one science is nothing without the other. Hence there arose those attempts at mystification of the sciences;[38] and the wonderful essence of philosophy sprang into being as a pure scientific element for a symmetrical basic norm of the sciences.[39] Others brought the concrete sciences into new relations, promoted their interchange, and sought to clarify their natural historical classification. And so it goes on. It is easy to estimate how promising might be this intimacy with the external and internal world, with the higher development of the understanding, and with the knowledge of the former and stimulation and culture of the latter. It is also easy to estimate how, under these circumstances, the storm will clear and the old heaven and the yearning for it – a living astronomy – must again appear.

Now let us turn to the political drama of our times. The old and new order are locked in struggle. The inadequacy and destitution of the previous political institutions has become apparent in frightful phenomena. If only the historical end of the war were, as in the

---

[38] 'Attempts at mystification of the sciences' (*Mystificationsversuche der Wissenschaften*): a reference to the *Naturphilosophie* of Schelling and others, which attempts to know the whole of nature through an intellectual intuition.

[39] 'Essence of philosophy' (*Wesen der Philosophie*): an allusion to Fichte's 'science of knowledge' (*Wissenschaftslehre*), which Novalis admired and characterized as the 'science of sciences' (*Wissenschaften der Wissenschaften*). See *Allgemeine Brouillon*, no. 56, *Schriften*, III, p. 249. The symmetrical basic norm for the sciences (*symmetrischen Grundfigur der Wissenschaften*) is probably the first principle of the *Wissenschaftslehre*, the proposition of identity '*Ich=Ich*'.

sciences, a more intimate and varied contact and connection
between the European states! If only there were a new stirring of
hitherto slumbering Europe! If only Europe wanted to awaken
again! And if only a state of states, a new political theory of science,
were impending.[40] Should perhaps the hierarchy, the symmetrical
basic figure of the sciences, be the principle of the union of states
as an intellectual intuition of the political ego? It is impossible that
worldly powers come into equilibrium by themselves; only a third
element, that is worldly and supernatural at the same time, can
achieve this task. No peace can be concluded among the conflicting
powers. All peace is only an illusion, only a temporary truce. From
the standpoint of the cabinets, and of common opinion, no unity
is conceivable.

Both sides have great and necessary claims and must put them
forward, driven by the spirit of the world and humanity. Both are
indestructible powers within the human breast. On the one hand,
there is veneration of the old world, loyalty to the historical constitution, love of the ancestral monuments and of the old glorious
royal family, and joy in obedience. On the other hand, there is the
rapturous feeling of freedom, the unlimited expectations of a more
potent sphere of action, the pleasure in what is new and young,
the informal contact with all fellow citizens, the pride in human
universality, the joy in personal rights and in the property of the
whole community, and the strong civic sense. Neither side should
hope to destroy the other. All conquests mean nothing, for the inner
capitol of that kingdom lies not behind earthen walls and cannot
be stormed.

Who knows whether there has been enough war, whether it will
ever cease, unless one seizes the palm branch, which a spiritual
power alone can offer. Blood will continue to flow in Europe until
the nations recognize their terrible madness. This will continue to
drive them into circles until, moved and calmed by sacred music,
they step before their past alters in a motley throng. Then they will
undertake works of peace, celebrating with hot tears a great banquet
of love as a festival of peace on the smoking battlefields. Only
religion can reawaken Europe, make the people secure, and install

---

[40] 'Political theory of science' (*politische Wissenschaftslehre*): Novalis' term for a political philosophy dealing with first principles, the fundamentals of all politics.

Christianity with new magnificence in its old peace making office, visible to the whole world.

Do not the nations possess everything of man – except his heart – his sacred organ? Do they not become friends, as people do around the coffin of their beloved? Do they not forget all hostility when divine pity speaks to them – and when one misfortune, one lament, one feeling, fills their eyes with tears? Are they not seized by sacrifice and surrender with almighty power, and do they not long to be friends and allies?

Where is that old, dear belief in the government of God on earth, which alone can bring redemption? Where is that sacred trust of men for one another, that sweet devotion in the effusions of an inspired mind, that all-embracing spirit of Christianity?

Christianity has three forms. One is the creative element of religion, the joy in all religion. Another is mediation in general, the belief in the capacity of everything earthly to be the wine and bread of eternal life.[41] Yet a third is the belief in Christ, his mother and the saints. Choose whichever you like. Choose all three. It is indifferent: you are then Christians, members of a single eternal, ineffably happy community.

The old catholic faith, the last of these forms, was applied Christianity come to life. Its omnipresence in life, its love for art, its deep humanity, the sanctity of its marriages, its philanthropic sense of community, its joy in poverty, obedience and loyalty, all make it unmistakable as genuine religion and contain the basic features of its constitution. It is purified through the stream of time; and in indivisible union with the other two forms of Christianity it will bless the earth.

Its accidental form is as good as destroyed. The old papacy lies in the grave, and for a second time Rome has become a ruin.[42] Should not Protestantism finally cease and give way to a new more lasting church?[43] The other parts of the world wait for Europe's

---

[41] On the doctrine of mediation, see *Pollen*, nos. 73 and 74, and *Universal Brouillon*, no. 398.

[42] 'For a second time Rome has become a ruin': an allusion to the events of February 1798 when Rome was sacked by French troops under Marshall Berthier. Pope Pius VI was taken prisoner and died 29 August, 1799.

[43] 'A new, more lasting church': the idea of a new church was a common theme of the time. In his *Religion within the Limits of Reason Alone*, Kant wrote of the idea of a church to unify all mankind in perpetuity, and that was to be a visible

reconciliation and resurrection to join with it and become fellow citizens of the kingdom of heaven. Should there not be soon again in Europe a number of truly sacred minds? Should not all kindred religious minds be full of yearning to see heaven on earth? And should they not eagerly meet to sing a holy chorus?

Christianity must again become alive and active, and again form a visible church without regard to national boundaries.[44] Once again it must receive into its bosom all hungry souls and become the mediator of the old and new world.

Christianity must again pour the old cornucopia of blessings over the nations. It will rise again from the bosom of a venerable European council, and the business of religious awakening will be pursued according to a comprehensible divine plan. No one will again protest against Christian and worldly coercion, for the essence of the church will be genuine freedom,[45] and all necessary reforms under its direction will be performed as peaceful and formal processes of state.

When and how soon? That is not to be asked. Have patience. It will and must come, the sacred age of eternal peace,[46] where the new Jerusalem will be the capitol. Until then be calm and brave amid the dangers of the age. Companions of my faith, proclaim by word and dead the divine gospel! Remain loyal to the true, eternal faith until death.

representation of the kingdom of God on earth. (See *Ak.* VI, p. 101). Hölderlin expressed a similar ideal in the first part of his *Hyperion*, *Sämtliche Werke*, I/I, p. 607. And in the fourth of his *Speeches*, Schleiermacher wrote of 'the inner, true church' (*KGA* II/I, pp. 269–70).

[44] 'A visible church'. Cf. Kant's definition in *Religion*: 'An ethical community under divine moral legislation is a church, which, in so far as it is not an object of possible experience, is called an invisible church (a mere idea of the union of all the righteous under a divine, immediate but moral world-government, as it serves as the model for every such government to be created by man). The visible church is the real unification of human beings into a whole that corresponds to that ideal' (*Ak.* VI, p. 101).

[45] 'Genuine freedom' (*ächte Freiheit*): the third characteristic of Kant's true, visible church. See *Ak.* VI, p. 102. This passage shows that Novalis did not intend to conflate church and state. Cf. *Pollen* no. 74.

[46] Cf. Lessing's *Education of the Human Race*: 'It will certainly come, the time of a new gospel' (*Sämmtliche Schriften*, XIII). In Novalis' notebooks from 1799 to 1800 Lessing is frequently mentioned. Novalis had plans to write a second half to Lessing's classic work. See *Fragmente und Studien*, *Schriften* III, p. 669, no. 609, and III, p. 682, no. 644.

Novalis
Fragments from the Notebooks

Philosophical Studies (1795–6)

421 The state is a person, just like the individual. What the individual is to himself the state is to individuals. States will differ among themselves as long as people do too. In essence the state is always the same, just as man always is.

497 Action according to principles is not valuable on account of the principles but on account of the constitution of the soul that it presupposes.[1] Whoever can act according to principles must be a worthy person. But his principles do not make him a worthy person. What does so is only what his principles are according to him: concepts of his manner of acting, forms of thought of his being.

617 No universal system of political economy is possible.

620 Only improvements in morals and character are real improvements. Everything else is only fashion, change, insignificant improvements.[2]

623 Dreams of the future – is a kingdom of a thousand years possible? – Will all vices ever disappear? Only when the education to reason is perfected.

The *Philosophical Studies* (*Philosophische Studien*), were probably written around 1795–6. They contain Novalis' excerpts of, and reflections on, Fichte's writings, which he had studied intensively since 1794. See *Schriften*, II, pp. 104–296.
The *Mixed Remarks* (*Vermischte Bemerkungen*) were the early draft for *Pollen*. See *Schriften*, II, pp. 412–70. Although the important fragment no. 122 was crossed out by Novalis, this was probably only on stylistic grounds, since it puts forward views he published and explicitly advanced elsewhere.
The Sketches (*Entwürte*) come from various collections of fragments that Novalis wrote in the first eight months of 1798. These collections include *Logologische Fragmente, Poëticismen, Teplitzerfragmente, Anekdoten* and the *Vermischte Fragmente*. See *Schriften*, II, pp. 522–61. These collections contain Novalis' reflections on a wide variety of topics: politics, philosophy, art, literature, mathematics and the philosophy of nature.
The *Universal Brouillon* (*Das Allgemeine Brouillon*) comprises some 1151 jottings that Novalis wrote down during his student years at Freiburg, September 1798 to early March 1799. Novalis' sketches were intended as materials for an encyclopedia that would unify all the sciences and lead to a single universal science. See *Schriften*, III, pp. 242–478.
Fragments and Studies (*Fragmente und Studien*) were Novalis' last collection of fragments, which he wrote from May 1799 to late autumn 1800. See *Schriften* III, pp. 556–694.
The numbering of all fragments is editorial and follows the critical edition.

[1] Here Novalis endorses Schiller's critique of Kant's moral philosophy: that the end of moral action is not to follow a certain principle but to become a certain kind of person. See Schiller, *Anmut und Würde*, *NA* xx, p. 283.
[2] Cf. *Pollen*, nos. 28, 32.

625 Do the people owe the aristocracy nothing? Are they mature enough to dispense with them?

652 Property in our legal sense is only a positive concept, i.e. it will end with the state of barbarism. Positive right must have a positive foundation a priori. Property is that which gives one the possibility of expressing freedom in the sensible world.

Mixed Remarks

122 Where the true majority decides, power rules over form; the converse is the case when the minority has the upper hand.

One cannot reproach the theoretical politicians for their boldness. It has not dawned on any of them to see whether monarchy and democracy, as elements of a true universal state, can and must be united.

A true democracy is an absolute minus state. A true monarchy is an absolute plus state.[3] The constitution of the monarchy is the character of the ruler. Its guarantee is his will.

Democracy, in the usual sense, is essentially not different from monarchy; its only that here the monarch consists in a mass of people. True democracy is Protestantism, the political state of nature, just as Protestantism in the narrow sense is the religious state of nature.

The moderate form of government is half state and half state of nature – an artificial and very fragile machine – hence totally contrary to all right thinking minds. Yet it is the hobby horse of our day. If this machine could only be transformed into a living, autonomous creature, then the greatest problem would be resolved. The unruliness of nature and the forced order of artifice would interpenetrate one another and be resolved into spirit. It is spirit that makes them both fluid. Spirit is always poetic. The poetic state is the true perfect state.

A very spiritual state would be poetic by itself. The more spirit, and spiritual interchange in the state, then the more it approaches the poetic form; then the more happy everyone will be out of love

---

[3] Absolute minus, absolute plus: Novalis applies the terminology of Schelling's *Naturphilosophie*, which analysed nature in terms of polarity, positive and negative forces.

for the beautiful great individual that is the state; then the more the individual will limit his own demands and be ready to make all necessary sacrifices; then the less the state will need him; and then the more akin will be the spirit of the state and that of some exemplary person, who has pronounced only a single law: be as good and as poetic as possible.

Sketches

104 In the past everything was an appearance of the spirit. Now we see nothing but a dead repetition that we do not understand. The meaning of the hieroglyph is missing. We still live from the fruit of better times.

105 The world must be romanticized. Then one will again find the original sense. Romanticizing is nothing more than a qualitative involution.[4] In this operation the lower self is identified with a better self. In the same manner we are such a qualitative series of powers. This operation is still completely unknown. When I give the commonplace a higher meaning, the customary a mysterious appearance, the known the dignity of the unknown, the finite the illusion of the infinite, I romanticize it. The operation is the converse for the higher, unknown, mystical and infinite; through this connection it becomes logarithimized. It receives a customary expression. Romantic philosophy. *Lingua romana*. Reciprocal elevation and debasement.

194 The first human being is a seer. To him everything appears to be a spirit. What are children but the first human beings? The fresh vision of a child is more fanciful than the presentiment of the most resolute seer.

195 It is only because of the weakness of our organs, and of our self-reflection, that we do not see into a fairy world. All fairy tales are only dreams of that home that is everywhere and nowhere. The

---

[4] 'A qualitative involution' (*qualitative Potenzirung*): Novalis uses a mathematical analogy to express the idea of the progressive intensification of a quality. In mathematics involution is the raising of a quantity to any given power. The terms *Potenzirung* and *Potenzen* were also prevalent in Schelling's *Naturphilosophie*. They express the ideas that nature consists in living power (*Kraft*), and that it has increasing degrees of organization and development (*Potenzen*). The more intense the power the higher the degree of organization and development.

higher powers in us that once, as genius, executed our will, are now muses that refreshen us with sweet memories during this dreary journey.

196. All poetry[5] interrupts our usual condition – our everyday life; almost like slumber, it renews us, and so keeps active our feeling for life.

269. Our states are almost nothing but legal institutions, organizations for defence. Educational establishments – academies – and societies for art: there are unfortunately none of these, or at best they are very deficient. People must therefore provide them through special coalitions. Even the lack of social organizations should be supplied through private connections.[6]

381 The heart is the key to the world and life. One lives in this helpless condition to love, and to be committed to others. Through imperfection one is capable of receiving the influence of *others*; and this alien influence is the goal. *In sickness* only *others should* and *can* help us. So is Christ, seen from this *standpoint*, certainly the *key to the world*.

The Universal Brouillon: Materials for an Encyclopædia

189 Politics. The complete citizen lives entirely in the state; he has no property outside the state. International law is the beginning of universal legislation for a universal state. On alliances – peace treaties – negotiations – unions – guarantees.[7]

Republic and monarchy are completely fused through an act of union. There must be several necessary steps with states, though they are joined through a union.

249 *Freedom* and *equality* make the highest character of the republic, a genuine harmony.

---

[5] Poetry (*Poesie*). Like Schlegel, Novalis uses the term in a very broad sense to refer to not only poetry (*Dichtung*) but any form of literature.

[6] Social organizations: *Polizeianstalten*, literally 'Police institutions'. In eighteenth-century German, however, *Polizei* refers to all matters of government policy relating to social welfare, such as roadworks, sanitation, public buildings and poor relief.

[7] Novalis seems to have in mind Kant's discussion in *Perpetual Peace*. See especially the 'Second Definitive Article': 'The right of nations shall be based upon a federation of free states.' See *Ak.* VIII, pp. 354–7; *PW*, p. 102.

250 A perfect constitution – determination of *the body of the state*, the soul of the state, the spirit of the state – makes all written laws superfluous. If the members are exactly determined, the laws are obvious. As long as the members are still not perfect members, still not exactly determined, there must be laws. With true culture in general the number of laws decreases. Laws are *the complement of deficient natures* and beings, and are therefore synthetic. If we determine more exactly the essence of a spirit, we do not need any more spiritual laws.[8]

Ethics. On the *moral law*. With perfect self-knowledge, knowledge of the world, and more perfect determination of myself and the world, the moral law disappears and the description of moral nature replaces the moral law. Laws are the data from which I *compose* my descriptions.

251 We are more closely joined with the invisible than the visible (the *mystical republican*).

261 Politics. Instinctively, the state has always been *divided* according to the *relative* insight into, and knowledge of, human nature. The state has always been a macroandropos.[9] The guilds = the members and individual powers; the estates = the powers. The aristocracy was the moral power; the priests, the religious power; the intellectuals, the intellect; and *the king, the will*. *Allegorical man*.

262 Politics. Resolution of the main political problem. Is a political life possible? Are unifications of opposed *political elements* possible a priori?[10] The *state of genius* (reunion of opposites).

306 Popular pedagogics. A people is like a child, an individual pedagogic problem. This or that people has, like this or that child, a special talent; but the others must not be forgotten in the attempt to develop this one. A talent cultivated in isolation withers early, because it lacks nourishment. This nourishment can come from only

---

[8] Here Novalis follows Fichte's view that laws are appropriate for only a lower stage of moral development. See Fichte, *Lectures on the Vocation of a Scholar*, *Werke*, VI, p. 306; *EPW*, p. 156.

[9] Macroandropos: literally, a great man, or man writ large, in Greek. This is the opposite of the idea that man is the microcosm of the universe.

[10] A Kantian-Fichtean formulation for the political problem. In his *Prolegomena to any Future Metaphysics* Kant raises the questions 'Is mathematics possible?', 'Is the pure science of nature possible?', and 'Is metaphysics possible?'. Under the influence of Fichte, Novalis poses these problems in terms of a unification of opposites. Fichte held that knowledge would be possible only if there were some point of unity between subject and object, which had opposing characteristics.

other talents. All of the talents make up, as it were, one body. If the body suffers at the expense of a single member, then afterwards that member suffers indirectly too.

320 The doctrine of the future for humanity. Everything that is predicated of God contains *the doctrine of the future for humanity*. Every machine, which lives from the great *Perpetuo mobili*, should itself become a *Perpetuum mobile*. Every person, who now lives from and through God, should himself become God.[11]

326 Politics. Man has attempted to make the state a cushion for his laziness; yet the state should be exactly the opposite. It should be the armature of his total activity. Its goal is to make man absolutely *powerful* – and not absolutely weak – not the laziest but the most active being. The state does not spare man any pains but increases his troubles to infinity – of course, not without increasing his power to infinity. The path to peace only goes through the temple (the territory) of comprehensive activity.

394 Political economy. Philosophy of *accise*.[12] Never is a population too large. The purposive, systematic employment of the mass of people is the chief problem of the politician. No class is displaced without another suffering. The more taxes the more the needs of the state, and so the more perfect it becomes. There should not be any tax that is not a gain for the individual. How much more must a person outside the state spend to have security, justice, good roads, etc. Only he who does not live *in* the state in the sense in which a person lives in his beloved will complain about taxes. Taxes are the greatest advantage. One can consider taxes as the payment of the state, that is, a very powerful, very fair, very clever and very amusing person.

Politics. The need of the state is the most pressing need of a person. To become and remain a person one has need of *a state*. The state has natural rights and duties just as the individual person. A person without a state is a savage. All culture springs from the relationship of a person with the state. The more cultivated one is, the more one is the *member* of a cultured state. There are *savage* states. There are cultivated states – moral and immoral – states of genius and philistine states. Education and development of the state. States educate themselves or are *educated* by other states.

[11] See Fichte, *Lectures on the Vocation of a Scholar*, *Werke* VI, p. 300; *EPW*, p. 152.
[12] *Accise*: a toll or tax.

398 Politics. The doctrine of a mediator bears application to politics.[13] Here too the monarch – or government officials – are *representatives of the state, mediators of the state*. What is true there is also true here. Here the converse of the physiological principle is true: the more spiritual and lively the members are, the more lively, the more personal the state. From every genuine citizen the *genius of the state* shines forth – just as in a religious community a personal God appears in a thousand forms. The state and God, like every spiritual being, appear not *singly*, but in a thousand, various forms. Only in pantheism does God appear *whole*; and only in pantheism is God *completely* everywhere, in every individual. So for the great 'I', the everyday 'I' and the everyday 'Thou' are only supplements.[14] Every 'Thou' is a supplement of the great 'I'. We are not at all the 'I' – but we can and should become it. We are germs to become the 'I'. We should transform everything into a 'Thou' – into a second 'I'; only by this means do we raise ourselves to the great 'I', which is the *one* and the all at the same time.

584 Political economy. Every community should have a treasury. A notice board in every city – a newspaper in the district.

762 How is community possible among people, if it is possible?

Absolute equality is the highest work of art – the ideal – but it is not natural. By *nature* people are only relatively equal, which is the old inequality. The stronger has also a stronger right. Likewise, people are not free by nature, but more or less bound to one another.

Few human beings are human beings; hence the rights of man are extremely *inappropriate* if they are represented as actually present.

Be a person, then human rights will come to you.

782 The whole state boils down to representation.

All of representation rests upon making present what is not present. (The magical powers of fiction.) My faith and love rests upon a *faith in representation*. Hence the assumptions: eternal peace is

---

[13] Cf. *Pollen* no. 74, *Universal Brouillon* no. 781.

[14] 'I' (*Ich*): a central term of Fichte's early philosophy, the 1794 *Wissenschaftslehre*. The pure 'I' or ego refers to the subject presupposed in all acts of knowing. Since it is the condition under which anything is individuated, determined to be this or that particular thing, it cannot be individuated itself and is therefore universal, the same in every individual subject. Hence Novalis remarks that the everyday 'I' and 'Thou' are only its parts or supplements.

already here, God is among us, here is America or nowhere, the golden age is here, we are magicians, we are moral, and so on.

857 Philosophy is really homesickness, *the urge to be at home everywhere in the world.*

1059 Of the Mercantile Spirit. The spirit of trade is the *spirit of the world.* It is absolutely the *splendid* spirit. It sets everything in motion and binds it together. It awakens countries and cities, nations and works of art. It is the spirit of culture, and the perfection of the human race. The *historical* spirit of trade, which slavishly conforms to *given needs* and the circumstances of time and place, is only a bastard of the true, *creative* spirit of trade.

1106 Marriage is for politics what the lever is for mechanics. The state consists not in individual persons, but in couples and societies. The estates of marriage are the estates of the state – man and wife. The woman is the so-called *uncultivated* part.

There is an ideal of this *estate* – Rousseau saw it exclusively in his apology for natural man. Rousseau's *philosophizing* is in general a feminine philosophy or theory of femininity – views from the female standpoint. Now the woman has become a slave.

1128 The dissolution of the constitution of the estates must be necessary when true inequality – disparity and corruption of the original estates – arises.

This can happen in various ways. 1. When the state of nature loses its purpose. 2. When this happens within the state of society. 3. When one grows or diminishes too much. 4. When the efficacy of one and the reciprocity of the other are not proportional. 5. When one part of the estate goes over to another without maintaining its rights and vice versa.

1129 For the sake of economy there is only one king. Should we not all have to be economical, we would all be kings.

1146 State and church stand and fall together. The philosophers or systematic thinkers are necessary – monarchists and the religious.

Fragments and Studies

21 A novel should be poetry through and through. Like philosophy, poetry is a harmonic mood of our spirit where everything is beautified, and where everything perceives its proper aspect, its suitable *accompaniment* and *environment.* In a genuine poetic book everything

seems so *natural* – yet so wonderful. One believes it could not be otherwise and that so far one has only dreamed in the world. Only now does one's proper sense for the world become alive. All memory and presentiment appear to come from this source – and that present moment too when one is caught in an illusion, those special hours when one, as it were, hides oneself in all objects that one considers, and when one feels the infinite, the inexpressible and simultaneous sensations of a harmonious plurality.

33 It seems to me that in our day one desire is universal: the desire to conceal the external world in an artistic husk, to be ashamed of open nature and to attribute to it a spiritual power through concealment and secrecy. This desire is certainly romantic – only not expedient for childlike innocence and clarity. This is especially noticeable in sexual relations.

89 In the state all civil law and property must be able to be documented. What does not *expressly* belong to someone belongs to the state. Like marriage, the state will be sealed under ecclesiastical sanction. It is a personal bond. What a private person has he receives from the *state*. Taxes are expenses to be reimbursed – payment of the state.

92 Women know nothing of the relationships in their community. Only through their husbands are they connected with state, church, public, etc. They live in a state of nature.[15]

106 State, church, marriage, society and public are mere concepts – that have the most appropriate reference to our proper *human* relations, that is, to our continued existence in an infinite association of rational beings.

126 Man is among animals, or in nature, what the state and philosophy are in their relations – the associative being.[16]

155 Politics is an erudite historical science and art.

160 The state is too little made *known* with us. There should be state heralds among us, preachers of patriotism. Nowadays most compatriots are on a very low, almost hostile footing with the state.

214 What forms a person but the *history of their life*? And so what forms the greatest people other than *world history*?

Many people live better with the past and future than the *present*.

---

[15] This is more a description than a prescription. Cf. *Brouillon*, no. 1106.
[16] Associative being: *das Associationswesen*. Cf. *Pollen*, no. 82.

But the present is not understandable without the *past* and a high degree of education – a saturation with, and digestion of, the greatest productions and the purest spirit of the age and the past. From this arises the human prophetic view, which the historian, the active idealistic compiler of historical data, cannot so easily dispense with as the grammarian and rhetorical *narrator*.

The historian must often be a speaker. He delivers a *gospel*, for all history is a gospel story.

218 That is the special attraction of a republic: that everything expresses itself more freely in it. Virtues and vices, talents and ineptitude, come more strongly to the fore, and so a republic is like a tropical climate, though without the regularity of the weather.

220 Proclamation regarding jurisprudence.

One must take jurisprudence itself to court.

Jurisprudence contains the principle of its improvement, purification, in itself.

The *Responsa Prudentum* and the *Jus consuetudinarium*[17] must be attacked.

571 The objects that make up the usual objects of entertainment are basically nothing more than local events. The rather similar standard of living, the same situation, the same education, the same moderate character, bring forth a considerable uniformity. Weather, city news, unusual events, newspapers, judgements and stories about well-known people, fashion, and at worst news of the residence, private life and society jokes, fill popular conversation. Broad and universal affairs interest no one and evoke boredom.

This is of course better in republics, where the state is the chief concern of every person. The life and needs, the activity and viewpoints, of everyone are bound up with the life and needs, the activity and viewpoints, of a more powerful and wide society; a person feels his life connected to a more potent life, and so his fantasy and intellect are broadened with, and exercised by, greater objects. He almost must forget his narrow self in the face of the immeasurable whole.

---

[17] *Responsa Prudentum*: judgement of reputable jurists. *Jus consuetudinarium*: customary law.

Essay on the Concept of Republicanism
occasioned by the Kantian Tract
'Perpetual Peace'
Friedrich Schlegel

The spirit that breathes in the Kantian essay *Perpetual Peace* must benefit every friend of justice, and even our most distant progeny will admire in this monument the elevated frame of mind of the venerable sage. His bold and dignified discourse is unaffected and candid, and it is spiced with a biting wit and a clever spirit. It contains a rich abundance of fruitful ideas and new insights for politics, morals and the history of humanity. For me, the opinion of the author concerning the nature of *republicanism*, and its relations to other kinds and conditions of the state, was especially interesting. The examination of it occasioned me to think through the subject anew. Hence arose the following remarks.

'The civil constitution', Kant says on p. 99,[1] 'of every state shall be republican. A republican constitution is founded firstly upon the principle of *freedom* for all members of a society (as men), secondly upon the principle of *dependence* of everyone upon a single common legislation (as subjects), and thirdly upon the principle of legal *equality* for everyone (as citizens).' It seems to me that this definition is unsatisfactory. If the concept of legal dependence already lies in the concept of a constitution in general (p. 99 note), then it cannot be the criterion of the *specific character* of a republican constitution. Since no principle is given for the division of a constitution in general into its various kinds, the question arises whether

Schlegel's 'Versuch über den Begriff des Republikanismus' was first published in J. F. Reichhardt's journal *Deutschland*, vol. III, Berlin 1796, pp. 10–41. Schlegel wrote the essay in the beginning of 1796. It was his first *published* work on political philosophy, though not the first he wrote (see note 18 below).

As the subtitle suggests, Schlegel's essay is a close commentary upon Kant's *Perpetual Peace*, which appeared in 1795. Schlegel's chief aim is to defend democracy against Kant's criticisms. He argues that democracy is not necessarily despotic, and that it provides the closest approximation to a republican constitution.

The essay marks the highpoint of Schlegel's early radicalism. It was indeed one of the most progressive political writings of the 1790s in Germany. Schlegel defends not only democracy, but also the right of rebellion and even a revolutionary dictatorship. He was far in advance of most of his contemporaries in defending a very broad franchise, which included women and the poor.

[1] Schlegel cites the first edition of Kant's work *Zum ewigen Frieden. Ein philosophischer Entwurf* (Königsberg: Friedrich Nicolovius, 1795). His references to this virtually inaccessible edition have been replaced by references to the more accessible Reiss edition (*PW*). Schlegel's citations of Kant's text frequently depart from the exact wording of the original. In these cases I have translated Schlegel's exact words, not the original text. In citing Reiss's edition, then, I am referring to the passages that correspond to Schlegel's citations, not reproducing Reiss's translation.

the attributes of freedom and equality exhaust the complete concept of a republican constitution. Both attributes are nothing positive but only negations. Now since every negation presupposes an affirmation, every condition something conditioned, there must be some attribute missing in the definition (and indeed the most important that contains the ground of the other two). A despotic constitution knows nothing of those two negative attributes (freedom and equality); hence it will be distinct from the republican constitution through some positive attribute. That republicanism and despotism are not forms of the state but of the constitution is presupposed without proof, and a constitution is never defined.[2]

The suggested deduction of republicanism (as defined above) is as little satisfactory as the definition. At least it appears, as maintained on pp. 99–100, that the republican constitution is necessary on practical grounds, because it is the only one that derives from the idea of the original contract. But upon what is this idea based other than the principles of freedom and equality? Is this not a circle?

All negations are limits of an affirmation. The deduction of their validity is the proof that the higher affirmation, from which the affirmation limited through it is derived, would destroy itself without this condition.[3] The practical necessity of political freedom and equality must therefore be deduced from the higher practical affirmation, which is the basis for the positive attribute of republicanism.

The definition of legal freedom – the right to do whatever one wants as long as one does no injustice to others – the author declares to be a tautology. He defines it instead as 'the right to obey no external laws except those to which the individual could have given

---

[2] See *Ak.* VIII, pp. 351–3; *PW*, pp. 100–1. Schlegel's distinction between the form of the state (*Staat*) and constitution (*Staatsverfassung*) corresponds to Kant's distinction between the form of sovereignty (*Form der Beherrschung, forma imperii*) and the form of government (*Form der Regierung, forma regiminis*). According to Kant, the form of sovereignty is the *number of persons* who exercise authority, whereas the form of government is *the way in which a nation is governed*, whether according to laws or the dictates of the ruler, whoever that might be. The only forms of government are either republican or despotic.

[3] As Schlegel later explains (p. 100), the higher affirmation is the proposition 'the ego should be'; the affirmation limited through it is 'the community should be'. In sum, Schlegel's argument is that freedom and equality are necessary conditions of the realization of the practical imperative 'the ego should be'.

his consent'.[4] To me, these definitions seem correct, but only with some qualification. Civil freedom is only an idea,[5] which can be made actual only through an infinite progressive approximation. Just as in every progression there is a first, last and middle term, so in the infinite progression to that idea there is a minimum, a medium and a maximum. The *minimum of civil freedom* is contained in the Kantian definition. The *medium* of civil freedom is the right to obey no external laws other than those which the (represented) majority of the nation has really willed and the (supposed) universality of the nation could will. The (unattainable) *maximum* of civil freedom is that of the criticized definition, which would be a tautology only if it spoke of moral and not political freedom. The highest political freedom would be equivalent to moral freedom, which is limited only by the moral law, completely independent of all coercive laws. Similarly, what Kant defines as external legal equality in general is only the minimum in the infinite progression to the unattainable idea of *political equality*. The *medium* consists in not allowing any differences among the rights and obligations of the citizens other than those which the majority of the nation has actually willed and the totality of the people could will. The maximum would be an absolute equality of rights and duties for all citizens, thus ending all domination and dependency.

But are these interrelated concepts not essential features of the state in general? The presupposition that the will of all individual citizens will not correspond always with the general will is the only basis for *political domination and dependence*. However universally true, its opposite is at least thinkable. Furthermore, this presupposition gives only an empirical condition which can more accurately limit the pure concept of the state, to be sure, but which for just this reason cannot be a defining characteristic of its pure concept. The empirical concept presupposes a more pure one, the determinate concept a more indeterminate, from which it is first derived. Hence not *every* state (p. 102) contains the relation of a superior to an inferior, but only that which is empirically limited by such factual data. We can conceive an *international state* [*Völkerstaat*] without this relation, and without all the different states having to be

---

[4] See *Ak*. VIII, p. 350 note: PW, p. 99, note.
[5] Schlegel uses the term 'idea' (*Idee*) in the technical Kantian sense. See note 3 to the *Oldest Systematic Programme*.

fused into one.[6] This would be (not a hypothetically, but a categorically purposive)[7] society determined not by any particular end, but striving for an indeterminate goal concerning the freedom of the individual and the equality of everyone within a majority or mass of politically independent nations. The idea of a *world republic* has practical validity and conceptual significance.

The *personale* of the executive power (p. 101), the number of rulers, can be a principle of division only when not the universal but the individual will is the basis of civil laws (in despotism). How does the claim 'republicanism is that principle of the state that separates the executive and legislative power' agree with Kant's first definition, and with the proposition that 'republicanism is possible only through representation' (p. 102)? If the whole executive power is not in the hands of the people's representatives but divided between an hereditary ruler and hereditary nobility, so that the former has the executive and the latter the legislative power, then, despite the separation of power, the constitution would not be representative but (according to the author's own definition) despotic, as the inheritability of state offices is incompatible with republicanism (pp. 99–100 note).

The legislator, executive and judge are indeed completely distinct *political* persons (p. 101); but it is physically possible that one *physical* person could unite these distinct political persons.[8] It is also *politically possible*, i.e. not contradictory, that the general will of the

---

[6] Kant distinguishes between a federation of peoples (*Volkerbund*) and an international state (*Volkerstaat*), *Ak.* VIII, p. 354; *PW*, p. 102. In the former nations retain their distinct identity and establish a civil constitution securing their rights. In the latter the nations fuse together and form a single state. Kant argues that the idea of an international state is self-contradictory, since the very idea of a state requires a relationship between a superior (the legislator) and inferior (the people obeying the law), which would not be possible if all the states became a single state.

[7] Schlegel alludes to Kant's famous distinction between hypothetical and categorical imperatives. See Kant, *Foundation of the Metaphysics of Morals, Ak.* IV, pp. 412–16. A hypothetical imperative prescribes an action as a means to an end. Since the end has only a conditional value, depending on whether we want it or not, the imperative is hypothetical in form ('If you want X, then do Y'). A categorical imperative prescribes an action as an end in itself. Since the end has an unconditional value, commanding our respect whether we like it or not, the imperative is categorical in form ('You ought to do Y').

[8] Schlegel's point is that the mere distinction in office or function between the legislative and executive does not preclude one and the same person performing them.

people decrees to delegate (not surrender) all power to one person for a definite time. Indisputably, the separation of powers is the rule of the republican state; but the exception to that rule, *dictatorship*, seems to be at least possible.[9] (Its splendid utility is especially evident from ancient history. The human race is indebted to this shrewd Greek invention for many of the greatest products ever created by the political genius.)[10] But dictatorship is necessarily a *transitory condition*; for if all power is transferred for an indefinite time, then that is not representation but a cession of political power. But a *cession of sovereignty* is politically impossible; for the general will cannot destroy itself through an act of the general will. The concept of a *dictatura perpetua*[11] is therefore as contradictory as that of a four-angled circle. But transitory dictatorship is *a politically possible form of representation* – therefore a *republican form* of representation essentially distinct from despotism.

In general, the author does not even suggest his principle for the division of the kinds and parts of states. The following provisional attempt at a *deduction of republicanism* and a *political classification a priori* appears to me not to be unworthy of a reader's examination.

By connecting the highest practical thesis (the object of the practical basic science)[12] with theoretical data concerning the limits and kinds of human powers, the pure practical imperative receives as many different modifications as human power in general has specific different powers. Each of these modifications is the foundation and subject matter of a special practical science. By means of the

---

[9] Here Schlegel defends temporary dictatorship for republican ends. He seems to wish to defend the terror and its apostle, Robespierre. On the romantic attitude toward Robespierre, see Schlegel, *Athenæum Fragments*, no. 422, p. 239; and Novalis, *Schriften* IV, p. 540.

[10] The reference is obscure. However, Schlegel seems to refer to the fact that in 594 BC Solon was appointed *archon* in Athens, having complete authority to reform its laws and establish its constitution. He is credited with having founded Athenian democracy. See Aristotle, *The Politics* 1273b35–74a21 and *The Constitution of Athens*, nos. 5–12.

[11] *Dictatura perpetua*: eternal, perpetual dictatorship.

[12] The highest practical thesis is the principle 'the ego should be' (*das Ich soll sein*), which is derived from Fichte's 1794 *Wissenschaftslehre*. The first principle of the *Wissenschaftslehre*, 'I am' (*Ich bin*) or 'I=I' (*Ich=Ich*), is given a regulative reading by Fichte so that it becomes 'The ego *should* be'. See Fichte, *Some Lectures concerning the Scholar's Vocation, Werke*, VI, pp. 296–300; *EPW*, pp. 148–53. According to Fichte, the ego's goal should be to achieve complete independence or autonomy, where all of nature conforms to purely rational ends.

theoretical datum that the human being, apart from the capacity it possesses as a pure isolated individual as such, has the *capacity of communication* in relation to other individuals of its species – that human individuals actually, or at least could, stand in a *relation* of reciprocal *natural influence* to one another – the pure practical imperative receives *a new specific modification*, which is the foundation and object of a new science. The proposition '*the ego should be*' means in this specific case '*the community of humanity should be*' or '*the ego should be communicated*'.[13] This derived practical thesis is the foundation and subject matter of *politics*, by which I understand not the art of using the mechanism of nature to govern human beings (p. 117), but (like the Greek philosophers) a *practical science* in the Kantian sense of the word,[14] whose object is the relation of practical individuals and species. Every human society, whose goal is the community of mankind (as an end in itself, or whose end is human society) is called a *state*. Since, however, the ego should be not only in the *relation* of all individuals but also in every *single* individual, and since it can be only under the condition of absolute independence of the will, *political freedom* is a necessary condition of the *political imperative*, and an essential characteristic of the concept of the state. For, otherwise, the pure practical imperative, from which the ethical as well as the political imperative is derived, would destroy itself. The ethical and political imperative are valid not merely for this or that individual, but for *every* individual; hence *political equality* is also a necessary condition of the political imperative, and an essential characteristic of the concept of the state.

The political imperative holds for *all* individuals; hence the state comprises an uninterrupted *mass*, a coexistent and successive *continuum* of human beings, the *totality* of which stand in a relation of physical influence to one another, eg. all inhabitants in a country, all descendants of a family. This characteristic is the *external criterion* by which the state is distinguished from political orders and associations, which have *special* ends, and therefore concern only

---

[13] Here Schlegel argues that the ideal of absolute independence or autonomy can be realized only in a community that grants liberty and equality to all.

[14] 'A practical science in the Kantian sense of the word' (*eine praktische Wissenschaft, im Kantischen Sinne dieses Worts*): Kant's ideal of science is a system organized according to a single idea or principle. See *CPR*, B 89–90, pp. 860–1.

certain particular individuals. All these societies comprise no mass, no total continuum, but connect only single scattered members.

Equality and freedom demand that the *general will* be the basis of all particular political activities (not only the laws, but also their application and execution). But just this is the character of *republicanism*. The despotism opposed to it, where the private will is the basis of all political activity, would therefore be no true state at all? It is indeed, and in the strictest sense of the word. Since, however, all political culture has its beginning in a special end, in force (cf. the splendid discussion p. 117) and in a private will – in short, in despotism – so that every *provisional government must be despotic*; since, moreover, despotism usurps the appearance of the general will and at least tolerates justice in civil and criminal cases in its interest; since, furthermore, despotism distinguishes itself from other societies by means of that continuity of membership characteristic of the state; and since, finally, it promotes, if only accidentally, the interest of the community along with its special ends,[a] and so against its knowledge and consent carries the germs of a genuine state within itself and gradually brings republicanism to fruition – so for all these reasons one could regard despotism as a *quasi-state*, not as a genuine form but as a *degenerate form of the state*.

But how is republicanism possible? The general will is its necessary condition; but the absolute general (and therefore absolute enduring) will does not occur in the realm of experience and exists only in the world of pure thought. The individual and universal are therefore separated from one another by an infinite gulf, over which one can jump only by a *salto mortale*.[15] There is no solution here other than, by means of a *fiction*, to regard an empirical will as the *surrogate* of the a priori absolute general will. Since a pure resolution of the political problem is impossible, we have to content ourselves with the *approximation* to this practical X.[16] Because the

---

[a] Every state that has a specific end is *despotic*, however innocent this end might appear at first. How many despots take physical self-preservation as their starting point? But whenever it is achieved it degenerates into oppression. The practical philosopher will not be surprised by this well-intentioned confusion of the conditioned with the unconditioned. The finite cannot usurp unpunished the rights of the infinite.

[15] *Salto mortale* (Italian): a mortal leap or jump.

[16] X, Kantian shorthand for something unknowable or unattainable in practice.

political imperative is categorical, and can be realized only in this manner (in an infinite approximation), the highest *fictio juris*[17] is not only justified but practically necessary. However, it is valid only when it does not contradict the political imperative (the foundation of its claims) and its essential conditions.

Since every empirical will (according to Heraclitus' dictum) is in *constant flux* and absolute universality found in *no one*, the despotic arrogance to sanction one's (paternal or divine) private will as the general will is not only a maximum of injustice, but also pure nonsense. But even the fiction that the private will of, for example, a certain family can be a surrogate for the general will for all future generations, is contradictory and invalid; for it would destroy the political imperative (whose essential condition is equality), which is its own foundation. The only valid political fiction is that based on the law of equality: *the will of the majority* should be the surrogate of the general will. *Republicanism is therefore necessarily democratic*; and the unproven paradox (p. 101) that democracy is necessarily despotic cannot be correct. Of course, there is a *legitimate aristocracy*, a *genuine patriciate*, which is completely distinct from the perverted hereditary aristocracy, whose absolute injustice has been so satisfactorily demonstrated by Kant (p. 99 note); but it is possible only in a democratic republic. In particular, the principle of determining the value of votes not according to their number but their weight (according to the degree of approximation of each individual to the absolute universality of the will) is perfectly compatible with the law of equality. Yet it must be not *presupposed* but truly proven that an individual has no free will, or that his will has no universality – [for example], the lack of freedom through childhood and madness, the lack of universality through crime or the direct contradiction with the general will. (Poverty and *presumed* corruptibility, femininity and *presumed* weakness, are indeed not legitimate grounds to exclude someone from the right to vote.) If the political fiction to regard an individual as a *political non-entity*, a person as a *thing*, were permitted, then it would thwart the opposite of the arbitrary presupposition,[18] and so conflict with the ethical impera-

---

[17] *Fictio juris*: a legal fiction.
[18] The opposite of the arbitrary presupposition (*das Gegenteil der willkürlichen Voraussetzung*): that is, the assumption that a person has a free will or that his will has universality.

tive, which is impossible, given that both rest on the pure practical imperative. The general will of the people can also never decree that the individual is a competent judge of the degree of universality of his own private will, and that he should have the right to make himself by his own authority into a patrician. The majority of the people must have willed the patriciate, determined its privileges and members, which should be regarded as the *political nobility* (those, whose private will best approximates the presumed general will). Perhaps it could give the elected nobility some share in the election of its future members, yet with the proviso that it could decide in the last resort; for sovereignty can never be surrendered.

That the majority of the people acts politically *in person* is in many cases impossible, and in almost all of them extremely disadvantageous. It can be very conveniently done through deputies and commisars. Hence *political representation* is certainly an indispensable organ of republicanism.

If one separates representation from political fiction, then there can be (even if technically extremely imperfect) republicanism even without representation. If one conceives of fiction as a form of representation, one goes astray to deny it of the ancient republics.[19] Their technical imperfection is notorious. But the more confused the prevalent conceptions of the inevitable corruption of their inner principle,[20] the more misleading the judgements of the political worth of these admirable (not only so-called but genuine) republics, which are based on the valid fiction of universality being represented through the majority. With regard to the *community of morals*, the political culture of the modern state is in a state of infancy compared to the ancient; and no state has reached a greater degree of freedom and equality than the Attic.[21] The ignorance of

[19] Here Schlegel takes issue with Kant's view of ancient republics, *Ak.* VIII, p. 354; *PW*, p. 102: 'None of the republics of antiquity employed a representative system, and they thus inevitably ended in despotism.'.

[20] The 'prevalent conceptions' (*allgemeineherrschenden Begriffe*): the view that the ancient republics degenerated into ochlocracy or mob rule. This was a prevalent view among the eighteenth century *Aufklärer*, who generally defended enlightened monarchy.

[21] In the *Kritische Ausgabe*, and most German editions, the text states *britische* instead of *attische*. Following the reading of Wolfgang Hecht (in *Friedrich Schlegel: Werke in Zwei Bänden* (Berlin: Aufbau Verlag, 1980, I, p. 327)), I have replaced *britische* with *attische*. The term *britische* is most probably a printer's error from the first edition. It is completely out of context and contrary to the meaning of the passage

the political culture of the Greeks and Romans is the source of unspeakable confusion in the history of humanity; and is even disadvantageous to the political philosophy of the moderns, which in these respects has much to learn from the ancients.[22] Even the reputed lack of representation is not true without qualification. The Attic nation could not perform the executive power in person; and in Rome at least part of the legislative and judicial power was managed through representatives (praetors, tribunes, censors, consuls).

The power of the majority of the people, as an approximation to universality and as a surrogate of the general will, is the *political power*. The highest classification of political phenomena (all the expressions of this power), like that of all phenomena, is according to the distinction between the *permanent* and *transitory*. The *constitution* is the totality of all *permanent* relations of political power and its components. The government, on the other hand, is the totality of all transitory manifestations of political power. The *components* of political power relate to one another and to their whole just as the different parts of the faculty of knowledge relate to one another and to their whole. The *constitutive* power corresponds to reason, the *legislative* to the understanding, the *judicial* to judgement and the *executive* to sensibility, the capacity of intuition. *The constitutive power is necessarily dictatorial*; for it would be contradictory to make the power of political principles, which is the foundation for all other political judgements and powers, to depend upon them, and hence to make it only *transitory*. Without *an act of acceptance* political power will not be represented but surrendered, which is impossible.

The constitution concerns the *form of fiction* and the *form of representation*. In republicanism there is indeed only one principle of political fiction, but *two distinct directions* of this single principle;

here. Schlegel's radical republicanism put him at odds with those German conservatives, such as A. W. Rehberg and Ernst Brandes, who praised the English constitution. Schlegel was highly critical of Rehberg's views. See his letter to his brother of 23 October 1793: *KA* XXIII, p. 145.

[22] Schlegel developed his views on the difference between early and modern republics in his essay *Ueber antiken und modernen Republiken*. Unfortunately, this essay has been lost. Schlegel mentions completing it in his letter to his brother of 4 July 1795: *KA* XXIII, p. 237. Since Schlegel's early political ideals were largely inspired by the ancient republics, which he preferred to modern ones, the loss of the essay is especially unfortunate.

and in their greatest possible divergence from one another there are not only two pure kinds but two opposed *extremes* of the republican constitution: the *aristocratic* and *democratic*. There are infinitely many different forms of representation (as mixtures of democratism and aristocratism)[23] but no pure kinds and no principle of division a priori. The constitution is the totality of everything politically permanent. Since one classifies a phenomenon according to its permanent attributes, not according to its transitory modifications, it would be nonsense to divide the genuine (republican state) according to the form of government.

In despotism there can be, properly speaking, not a political but only a *physical* constitution. That is, there cannot be relations of political power and their essential constituents that are absolutely permanent, but only such as are relatively permanent. Where there is no political constitution one can only classify the form of constitution dynamically, for physical modifications give no pure classes.

The single pure classification is furnished by the mathematical principle of the numerical quantity of the despotic persons.

The single (physically) permanent quality of despotism determines the *dynamic* (not political) *form of despotic government*. It is either *tyrannical, oligarchic* or *ochlocratic* depending on whether an individual, an estate (order, corps, caste), or mass rules. If *all* rule (p. 101) then who will be ruled? Furthermore, Kant's concept of democracy seems more adequate to ochlocracy. *Ochlocracy* is the despotism of the majority over the minority. Its *criterion* is the patent contradiction between the majority, in its function as a political fiction, with the general will, whose surrogate it should be. Among all political aberrations, it is – along with tyranny, given that the Neroes of the world could easily compete with Sansculottism[24] – the greatest physical evil (p. 101).[b]

On the other hand, oligarchy – the Oriental caste system, the European feudal system – is incomparably much more dangerous

---

[b] If this were the place, it would not be difficult to explain why among the ancients ochlocracy evolved into tyranny, and to prove with the highest degree of evidence that with the moderns it evolves into democracy, and hence is much less dangerous to humanity than oligarchy.

[23] 'Democratism and aristocratism': *Demokratismus und Aristokratismus*. In this context Schlegel means the pure principles or concepts of democracy or aristocracy.

[24] *Sansculottism (Sanskulottismus)*: a term popular in the 1790s to refer to the violence and excesses of the Paris mob and French radicals, the so-called *sansculottes*.

to humanity; for the very ponderousness of its artificial mechanism, gives it a colossal solidity. The concentration of those bonded together by similar interests isolates one caste from the human race and creates a resolute *esprit de corps*. The spiritual friction of the mass brings to early fruition the devilish art that makes the ennoblement of humanity impossible.

With suspicious glances the oligarchy detects every aspiring stirring of humanity and crushes it in the bud. On the other hand, *tyranny* is an uncaring monster, which often turns a blind eye to individual cases of the highest freedom, indeed even of the most perfect justice. The very clumsy machine *hangs on a single spring*; and if this is weak, it collapses with the first strong shove.

If the *form of government* is *despotic*, but the spirit representative or republican (see the excellent remark p. 101), then *monarchy* arises. (In ochlocracy the spirit of the government cannot be republican; otherwise, it would necessarily also be the form of the state. In pure oligarchy the spirit of the estate[25] must be despotic, if the form is not that of a legitimate democratic aristocracy; the republican spirit of individual members helps nothing, for it is the estate, as such, that rules.) Chance can provide a legitimate monarch with despotic power. He can govern in a republican manner, and still retain the despotic form of the state, that is, if the degree of political culture or the political condition of the state makes a provisional (therefore despotic) government necessary, and if the general will could approve it. The *criterion of monarchy* (that which distinguishes it from despotism) is the greatest possible promotion of republicanism. The degree of approximation of the private will of the monarch to the absolute universality of the will determines the degree of its perfection. The monarchical form is perfectly adequate to some degrees of political culture, since the republican principle is either in its infancy (as in heroic prehistory) or has completely faded (as in the time of the Roman Caesars). It provides great and obvious advantages in rare but real cases, such as *Friedrich* and *Marcus Aurelius*,[26] so that it is understandable why it has been,

[25] 'Estate': *Stand*. This broad term can also be rendered 'position', 'standing' or 'condition'. Here Schlegel opposes the old hierarchic society of estates (*Ständegesellschaft*).
[26] Marcus Aurelius, Roman emperor from AD 161 to 180, and Friedrich II, Prussian monarch from 1740 to 1786. Both were admired by the *Aufklärer* as examples of wise rulers, as 'philosophers on the throne'.

and still is, the favourite of so many political philosophers. Following Kant's excellent point (p. 102 note), one must not ascribe the spirit of a government to its bad (and illegitimate, pp. 99–100 note) form.

The *sacred* is only that which can be infinitely violated, something like freedom and equality, or the general will. How Kant can find the majesty of the people absurd I do not understand.[27] The *majority of the people*, as the single valid surrogate of the general will, is in its role as a political fiction equally sacred; and every other political title and dignity is only a product of the *sacredness of the people*. The very sacred *tribune*,[28] for example, was so only in the name of the people, not on his own. He reveals the sacred idea of freedom only in a mediate way; he is not a surrogate, but only a representative of the sacred holy will.

The state should exist, and it should be republican. Republican states have an absolute worth simply because they strive toward just and absolutely commanded ends. In this respect their worth is all equal. But they can be very different in their degree of approximation to the unattainable ends. In this respect their worth can be determined in two different ways.

The *technical perfection* of the republican state divides itself into the perfection of the constitution and the government. The technical perfection of the constitution is measured by the degree of approximation of its individual form of fiction and representation to the absolute (though impossible) adequacy of fiction to the fictionalized, the representation to the represented. (This agrees with the trenchant observation on pp. 101–102, if by a 'representation' the author also means a fiction. May a pragmatic politician fill a gap in our knowledge with a theory of the means to extend fiction and representation both extensively and intensively! The Kantian remark concerning the persons of state power (p. 101)[29] may perhaps hold only for the executive and, under certain circumstances, constitutive power; but for the legislative and judicial power

[27] See *Ak.* VIII, p. 354; *PW*, p. 103: '... it would be absurd to speak of the majesty of the people ...'.

[28] Tribune: a Roman magistrate, who had various kinds of duties. The office was established in 494 BC to defend plebeian interests.

[29] See *Ak.* VIII, p. 353; *PW*, p. 101: 'We can therefore say that the smaller number of ruling persons in a state and the greater their powers of representation, the more the constitution will approximate to its republican potentiality.'

experience seems to show that the college and jury system are the best.) The negative technical perfection of a government is measured by the degree of harmony with the constitution; the positive by the degree of positive power with which the constitution is actually executed.

The *political worth* of a republican state is determined by the extensive and intensive degree of the actually achieved community, freedom and equality. Of course, the moral culture of a nation is not possible before the state is organized on republican lines and has reached at least a certain degree of technical perfection (p. 113); but, on the other hand, the *reign of morality* is the necessary condition of the *absolute perfection* (the maximum of community, freedom and equality) of the state, indeed even of every degree of higher political excellence.

Hitherto we have considered only the *partial* republicanism of a single state and nation. But only through a *universal* republicanism can the political imperative be fully realized. The concept is therefore no will-of-the-wisp of dreaming mystics, but practically necessary, as much so as the political imperative itself. Its components are:

1) *Politicization of all nations*;
2) *Republicanism of everything politicized*;
3) *Fraternity of all republicans*;
4) *The autonomy of each individual state, and the isonomy*[30] *of all.*

Only a universal and perfect republicanism would be valid, but also the only sufficient *definitive article for eternal peace*. As long as the constitution and government are not completely perfect, it would still remain *possible*, even in republican states, whose peaceful inclinations have been so splendidly shown by Kant, for there to be an unjust and unnecessary war. The first Kantian article for definitive peace demands indeed the republicanism of *all* states; but *federalism*, whose practicality (p. 104) has been so cogently proven by Kant, cannot by its very *concept* comprise *all* states; otherwise it would be, contrary to Kant's opinion (pp. 102–5), a universal international state. The aim of the pacific federation to secure the freedom of the republican states (p. 104) presupposes that there is

---

[30] 'Isonomy' (*Isonomie*): equality of laws, rights or privileges.

a danger to them from states of a warlike tendency, i.e. *despotic states*. The cosmopolitan hospitality, whose origin and stimulus through the spirit of commerce has been so thoughtfully developed by Kant (p. 114), seems to presuppose even *unpoliticized nations*. But as long as there are still despotic states and unpoliticized nations there will still remain cause for war.

1) *The republicanism of cultivated nations*;
2) *The federalism of republican states*;
3) *The cosmopolitan hospitality of the federated*;

will therefore be only *valid definitive articles to the first genuine and permanent*, though only partial, peace, instead of the hitherto falsely named 'peace pacts', which are really only truces (p. 130).

One can also regard them as *preliminary articles to eternal peace*, which they intend to achieve, and which cannot even be thought of before the first genuine peace.

Universal perfect republicanism and eternal peace are inseparable complementary concepts. The latter is as *politically necessary* as the former. But how do things stand with its historical necessity or possibility? Which is the *guarantee of eternal peace*?

'Perpetual peace is *guaranteed* by no less authority than the great artist, nature herself', Kant says on p. 108. As ingenious as the development of this splendid idea is, I still frankly want to confess what I find missing in it. It is not enough to show the *means* of its possibility, the *external occasions of fate* that lead to the gradual realization of eternal peace. One expects an answer to the question *whether the inner development of humanity* leads to it? The (postulated) *purposiveness of nature* (however beautiful, and indeed necessary this view might be in other respects) is here completely beside the point; only the (actual) *necessary laws of experience* can provide a guarantee for future success. *The laws of political history*, and the *principles of political culture*, are the only basis from which we can show 'that eternal peace is no empty idea but a task which, as solutions are gradually found, constantly draws near to fulfilment' (p. 130). Although we cannot *prophetize* from them categorically and according to all circumstances of time and place, we can perhaps theoretically (if only hypothetically) determine beforehand with certainty the future reality of peace and the manner of approximating it.

Kant avoids here (as is only to be expected) any transcendent use of the teleological principle in the history of humanity[31] (which even critical philosophers have allowed themselves). However, in one place it seems to me the practical concept of the unconditional freedom of will has wrongly been drawn into the theoretical domain of the history of humanity. If moral theology can and must raise the question 'What is the intelligible ground of immortality?' – whether it can and must I will not consider here – then I know no other answer than original sin in the Kantian sense.[32] But the history of humanity has to deal with only the *empirical causes of the phenomenon of immorality*; the intelligible concept of original evil is empty and without all meaning in the realm of experience. The purported fact (pp. 120–1 note) that there is absolutely no belief in human virtue is unproven; and how can the obvious evil in the external relations of states (p. 121 note) – the immorality of a small human group[33] that, for easily understood reasons, consists in the dross of the human race – be an argument against human nature in general?

It is an unfruitful standpoint here to consider the perfect constitution not as a phenomenon of political experience but as a problem of the political art (p. 113), for we want to know not about its possibility but its future reality and its law of progression toward political culture.

It is only from *historical principles of political development*, from the *theory of political history*, that we can discover a satisfactory *result concerning the relation of political reason and political experience*. Instead of this Kant has devoted an appendix to the inessential border disputes between morals and politics, which arise only accidentally from incompetence. He understands by *politics* not practical science, whose foundation and object is the political imperative, and also not political art, that is, the skill in realizing that imperative.

[31] 'Transcendent use of the teleological principle' (*transzendenten Gebrauch von dem teleologischen Prinzip*): in this context, the assumption that we *know* that the purpose of nature is the realization of eternal peace.

[32] On Kant's concept of sin, see *Religion within the Limits of Reason Alone*: 'The proposition "man is evil" can mean ... only that he is conscious of the moral law but adopts into his maxim a deviation from it. He is evil *by nature* means that this is true of him considered as a species; not that such a quality can be deduced from the very concept of his species (that of mankind in general) ... but that he cannot be judged otherwise from what we know of him in our experience.' See *Ak.* VI, p. 32.

[33] 'A small human group' (*eine kleine Menschenklasse*): a reference to the princes.

Rather, he regards politics as the despotic aptitude, which is no political art but really a *political bungling*.[34]

The two pure types of all conceivable constitutions (both politically necessary and possible) are republicanism and despotism. In addition, though, there are also two, at first glance very analogous but in essence completely distinct, *formless political conditions*, which should not be ignored as *limiting concepts*[35] in the analysis of republicanism. Only one is politically possible; the other is merely historically possible.

Insurrection is not politically impossible or absolutely illegitimate (as is maintained pp. 126–7); for it is not completely incompatible with publicity. Concerning the (perhaps illegitimate) ruler what Kant says on p. 129 holds: 'The person who has decisive sovereignty has no need to conceal his maxims.' A constitution that allowed every individual to rebel *whenever it seemed right to him* would surely destroy itself. On the other hand, a constitution containing an article that, in certain cases, *peremptorily commanded* revolution would indeed not destroy itself. Yet this single article would be *null* and void; for a constitution cannot command anything if it ceases to exist. Insurrection can be legitimate only when the constitution has been already destroyed. It is indeed possible that an article in the constitution determines the cases in which the constitutive power can be regarded as *de facto nullified*, so that insurrection can be *allowed* for every individual. Such cases occur when, for example, the dictator keeps his power beyond the specified time; when the constituted power destroys the constitution, the foundation of its legal existence; and so forth. Since the general will cannot will such a destruction of republicanism through usurpation, and necessarily wills republicanism, it must also permit the only means to destroy usurpation (insurrection) and to organize republicanism anew (provisional government). Hence that insurrection is *legitimate* whose motive is the destruction of the constitution, whose

---

[34] See *Ak.* VIII, p. 377; *PW*, p. 122. Here Schlegel takes issue with Kant's conservative approach to political reform, which should come from above and only as opportunities present themselves to the ruler.

[35] 'Limiting concepts' (*Grenzbegriffe*): in Kant, a limiting concept is one whose function is to limit the concepts of understanding, and the intuitions of sensibility, to experience and to prevent their application to noumena. See *CPR*, B, pp. 310–11. Schlegel uses the term here in an extended and analogical sense.

government is a merely provisional organ, and whose goal is the organization of republicanism.

The second valid motive for a legitimate insurrection is the existence of an *absolute* despotism, ie. not one which is provisional and therefore can be conditionally permitted, but one which strives to crush and destroy the republican principle of development (through whose free development alone the political imperative can be gradually realized), and which is absolutely impermissible i.e. could never be permitted by the general will. Absolute despotism is not even a quasistate, but rather an *antistate*, and (even if perhaps physically more tolerable) an incomparably greater evil than *anarchy*. The latter is only a negation of the politically positive; the former an affirmation of the politically negative. Anarchy is either a *fluid despotism*, in which the persons of the ruling power as well as the borders of the ruled masses constantly change, or an ungenuine and *permanent insurrection*; for the genuine and politically possible is necessarily transitory.

Athenæum Fragments
Friedrich Schlegel

5 What is called good society is usually only a mosaic of polished caricatures.

15 Suicide is usually only an event, not an action. If it is the former, the perpetrator is always wrong; it is like a child trying to free itself. But if it is an action, then there can be no question of right and wrong, but only one of decorum. For matters of decorum are subject to only the will. The will should determine everything that is not laid down precisely by the pure law, such as the here and now; and it may determine everything that does not destroy the free will of others and that of oneself. It is not wrong to die voluntarily; but it is often indecent to live longer.

27 Most people are, like Leibniz's possible worlds, only equally justified pretenders to existence. There are few who actually exist.

31 Prudery is the pretension to innocence without innocence. Women will probably have to remain prudish as long as men remain sentimental, stupid and bad enough to demand for them eternal innocence and a lack of education. For innocence is the only thing that can ennoble the loss of education.[1]

34 Almost all marriages are only concubinages, morganatic marriages,[2] or rather provisional attempts and distant approximations

---

The *Athenaeum Fragments* (*Fragmente*) first appeared in June 1798 in the *Athenaeum, Band* I, Zweites Stück, pp. 1–146. Originally, there were 451 aphorisms written by different authors: 85 were by A. W. Schlegel, 29 by Schleiermacher, 13 by Novalis; 4 were jointly written. The remaining 320 aphorisms were by Friedrich Schlegel. The aphorisms translated here are all those by Friedrich Schlegel dealing directly with social, political and cultural themes. The numbers are not Schlegel's own but are customary in all editions of his works.

The *Fragments* are in part a manifesto for sexual equality, the emancipation of the senses, and the sovereign rights of the individual to lead his or her life as he or she wants, regardless of social conventions and antiquated laws. But its social radicalism is balanced by a growing political conservatism. In recognizing the need for elite rule (no. 214), in permitting some degree of arbitrary power in the state (no. 385), and in characterizing the Revolution as a grotesque and tragi-comedy (no. 424), Schlegel tempers and qualifies the more radical standpoint of the *Essay on Republicanism*.

[1] In his early essay 'Ueber die Diotima' (1795), Schlegel praised some of the ancient Greek philosophers – Plato, Diogenes, Zeno and Chrysippus – for including women within their schemes of education. He contended that many apparently natural sexual differences – such as 'the dominating impetuousness of the man', 'the selfless abandonment of the woman' – were the product of modern education, which repressed the potentialities of men and women alike. See *KA* I, pp. 70–115, esp. 99–100, 107.

[2] Morganatic marriages (*Ehen an der linken Hand*): marriage between a royal or noble person and someone of inferior social rank with the provision that neither the spouse nor the children may claim to the property.

to a real marriage, whose true essence – according to not the paradoxes of this or that system but all spiritual and worldly rights – consists in several persons becoming one. A nice idea, whose realization seems to be beset with great difficulties. For this reason the will, which surely should have a say when it comes to deciding whether to be an independent individual or an integral part of a common personality, should be restricted as little as possible.[3] It is hard to see what solid objection could be made against a marriage *à quatre*. But if the state wants to hold together with force even unhappy attempts at marriage, it hinders the possibility of true marriage, which could be promoted through new, perhaps more successful experiments.

49 Women are treated as unjustly in poetry as in life. The feminine is not ideal, and the ideal is not feminine.

63 Every uncultivated person is a caricature of himself.

64 The ethic of moderation is the spirit of castrated intolerance.

80 The historian is a prophet facing backwards.

86 Real sympathy concerns itself with promoting the freedom of others, not with securing their animal pleasures.

87 The first principle in love is to have a sense for another, and the highest principle is to have faith in one another. Devotion is the expression of faith, and pleasure can enliven and intensify the senses, even if it cannot create them, which is the common opinion. Hence, for a short while, sensuality can deceive bad people into thinking that they love one another.

90 The subject of history is the realization of everything that is practically necessary.

102 Women have absolutely no sense for art, but certainly for poetry. They have no capacity for science, but probably for philosophy. For speculation, the inner intuition of the universe, they are lacking nothing. They are missing only in the power of abstraction, which can be more easily learned.

116 Romantic poetry is a progressive universal poetry. Its goal is not merely to reunite all the separate forms of poetry, and to put

---

[3] A critique of the severe restrictions upon divorce in late eighteenth century Prussia. Such criticism was a *leitmotif* of the romantic school. It is also found in Wilhelm von Humboldt, who participated in the romantic salons in Berlin. See his *Ideen zu einem Versuch, die Gränzen der Wirksamkeit des Staats zu bestimmen, Werke*, I, pp. 78–82.

poetry in contact with philosophy and rhetoric. It also wants to and should now mix, and then fuse, poetry and prose, inspiration and criticism, the poetry of art and that of nature; to make poetry lively and social and to make life and society poetic; to poeticize wit and to fill and saturate the forms of art with very kind of solid material for instruction, and then to animate them with the pulsations of humour. It embraces everything that is only poetic, from the great system of art, which encompasses all systems within itself, to the sigh and kiss that the poetic child breathes in artless song. It can so lose itself in its object that one would like to think that its one-and-all is to characterize poetic individuals of every kind; and still there is no form that is perfectly made to express perfectly the spirit of the author, so that many artists, who only wanted to write a novel, have only by accident portrayed themselves. Only it can be, like the epic, a mirror of the whole surrounding world, a portrait of the age. And yet, on the wings of reflection, it can hover in the middle between the portrayed and the portrayer, free from all real and ideal interests, and then raise that reflection to a higher power in an endless series of mirrors. It is capable of the highest and most diverse development, not merely from the inside out but also from the outside in; for, in what should be the whole of its creation, it organizes all parts alike, so that the view is opened up of an endlessly expanding classicism. Among the arts, romantic poetry is what wit is to philosophy, and what society company, friendship and love are to life. Other kinds of poetry are fixed and can be completely analysed. Romantic poetry is still in a process of becoming; indeed, that is its true essence, that it can only eternally become and never be perfected. It cannot be exhausted by any theory, and only a prophetic criticism may dare to characterize its ideal. It alone is infinite, just as it alone is free; it recognizes as its first law, that the will of the artist does not suffer any law above himself. The romantic form of poetry is the only one that is more than a form and is, as it were, poetry itself; for in a certain sense all poetry is or should be romantic.

211 Not to respect the masses is moral; but to honour them is lawful.

212 Perhaps no people deserves freedom; but that is a matter for the *forum dei*.[4]

---

[4] *Forum dei*: the divine tribunal, judgement seat of God.

213 Only that state deserves to be called an aristocracy in which at least the smaller mass that despotizes over the larger has a republican constitution.

214 The perfect republic must be not only democratic but also aristocratic and monarchical. Within the realm of freedom and equality, the educated must outweigh and guide the uneducated and organize everything into an absolute whole.

215 Can legislation be called moral when it punishes attacks on the honour of its citizens less severely than attacks on their lives?

216 The French Revolution, Fichte's *Wissenschaftslehre*, and Goethe's *Meister* are the great tendencies of the age.[5] Whoever is offended by this juxtaposition, whoever takes seriously only a revolution that is noisy and materialistic, has still not elevated themselves to the broader, higher perspective on the history of mankind. Even in our shabby histories of civilization, which usually resemble a collection of variants with running commentary for a lost classical text, many a little book has played a larger role than anything done by the noisy rabble, who took no notice of it at the time.

222 The revolutionary wish to realize the kingdom of God on earth is the elastic point of progressive development, and the beginning of modern history. What stands in no relation to the kingdom of God is only of secondary importance in it.

227 The appearance of lawlessness in the history of mankind arises only from the collisions between heterogeneous spheres of nature, which all coincide and interconnect. For, otherwise, the absolute will has, in this realm of free necessity and necessary freedom, neither constitutive nor legislative power and only the deceptive title of the executive and judicial. The sketchy idea of an historical dynamic does as much credit to Condorcet's mind as his more than French enthusiasm for the now almost trivial idea of infinite perfection does to his heart.[6]

228 The historical tendency of his actions determines the positive morality of the statesman and cosmopolitan.

---

[5] The earlier version of this much quoted fragment adds: 'But they are all still only tendencies and not thoroughly executed.' See *Philosophical Fragments*, Epoche I, no. 662, *KA* XVIII, p. 85.

[6] Schlegel refers to Condorcet's *Esquisse d'un tableau historique des progres de l'esprit humain*, which was written in 1794 and published posthumously. Schlegel reviewed this work in the *Philosophisches Journal* III (1795), pp. 161–72. His review is reprinted in *KA* VII, pp. 3–10.

230 Through the unceasing conflict in which they involve reason and faith, the mysteries of Christianity must lead to either a sceptical resignation in all non-empirical knowledge or critical idealism.[7]

231 Catholicism is naive Christianity. Protestantism is sentimental Christianity. Besides its polemical revolutionary contribution, Protestantism, through its worship of the Bible, has also had the positive result of giving rise to philology, which is essential to any universal and progressive religion.[8] Perhaps Protestant Christianity is still missing only urbanity. To travesty some biblical stories in a Homeric epic, to describe others with the candour of Herodotus or the strictness of Tacitus in classical style, or to review the whole Bible as the work of one author: that would be paradoxical to everyone, annoying to many, and superfluous and improper to a few. But should something seem superfluous that makes religion more liberal?

233 Religion is mostly only a supplement or surrogate for education. Nothing is religious in the strict sense that is not a product of freedom. One can therefore say: the more free, the more religious; and the more education, the less religion.

234 It is very one-sided and presumptuous to say that there should be only one mediator. For the perfect Christian, whom in this respect the peerless Spinoza comes closest to, everything must be a mediator.[9]

235 Nowadays Christ has been deduced a priori in various ways. But should not the Madonna have as much claim to be an original, eternal and necessary ideal, if not of pure at least of feminine and masculine reason?

251 How many people there are nowadays who are too soft and good-natured to see tragedies and too noble and dignified to hear comedies – a perfect proof of the tender sensibility of our age, which wanted only to slander the French Revolution.

262 Every good person becomes more and more God. To become God, to be human, to cultivate oneself, are expressions that all mean the same thing.

[7] Cf. *Philosophical Apprenticeship*, *KA* xviii, para. 84, no. 658: 'With only a gleam of philosophy Christianity leads to the critical philosophy. To accept the concept of a mediator one must be a critical philosopher or crazy. . . For only in absolute idealism can one conceive the proposition "To be at once God and man".'

[8] Cf. Novalis, *Christianity or Europe*, p. 66.

[9] Cf. Novalis, *Pollen*, no. 74; *Universal Brouillon*, no. 398.

263 Genuine mysticism is morals in its highest dignity.

272 Why should there not be immoral people, just as there are unphilosophical and unpoetic ones? Only anti-political or unlawful people cannot be tolerated.

369 The deputy is something quite different from the representative. The representative, whether elected or not, is he who symbolizes the political whole in his person, and is as it were identical with it; he is the visible soul of the state. This idea, which obviously was not seldom the spirit behind monarchies, was perhaps never so purely and consistently practised as in Sparta. The Spartan kings were the first priests, directors and presidents of public education. With the actual administration they had little to do; they were nothing but kings in the representative sense. The power of a priest, a director or an educator, is by its very nature indeterminate and universal, more or less a kind of lawful despotism. Only through the spirit of representation can it be softened and legitimated.

370 Is it not an absolute monarchy when everything essential happens secretly in a cabinet, and where a Parliament may speak and dispute publicly with pomp over formalities? An absolute monarchy could very easily have a kind of constitution, which appears even republican to the uninitiated.

397 Does the state have a right, purely arbitrarily, to make change of a constitution more sacred than other contracts, and so to deprive them of their force?

385 In the deeds and decisions that are necessary for the legislative, executive and judicial powers to achieve their ends, there is often something purely arbitrary, which is unavoidable and not deducible from the pure concept of those powers, and which therefore seems to be unjustifiable. But is the authority for it not borrowed from the constitutive power, which therefore must necessarily have a veto and not merely a right of interdiction? Are not all absolutely arbitrary decisions in a state in virtue of a constitutive power?

406 If every infinite individual is God, then there are as many gods as ideals. Even the relationship of the true artist, and the true human being, to his ideals is completely religious. Whoever makes this inner worship the goal and business of their life is a priest; everyone can and should become one.

414 If there is an invisible church,[10] then it is that of the great paradox, which is inseparable from morality, and which must be distinguished from the merely philosophical. People who are so eccentric that they are completely serious in being and becoming virtuous understand one another in everything, find one another easily, and form a silent opposition against the prevailing immorality that pretends to be morality. A certain mysticism of expression, which, joined with romantic fantasy and grammatical understanding, can be something very charming and good, often serves as a symbol of their beautiful secrets.[11]

420 Whether an educated woman, whose morality is questioned, is corrupt or pure can be very clearly decided. If she follows the general trend, if the external appearance of energy and spirit, and whatever relates to it, is her be-and-end-all, then she is corrupt. If she knows something greater than 'greatness'; if she can smile at her natural liking for energy; if she, in a word, is capable of enthusiasm; then she is innocent in the moral sense. In this respect, one can say that all virtue in a woman is religious. But that women might believe more in God or Christ than men, that good and beautiful free-thinking suits them less than men, is only one of the infinitely many platitudes that Rousseau built into a systematic theory of femininity.[12] Its nonsense was so purified and refined that it had to gain universal acclaim.

422 Mirabeau played a great role in the Revolution because his character and spirit were revolutionary; Robespierre because he obeyed the Revolution unconditionally, devoted himself to it entirely, prayed to it and regarded himself as its god; and Napoleon

---

[10] Invisible church (*unsichtbare Kirche*): cf. Novalis, *Pollen*, no. 43, note 22, and *Philosophical Lectures*, note 5.

[11] Cf. Novalis, *Faith and Love*, no. 2.

[12] Schlegel criticizes book V of Rousseau's *Emile*, especially the following passage: 'Due to the very fact that in her conduct woman is enslaved by public opinion, in her belief she is enslaved by authority. Every girl ought to have her mother's religion, and every woman her husband's . . . Since women are not in a position to be judges themselves, they ought to receive the decision of fathers and husbands like that of the Church.' See *Emile* edited and translated by Allan Bloom (New York: Basic Books, 1979), p. 377. In general, Schlegel's theory of femininity could be regarded as a reaction to book V of the *Emile*. According to Rousseau, women are made to be pleasing to men, and because they have very different natures from men they should receive a different education.

because he can create and shape revolutions and annhilate himself.

423 Does not the present French character begin with Cardinal Richelieu?[13] His strange and almost tasteless universality reminds one of many of the most remarkable French phenomena after him.

424 One can regard the French Revolution as the greatest and most remarkable phenomenon in the history of states, as an almost universal earthquake, as an immeasurable flood in the political world, or as the model of revolutions, as *the* revolution. These are the usual standpoints. But one can also regard it as the centre and summit of the French national character, in which all its paradoxes are compressed together; or as the most horrible grotesque of the age, where all the most profound prejudices and their most powerful forebodings are mixed together in a terrible chaos and woven together as bizarrely as possible into a gigantic tragicomedy of humanity. One finds only isolated instances where these historical views are developed.

441 The liberal is he who is spontaneously free from all sides and directions; who lives in his whole humanity; who regards everything as holy that acts, is and becomes in the full measure of its powers; and who takes part in all life without letting himself become seduced by partial standpoints into hating or disparaging it.

---

[13] Armand Jean Richelieu (1585–1642), French cardinal and chief minister of Louis XIII. Although he had pretensions to culture and piety, he had a reputation for cunning, ruthlessness and extravagance. It has been said that his own religion was 'reason of state'.

Ideas
Friedrich Schlegel

1 The demands for, and anticipations of, a new morals, which would be more than merely the practical part of philosophy, have grown steadily louder and clearer. Already there is talk even of religion. It is time to tear away the veil of Isis and to reveal the mystery. He who cannot bear the sight of the goddess should flee or perish.

2 A priest is whoever lives only in the invisible world, and for whom everything visible has only the truth of an allegory.

3 Only in relation to the infinite is there meaning and purpose; what does not relate to it is completely meaningless and useless.

4 Religion is the animating world-soul of culture, the fourth invisible element with philosophy, morals and poetry. It is like fire: bound to one place, it quietly warms everything around it; only through force or an external stimulus does it break out in terrible destruction.

5 The mind understands something only by absorbing it, nourishing it and letting it grow to blossom and fruit. So scatter holy seeds on to the soil of the spirit, without affectation and idle distractions.[1]

6 Eternal life and the invisible world is to be sought only in God. All spirits dwell in him; he is the abyss of individuality, the only infinite fullness.

7 Liberate religion, and a new humanity will begin.

8 The intellect, the author of the *Speeches on Religion* says,[2] knows only the universe; but if fantasy rules, then you will have a God. Quite right, for fantasy is the organ of man for divinity.

9 The true priest always feels something greater than sympathy.

10 Ideas are infinite, independent divine thoughts, always moving in themselves.

Schlegel completed the manuscript of the *Ideas* (*Ideen*) in August 1799. The *Ideas* first appeared in March 1800 in the *Athenaeum*, vol. III, part 1, pp. 4–33. The translation is based on *KA* II, pp. 256–72.

The *Ideas* marks the beginning of Schlegel's turn toward religion as a source for social and cultural renewal. Religion now takes over the role of art as the chief source of *Bildung*. Like Novalis in *Christianity or Europe*, Schlegel writes under the influence of Schleiermacher's *Speeches*, as is clear from nos. 8, 112, 125, 150.

[1] Cf. Novalis, *Pollen*, the motto.
[2] Cf. Novalis' references to the *Speeches* in *Christianity or Europe*, p. 75.

11 Only through religion does logic become philosophy; only from it comes everything that makes philosophy more than a science. Without it we have, instead of an eternal, complete and infinite poetry, only novels, or the frivolity that now passes for fine art.

12 Is there Enlightenment?[3] One could use the term only if there is a principle in the spirit of man, like light in the cosmos, that one could set into activity at will, even if it could not be produced by artificial means.

13 Only he who has his own religion, an original view of the infinite, is an artist.

14 Religion is not merely one part of education, one limb of humanity, but the centre of all others, everywhere the first and highest, the absolutely original.

15 Every concept of God is empty chatter. But the idea of divinity is the idea of all ideas.

16 The priest as such exists only in the invisible world. How does he appear among men? He wants nothing on earth but to form the finite into the eternal; and so he must be and remain – whatever they want to call his profession – an artist.

17 If the ideas became gods, then the consciousness of [their] harmony would become devotion, humility and hope.

18 Religion must permeate everywhere the spirit of moral man, as if it were his element. This lucid chaos of divine thoughts and feelings we call enthusiasm.

19 To have genius is the natural condition of mankind; but it too must come healthy from the hands of nature. And since love is for women what genius is for men, we must think of the golden age as that where love and genius are universal.

20 An artist is everyone who makes the goal and centre of his existence the development of his mind.

21 It is characteristic of humanity that it must rise above humanity.

22 What do the few remaining mystics do? They more or less form the raw chaos of still existing religions. But only individually, on a small scale, through some feeble efforts. But act on a grand

---

[3] Schlegel alludes to the famous debate concerning the nature of the Enlightenment, which began in 1784 in the *Berlinische Monatsschrift*. Among the contributors to the debate were Kant, Hamann and Mendelssohn.

scale from all sides and with great masses; let us awaken all religions from their graves, and through the omnipotence of science and art enliven and create anew the immortal.

23 Virtue is reason formed into energy.

24 The symmetry and organization of history teaches us that humanity, for as long as it existed and developed, has really always been and become one individual, one person. To the great person of humanity God became man.

25 The life and energy of poetry consists in its going outside itself, tearing off a piece of religion, and then returning into itself by absorbing it. The same is true for philosophy.

26 Wit is the appearance, the external flash, of fantasy.[4] Hence its divinity and the similarity to the wit of mysticism.

27 Plato's philosophy is a worthy preface to a future religion.

28 Man is nature's creative backward glance upon itself.

29 Man is free when he produces God or makes him visible. In this way he becomes immortal.

30 Religion is absolutely unfathomable. Everywhere one can probe deeper into it *ad infinitum.*

31 Religion is the centripetal and centrifugal power of the human spirit, and what unites both.

32 Whether the salvation of the world is to be expected from intellectuals? I do not know. But it is time that all artists meet as sworn brothers in an eternal alliance.

33 What is moral in a writing lies not in its subject matter, or in the relation of the speaker to his audience, but in the spirit of its execution. If this breathes the whole wealth of humanity, then it is moral. But if it is only the work of an isolated power or art, then it is not.

34 Whoever has religion will speak in verse. But, to seek and discover religion, philosophy is the instrument.

35 Just as the ancient generals spoke to their warriors before battle, so the moralist should speak to people in the struggle of our age.

36 Every complete person has genius. True virtue is geniality.

37 The highest good, and all that is useful, is culture. [*Bildung*]

---

[4] On the concept of wit, see *Pollen*, note 18.

38 In the world of language or, what means the same, in the world of art and culture, religion appears necessarily as mythology or the Bible.

39 The duty of the Kantian relates to the command of honour, the voice of our calling and the divinity in us, as the dried plant to the fresh flower on the living stem.

40 A limited relation to the divinity must be as unbearable to the mystic as a limited view or concept of it.

41 There is no greater need of the moment than a spiritual counterweight against the Revolution, and against the despotism that it exercises over minds by the concentration of the highest worldly interests. Where should we seek and find this counter-weight? The answer is not difficult. Indisputably, within ourselves. And whoever has grasped the centre of humanity there, he will also have found the centre of modern culture and the harmony of all hitherto divided and conflicting sciences and arts.

42 If one believes the philosophers, then what we call religion is only an intentionally more popular, or an instinctively primitive, form of philosophy. The poets seem to regard religion as a degener-ate form of poetry, which fails to understand its beautiful game by taking itself too seriously and one-sidedly. Nevertheless, the philos-ophers confess and recognize that they begin and perfect themselves only with religion; and poetry strives only after the infinite and despises mundane utility and culture, which are the exact opposites of religion. So eternal peace among artists is not far away.

43 What human beings are among the creations of the earth art-ists are among human beings.

44 We do not see God; but we see the divine everywhere. We see it initially and most properly, however, in the heart of a sensitive soul or in the depths of a living human creation. You can immedi-ately feel, or immediately think, nature or the universe, but not therefore divinity. Only among people can a person write divine poetry, have divine thoughts or live with religion. No person can be the direct mediator for himself, even for his own spirit, because this mediator must be purely objective, having his centre outside the perceiving subject. A person can select and appoint his mediator; but he can select and appoint only those who have selec-ted themselves. A mediator is whoever perceives the divine in him-self, and whoever sacrifices himself to preach, proclaim and present

the divine to everyone through morals and actions, words and deeds. If this impulse does not arise, then what was perceived was neither the divine nor one's own. To mediate, and to be mediated, is the whole higher life of man, and every artist is a mediator for all others.[5]

45 An artist is whoever has his centre within himself. Whoever fails to find it there must select a particular leader and mediator outside himself; of course, not forever but only at first. For without a living centre a person cannot exist; and if someone does not have this in himself, then he must seek it only in another person; only another person's centre can excite and awaken his own.

46 Poetry and philosophy are, according to how one takes them, different spheres, different forms or even the factors of religion. For just try to join them and you will get nothing other than religion.

47 God is everything purely original and supreme, therefore the individual himself in his highest power. But are not nature and the world individuals?

48 Where philosophy stops, poetry must begin. A common standpoint – a natural way of thinking solely in opposition to art and culture, living just to exist – should not exist at all, i.e. no realm of crudity should be conceived beyond the limits of culture. Every thinking member of an organization feels his limits only with his unity in relation to the whole. One should contrast philosophy, for example, not only with non-philosophy but poetry.

49 To give the league of artists a specific end means to replace an eternal union with a meagre institute; in other words, it reduces the community of saints to a state.

50 You marvel at the age, at its seething gigantic energy, at its convulsions, and do not know what new births to expect. But do not mistake yourselves and answer the question: whether anything can happen to humanity that does not already have its basis in humanity? Must not all movement come from the centre; and where lies the centre? The answer is clear, and the appearances also indicate that there will be a great resurrection of religion, a universal metamorphosis. Of course, religion in itself is eternal, constant and unchanging like the divinity itself, but for just this reason it appears newly shaped and transformed.

[5] On the doctrine of mediation, see Novalis, *Pollen*, no. 74 and *Universal Brouillon*, no. 398.

51 We do not know what a human being is until we explain from the essence of humanity why some people have sense and spirit and not others.

52 To come forward as the representative of a religion is more sacrilegious than to want to found a new religion.

53 No activity is so human as one that simply completes, unites and fosters.

54 The artist should want to rule as little as serve. He can only create, do nothing but create; and so for the state he can only create masters and servants and elevate politicians and economists to artists.

55 Many-sidedness requires not only a comprehensive system, but also a sense for the chaos outside it; just as humanity requires a sense for what is beyond humanity.

56 Just as the Romans were the only nation that was entirely a nation, so our age is the first true age.

57 You will find a wealth of culture in our highest poetry; but the depths of humanity should be found only with philosophers.

58 Even the so-called teachers of the people hired by the state should become priests and spiritually minded; but they can become so only if they attach themselves to a higher culture.

59 Nothing is more witty and grotesque than the old mythology and Christianity. That is because both are so mystical.

60 Precisely individuality is the original and eternal in human beings. Personality is not so important. To pursue the education and development of this individuality as the highest calling would be divine egoism.

61 One has talked for a long time about the power of the letter without really knowing what one is saying. It is time for it to be taken seriously, so that the spirit awakens and grasps again the lost magical wand.

62 One has only as much morals as one has philosophy and poetry.

63 The really central intuition of Christianity is sin.

64 Through artists humanity will become one individual, since they connect the past and future with the present. They are the higher organ of the soul, where the living spirits of outer humanity meet, and in which inner humanity begins to act.

65 Only through education does a human being, who is wholly that, become everywhere a human being and penetrated by humanity.

66 The original Protestants wanted to live faithfully according to Scripture, to take it alone seriously and to destroy everything else.

67 Religion and morals are symmetrically opposed, like poetry and philosophy.

68 If you make your life human you have done enough; but the heights of art, and the depths of science, you will never attain without something divine.

69 Irony is the clear consciousness of eternal agility, of the infinitely abundant chaos.

70 Music is more closely related to morals, history to religion; for rhythm is the idea of music, but history concerns the primitive.

71 Only from confusion that is chaotic can a world spring.

72 It is in vain to seek in what you call aesthetics the harmonic wealth of humanity, the beginning and end of culture [*Bildung*]. Try to recognize the elements of culture and humanity and worship them, especially fire.

73 There is no dualism without primacy; hence morals is not equal to religion but subordinate to it.

74 Join the extremes, and then you have the true middle.

75 As the most beautiful blossom of a particular organization, poetry is very local; the philosophy of different planets need not be so different.

76 Morality without a sense for paradox is vulgar.

77 Honour is the mysticism of legality.

78 All thought of a religious person is etymological, a tracing back of all concepts to the original intuition, to what is singular.

79 There is only one sense, and in that one lie all others. The most spiritual is the original, and all the others are derived from it.

80 Here we agree because we are of one sense; but here we disagree because you or me are missing some sense. Who is right, and how can we agree? Only through an education that broadens every particular sense to the universal infinite sense. And only through our faith in this sense, or in religion, are we already now that which we will become.

81 Every relation of man to the infinite is religion, that is, of man in the fullness of his humanity. When the mathematician calculates

infinite quantity that is of course not religion. The infinite thought in that fullness is the divinity.

82 A person lives only in so far as he lives according to his own ideas. The principles are the means, the calling the end in itself.

83 Only through love, and the consciousness of love, does a human being become a human being.

84 To strive after morality is probably one of the greatest wastes of time, excepting exercises in piety. Could you grow accustomed to having a soul, a spirit? So it is with religion and morals, which should not influence the economy and politics of life without mediation.

85 The core, the centre of poetry is found in mythology, and in the mysteries of the ancients. Satiate the feeling of life with the idea of the infinite and you will understand the ancients and poetry.

86 Beauty is what reminds us of nature, and therefore excites the feeling of the infinite fullness of life. Nature is organic, and the highest beauty is therefore eternal and always vegetable. And the same holds for morals and love.

87 A true person is he who has come to the middle point of humanity.

88 There is a beautiful openness that, like a flower, opens only to be fragrant.

89 How should morals belong merely to philosophy, since the greatest part of poetry relates to the art of life and to the knowledge of the people? Is morals therefore independent of both and something for itself? Or is it that, like religion, it cannot ever appear isolated?

90 You want to destroy philosophy and poetry to make room for religion and morals, which you fail to understand? But you have not been able to destroy anything but yourself.

91 In its ultimate origins, all life is not natural, but divine and human; for it must spring from love, just as there can be no intellect without spirit.

92 The only significant opposition against the religion of man and artist now emerging everywhere is to be expected from the few remaining real Christians. But even they, when the morning sun really rises, will fall on their knees and pray.

93 Polemics can only sharpen the intellect, and should destroy irrationality. It is completely philosophical. Boundless religious

wrath and fury loses its dignity when it appears as polemic, having a definite direction toward a single object and goal.

94 The few revolutionaries that were in the Revolution were mystics, as only the French of our age can be. They made their characters and actions into a religion. But in the future it will seem the highest destiny and dignity of the Revolution that it was the most violent incitement to slumbering religion.

95 The new gospel will appear as a Bible, as Lessing prophesied,[6] but not as a single book in the customary sense. Even what we call the Bible is only a system of books. And that is not arbitrary usage! Or is there another word besides 'Bible', say 'the book', 'the absolute book', to distinguish the idea of an infinite book from a common one? Surely there is an eternal, and even a practical difference if a book is merely a means to an end or an independent work, an individual in its own right, a personified idea. A book cannot have such status without the divine, and here our esoteric concept agrees with our exoteric; moreover, no idea is isolated but is what it is only among all other ideas. An example will explain my meaning. All classical poems are connected and inseparable, forming an organic whole; seen properly, they are only one poem, the only one in which poetry appears in perfection. Similarly, in a perfect literature all books should be one book; and in such an eternally developing book the gospel of humanity and culture will be revealed.

96 All philosophy is idealism, and there is no true realism other than in poetry. But poetry and philosophy are only extremes. If one says that some are uncompromising idealists while others are determined realists, then that is a true remark. Put differently, it means that there are no completely cultivated human beings, that there is no religion.

97 A good omen that even a physicist – the profound Baader[7] – has raised himself from the midst of physics to anticipate poetry, to honour the elements as organic individuals, and to point at the divine in the very heart of matter!

---

[6] Lessing, *Education of the Human Race*, no. 86: 'It will certainly come, the age of a new gospel, which has been promised to us in the elementary books of the New Testament'. Lessing refers to John 14: 6.

[7] Franz von Baader (1765–1841), Bavarian *Naturphilosoph*. Schlegel probably has in mind Baader's *Ueber das pythagoräische Quadrat in der Natur oder die vier Weltgegenden* (1798). See Novalis to Schlegel, 20 January 1799, *Schriften*, IV, p. 273.

98 Think of something finite formed into the infinite, and you think of a human being.

99 If you want to penetrate the heart of physics, then consecrate yourself to the mysteries of poetry.

100 We will know people when we know the centre of the earth.

101 Where there is politics or economics there is no morals.

102 The first among us who had an intellectual intuition of morals, and who recognized and proclaimed under divine inspiration the model of perfect humanity in the forms of art and antiquity, was the holy Winckelmann.[8]

103 Whoever does not know nature through love will never know her.

104 Primal love appears never pure but in various shapes and guises: as trust, humility, devotion, serenity, loyalty, shame and gratitude; but mostly as longing and as quiet melancholy.

105 Fichte is supposed to have attacked religion?[9] If the interest in the supersensible is the essence of religion, his whole doctrine is religion in the form of philosophy.

106 Do not squander your faith and love on the political world, but sacrifice your inner self to the world of science and art in a holy firestorm of eternal creation.[10]

107 In undisturbed harmony Hülsen's muse creates beautiful, sublime thoughts about culture, humanity and love.[11] It is morals in the higher sense, but morals permeated by religion, moving from the artificial flux of the syllogism into the free stream of the epic.

---

[8] J. J. Winckelmann (1717–1768), German classicist. His works on Greek art, especially his *Gedanken ueber die Nachahmung der griechischen Werke in der Mahlerey und Bildhauer Kunst* (1755), were an important influence on the young Schlegel.

[9] Schlegel refers to 'the atheism controversy', which arose in 1799 when Fichte was removed from his position at Jena on the grounds that he had preached atheism. On the details of this debate, see Breazeale, *Fichte, Early Philosophical Writings*, pp. 40–4, 427–32. Schlegel and Novalis defended Fichte, arguing that he was not an atheist, and that, in any case, he had a full right to express his views.

[10] This aphorism was written to console Novalis for the hostile reception of *Faith and Love*. In his marginal notes to the *Ideen*, Novalis wrote: 'I heed your advice, dear friend.' See Novalis, *Schriften*, III, p. 492.

[11] August Ludwig Hülsen (1765–1810), educator and philosopher, also an occasional contributor to the *Athenaeum*. Schlegel perhaps refers to his 'Ueber die natürliche Gleichheit der Menschen', which appeared in 1799 in the *Athenæum*, vol. II, part 1, pp. 152–80.

108 What can be done, as long as philosophy and poetry are separated, is done and perfected. So it is time to unite them both.

109 Fantasy and wit are for you the one and all: Interpret the pleasing illusion and take the game seriously. You will then grasp the heart of things and see your revered art in a higher light.

110 The distinction between religion and morals lays quite simply in the old division of all things into sacred and human, provided that one only correctly understands it.

111 Your goal is art and science, your life love and culture [*Bildung*]. Without knowing it, you are on the way to religion. Recognize this and you will be sure of achieving your goal.

112 In our age, or any other, nothing better can be said in praise of Christianity other than that the author of the *Speeches on Religion* is a Christian.

113 The artist who does not sacrifice his whole self is a useless servant.

114 No artist should be by himself alone the artist of artists, the central artist, the director of all others; but all should be it, each from their own standpoint. None should be merely a representative of his kind, but should relate himself and his kind to the whole, which he should direct and rule. Like the Roman senators, true artists are a nation of kings.

115 If you want to act on a grand scale, then inspire and educate young men and women. This is still the first place to find fresh energy and health; and in this way the most important reformations have been achieved.

116 Outer nobility is to genius in the man, as beauty is to the ability to love or the soul in the woman.

117 Philosophy is an ellipse. The centre, which we are closer to now, is the autonomy of reason. The other centre is the idea of the universe, and here philosophy and religion intersect.

118 The blind ones who talk of atheism! Are there any more theists? Is any human mind master of the idea of divinity?

119 Honour the true philologists! They do something divine, for they spread a feeling for art over the whole domain of scholarship. No scholar should be merely a craftsman.

120 As long as we remain Germans, the spirit of the old heroes of German art and science should be ours too. The German artist

has either no character or that of an Albrecht Dürer, Kepler, Hans Sachs, Luther or Jakob Boehme. This character is fair, sincere, thorough, exact and profound, but therefore innocent and somewhat clumsy. Only among the Germans is it a national characteristic to honour art and science purely for the sake of art and science.

121 If you only listen to me now and see why you cannot understand one another, then I have achieved my goal. When the sense for harmony has been aroused, then it will be time to say more harmoniously the one thing that will always have to be said again.

122 Where the artists form a family, there are the original assemblies of humanity.

123 False universality is that which grinds off all the individual forms of culture and rests upon the mediocre average. On the other hand, through a true universality art, for example, will become more artistic than it has been on its own, poetry will become more poetic, criticism more critical, history more historical, and so on. This universality can arise when a simple ray of religion and morality touches and impregnates a chaos of combinative wit. Then the highest poetry and philosophy will blossom by itself.

124 Why does the highest express itself so often now as a false tendency? Because no one can understand himself who does not understand his fellows. You must first believe that you are not alone, you must intuit everywhere infinitely much, and you must not grow tired of cultivating your sense until you have at last found the original and essential. Then the genius of time will appear to you and will softly tell you what is proper and what is not.

125 Whoever intuits the highest in himself and does not know how to interpret it should read the *Speeches on Religion*, and what he feels will become clear to him to the point of putting it in word and speech.

126 A family can form itself only around a loving woman.

127 Women need the poetry of poets much less, because their inner essence is poetry.

128 Mysteries are feminine. They veil themselves gladly, but they want to be seen and solved.

129 In religion there is always morning and the rosy light of dawn.

130 Only he who is at one with himself can be at one with the world.

131 The secret meaning of sacrifice is the destruction of the finite because it is finite. To prove that it happens only for this reason the most noble and beautiful must be selected, above all a human being, the flower of the earth. Human sacrifice is the most natural sacrifice. But a human being is more than the flower of the earth; he is rational and nothing more than an eternal self-determining to infinity. Hence man can sacrifice only himself, and he does so in an omnipresent sanctum of which the rabble sees nothing. All artists are Decians,[12] and to become an artist means nothing other than to consecrate onself to the subterranean divinities. In the enthusiasm of destruction the meaning of divine creation first reveals itself. Only in the midst of death is the spark of eternal life ignited.

132. Separate religion entirely from morals and you have the real force of evil in man, the frightening cruel, raging and inhuman principle, which lies originally in his spirit. Here the separation of the inseparable is punished most horribly.

133. To begin with I speak only with those who are facing the Orient.

134. You suspect something higher in me and ask why I am silent right at the threshold? This is because it is still so early in the day.

135. The national gods of the Germans are not Hermann and Wotan, but art and science. Think again of Kepler, Dürer, Luther, Boehme, and then of Lessing, Winckelmann, Goethe and Fichte. Virtue is applicable not to morals alone; it holds also for art and science, which have their rights and duties. And this spirit, this power and virtue, distinguishes the Germans in their treatment of art and science.

136. Of what am I proud, and of what may I be proud, as an artist? Of the decision that eternally separates and isolates me from everything common; of that work that divinely surpasses every intention and whose intention no one will fathom completely; of the capacity to worship the perfect that faces me; of the consciousness that I can inspire my fellows to do their best, and that everything they create is a gain for me.

---

[12] Decians: a Roman family, the Decii, of which a grandfather, father and son gave their lives for Rome.

137. The devotion of the philosophers is theory, the pure intuition of the divine, reflective, peaceful and serene in quiet solitude. Spinoza is the ideal for this. The religious state of the poet is more passionate and communicative. At the beginning there is enthusiasm, at the end there remains mythology. What lies in the middle has the character of life, including even sexual differences. Mysteries are, as said before, feminine; and orgies seek, in the exuberance of masculine power, to conquer everything around them or to impregnate it.

138 Just because Christianity is a religion of death it must be treated with the greatest realism; it could have its orgies as well as the old religion of nature and life.

139 There is no self-knowledge other than the historical. No one knows who he is who does not know who his fellows are, especially the highest fellow of the brotherhood, the master of masters, the genius of the age.

140 One of the most important concerns of the brotherhood is to remove again all the outsiders who have sneaked into its ranks. Bungling should no longer be tolerated.

141 Oh, how miserable are your concepts of genius (and here I mean the best among you). Where you find genius I find not seldom a wealth of false tendencies, the very soul of incompetence. Some talent and much bombast is praised by all and they pride themselves on knowing that the genius is incorrect and that he must be so. So is this idea also lost? Is not the thoughtful person the one most fit to perceive the word of the spirit? Only the spiritual has a spirit, a genius, and every genius is universal. Whoever is only representative has only talent.

142 Like the merchants of the Middle Ages, the artists today should join together into a Hansa to defend one another to some extent.

143 There is no great world but the world of the artists. They lead a noble life. But they still lack good manners. This they could develop if everyone expressed themselves freely and happily, and if they fully felt and understood the worth of the others.

144 You demand, once and for all, an original mind from a thinker, and a certain amount of inspiration you even permit the poet. But do you know what that means? Without knowing it, you have trespassed on sacred ground; you are ours.

145 All human beings are somewhat ridiculous and grotesque, merely because they are human; and in this respect artists are doubly human. So it is, so it was, and so it will be.

146 Even in the most external practices, the way of life of artists should differ completely from the way of life of other people. They are Brahmins, a higher caste, but ennobled not through birth but self-consecration.

147 What the free person absolutely creates, that to which the unfree person relates everything, that is his religion. There is a deep meaning to the expression (and other similar ones): this or that is his god, or his idol.

148 Who unseals the magical book of art and frees the captive holy spirit? Only a fellow spirit.

149 Without poetry religion will be dark, false and evil; without philosophy it will be indulgent in its lechery, and lustful to the point of self-emasculation.

150 One can neither explain nor conceive the universe, only intuit or reveal it. Only stop calling the system of empiricism the universe; and for the present, if you have not already understood Spinoza, learn its true religious idea in the *Speeches on Religion*.

151 In all forms of feeling religion can break out. Wild rage and the sweetest pain border immediately next to one another, as do consuming hatred and the innocent smile of happy humility.

152 If you want to see complete humanity, seek a family. In a family souls organically grow into one; and for just this reason it is pure poetry.

153 All independence is original, and all originality is moral, the originality of the whole person. Without it there is no energy of reason or beauty of soul.

154 One first speaks completely frankly, totally carefree and exactly to the point of the highest.

155 I have stated some ideas that point to the centre of things. I have greeted the dawn in my opinion, from my point of view. Whoever knows the way, do the same in your opinion, from your point of view.

To Novalis

You do not hesitate before the threshhold, but in your spirit poetry and philosophy have deeply interpenetrated one another. Your spirit stood closest to me with these images of the inconceivable truth. What you have thought, I think; what I thought, you will think, or you have already thought it. There are misunderstandings that only confirm the highest understanding of one another. Every doctrine of the eternal Orient belongs to all artists. I name you instead of all the others.

Philosophical Lectures:
Transcendental Philosophy (excerpts)
Jena, 1800–1801
Friedrich Schlegel

II: Theory of Human Nature

When we speak now of a theory of human nature, we do not refer to what is usually understood by that name, namely everything that a person who begins to reflect wants to know. Our theory concerns the vocation of man. According to it, there is no universal vocation of man, because every person has his own ideal; and only the striving after this ideal will make him moral.

The opposite theory or a universal one would be only formal and would not bring people any further in a moral respect.

The vocation of man should be stated as a whole; and this can be found, because every individual presents the whole. Man should be considered as human society, or as the relation of man to man. The universal schematism[1] for the theory of man is: all human society can be reduced to *family*, *hierarchy* and *republic*.

Preliminary Reminder. One should not expect here the customary theory of natural right.[2] One cannot derive the concepts of *family*

The lectures on transcendental philosophy were delivered during the winter semester of 1800–1801 at the University of Jena. Schlegel completed the lectures on 24 March, 1801.

These lectures represent Schlegel's most systematic early reflections on political philosophy. They are an epitome of some of the fundamental early romantic doctrines: an ethic of love, the value of community and individuality, a social conception of the self and right, and an idealism and optimism regarding the future. Although the lectures still defend a republican point of view, their defence of aristocracy and the hierarchy give further evidence of a growing conservatism.

What follows are excerpts from part II, the 'Theory of Human Nature'. In part I, the 'Theory of the World,' Schlegel developed the general principles of his metaphysics, epistemology and philosophy of nature. Part III, 'Return of Philosophy into Itself', considers methodological issues in transcendental philosophy.

The translation follows the text in *KA* XII, 1–105. All the titles in the text, unless indicated by brackets, are Schlegel's own. I have excerpted that material most directly relevant to Schlegel's political thought. Footnotes followed by letters are Schlegel's own.

[1] Schematism (*Schematismus*): a Kantian technical term. The schema is a representation of the imagination that mediates between the pure a priori concepts of the understanding and the intuitions of sensibility to show which instances the concept applies to in experience. See *CPR*, B, pp. 178–80.

[2] Natural right (*Naturrecht*): the German term is ambiguous; it can refer to either natural right or natural law. According to customary natural law theories, such as those of Hobbes and Locke, the state is justified on the basis of natural law, by its agreement with principles that are valid of human nature as such apart from any society or state. Schlegel argues here, however, that natural law must be placed within a social and political context and that it is justified only from within it.

and *republic* from the concepts of right; they stand much higher. The concept of a republic implies something that is an end in itself, something that presents the vocation of man in its perfection, when that vocation rests upon the agreement of everyone. The republic will be derived from the vocation of man, and from the fact that the vocation of man is achieved only in society and the community of everyone.

In general, we doubt that natural right is a science.[a] Its first principle – the concept of right, of equality – is not scientific; it is a priori. It can be derived from the concept of human society, and this is constructed[3] through the task of constructing the vocation of man. But from that no science can be derived. If one wants to raise natural right to a science, then one must know all the circumstances that can take place among men. Natural right is nothing more than – positive jurisprudence, philosophically treated. This cannot take place systematically.

In constructing our concepts we have to abstract entirely from the empirical. This is true of all three concepts, the family, republic and hierarchy. For we should construct the concepts. But, on the other hand, it is also not our aim to set up ideals, e.g. of a state. If one wants to give rules about how to create a perfect state, one enters the realm of practice, where it is empty and not applicable.

The common centre from which the three concepts are to be constructed is *human society*. This relates to the task of characterizing the *vocation of man*, for the vocation of man is attainable only through human society – a condition to which man as man is bound, and from which morals proceeds and what determines the proper character of man, and rationality.

Now the essence of man consists in his vocation, and the possibility of attaining it.

---

[a] One should call natural right *rational right*. Its foundation is *equality*.

[3] 'Constructed' (*konstruiert*): a Kantian technical term for the method of mathematics. See *CPR*, p. B, 741. We construct a concept when it is presented or exhibited a priori to our intuition. To construct a triangle, for example, is to draw on the basis of a general definition an enclosed three-sided figure. In extending the method to philosophy, Schlegel followed the practice of Schelling, who had used the method extensively in his *Naturphilosophie*. See Schelling, 'Ueber die Konstruktion in der Philosophie', *Werke*, III, pp. 545–71.

Whoever grasps the basic concepts of human society therefore knows man entirely. He knows him according to his external conditions and relations. His knowledge is objective, and therefore universal.

A theory of the inner human powers is only subjective; it is, as it were, the expression of experiments with oneself, and for just this reason subjective. But the proper knowledge of man consists in the correct knowledge of the external relations of men among one another.

The theory of inner powers leads us theoretically to a description of consciousness. This can be also considered practically if it has the aim of presenting inner development, the power that is only possible, through a universal schematism. But this is only subjective. Hence no schematism has priority. What is objective in it is merely that there is some kind of schematism. A history of consciousness is indeed necessary, but it still does not give knowledge of man, because the single higher power is dissipated. He who wants to know man as a whole must consider him in society, for here he acts with all his powers.

We now have to seek the *categories of society*. In the concept of society lies immediately the concept *community* and the concept *freedom*.

Society is unity in multiplicity and multiplicity in unity. But if freedom were absolute there could be no community, and vice versa. We therefore must seek a mediating concept that unites both concepts and makes them possible. This is the *concept of equality*, the foundation of rational right. Here we speak not of physical but *moral* equality.

Our three concepts follow from the proposition concerning the vocation of man: *that a person can be a person only among people.*

It is an important question whether those categories of society – *community*, *freedom* and *equality* – are applicable to all three societies [family, hierarchy, republic] or if any is applicable only to one.

The answer to this question will shed some light on the forms of government and their relation to the original society. The opposition between family and hierarchy is very clear, since one is a natural and the other a spiritual relationship. Every human association that has only a spiritual end has a character that is different from the character of the state, and we find community with the concept of hierarchy. (The relationship between the political philosopher and positive jurisprudence is approximately as follows: the philosopher should be the legal counsel at the highest tribunal.)

The church should be a completely spiritual community. But every society that is based upon a completely spiritual community is not capable of any fixed laws and constitution. It rests upon absolute freedom, and is progressive ad infinitum.[b]

The construction of the three fundamental political concepts is the proper answer to the question of the vocation of man, and to know this vocation is the *knowledge of man.*

The doctrine of the *highest good* is completely identical with the theory of human nature.[4] The highest good should be, and determines, the *end of all ends.*[c] Taken subjectively, the question of the highest good is probably not capable of a definite answer. One could only say: man should strive to be himself. Then everyone has their highest good and it lacks objectivity.

On the other hand, an objective determination of the question of the highest good is possible if we relate it to the three basic concepts. The highest good may not be applied to the *supersensible.* It is the source of the useful, of right, and it corresponds to morality. But the supersensible is above all these things.

The highest good is community and freedom. Hence he who promotes community and freedom has done service for humanity.

Our concepts must be completely separated from all experience.

---

[b] Here a writing by Lessing should be noted: *Conversations on Free Masonry.*[5] Lessing was on the path toward philosophy. This is shown by his valuable book *On the Education of the Human Race.* It is to be regretted that he did not live another twelve years. Surely, he would become for philosophy what Goethe was for poetry.

[c] Politics is the science of the highest good.

[4] Highest good (*höchsten Gut*): a term introduced by Kant, *CPR*, B, p. 838, for the perfect correspondence between happiness and the worthiness for happiness or virtue in the design of nature. Following Fichte, Schlegel regards this ideal as a goal to be achieved by human action, not as a reality that is an object of faith.

[5] Lessing, *Ernst und Falk, Gespräche für Freimaurer*, first appeared anonymously in 1778. The work was basic to Schlegel's conception of the invisible church. See *Philosophical Fragments, KA* xviii, p. 250: 'Lessing's Free Masonry is the ideal of the church' (no. 678).

Concerning the republic. One should not think here of the constitution of a state, as it is now or has been. It is possible that all
states suffer a revolution; on the other hand, the revolutions that
have occurred amount to nothing at all. All states are based upon
money; but money does not arise by accident; it could be therefore
taken away, so that the states were deprived of their foundation.
All the present states would collapse in ruins.

Concerning hierarchy. This concept must be abstracted from *the
papacy.* If the hierarchy is aristocratic, or has a worldly power, then
it is diametrically opposed to the true concept. It therefore is to be
abstracted from all experience.

Concerning the family. This concept too must be abstracted from
all experience. This seems to be most difficult. But this relationship,
too, as it is given in experience, does not exhaust the concept. It
therefore must be able to give a new relationship. From the present
relationship of a family no republic can arise. A change of the family
relationship could be effected by chance if a legislator could over-
turn the laws of inheritance so that the daughter inherited the goods
and the sons were provided for. In the present family relations general morality is oppressed and it can take place only by chance on
an individual basis.[6]

Hence for our three basic concepts we must abstract entirely from
experience. They must be thought as only the schematism of
society. With our a priori construction concerning them our investi-
gation is brought to a close.

[Principles of Morals]

To bring clarity to our whole exposition, we must anticipate the
principles of morals.

In the very concept of morals lies a relation to life. Morals is a
philosophy of life. But perhaps it is not the whole philosophy of
life. There is something in life that it does not consider. This is
something completely different from practice. Practice relates to the
outer person, but this relates to the inner person. We can easily
distinguish between a *higher life of the inner person* and its external

[6] Here Schlegel criticizes the prevailing system of primogeniture, according to
which the eldest son had an exclusive right to inherit his father's estate.

relations or practice, everyday life. This latter is what is meant when we speak of morals as a philosophy of life. – The philosophy of the inner person is *religion*, or the philosophy of religion.

If we will grant it initially only as an hypothesis that the *principles of the philosophy of life, or morals*, are applicable to infinitely many objects, then we must find a centre from which we can proceed to the infinite and go back again.

What offers itself to us here is the analogy of philosophy itself.

With the construction of philosophy we had two basic concepts and a final proposition, by which we could construct philosophy itself.

In just the same manner we will proceed in the constitution of the principles of morals.

The two basic concepts of morality are *education* [*Bildung*] and *honour*.

(Concerning education, we speak not of external culture, but *the development of independence*.)

What is the basic proposition, the first principle of morality?

The universal formulae of ethics cannot help us. Kant placed the first principle of morality in *universality*. Only our principle must be diametrically opposed to universality, because it derives from the concepts of education and honour. It therefore must be: *individuality, originality*.

Only honour gives morality to people.[d] Only it takes them further.

Genetic Presentation of the Whole

We began philosophy with the demand that it be a science of the whole human being. It therefore must produce itself from within and then go outside itself. In this way arises a philosophy of life, where only the guidelines, the first principles, can be given, *because its applicability is infinite*. Precisely that the philosophy of life cannot be completed, that its application is infinite, that is the motif of philosophy that compels it to return into itself.

The theory of human nature should teach what is real in the totality of a person. What we should expect from it is not a theory of the inner person, but an answer to the question of the vocation of man. In answering it we came to the concept of

---

[d] The principles and feelings of morality are objective.

society. We also found *a schematism* for society, where its basic concepts were determined according to their relationship and categories. One could call the basic principles also *principles of politics* if politics should be a science. In these basic concepts we will find the basic concepts from which alone right can be derived by reason.

Hence here politics is given priority and the doctrine of natural right is the applied, the derived, because the basic concepts so relate to one another. There could be a society even if there were no right, namely that which would be superior to right.

Similarly, in the doctrine of natural right only the first principles are derived, namely from the basic political concepts. The applicability is then infinite. In the doctrine of natural right this is even more the case than in other fields, e.g. morals.

The principles of *politics* – *morals* – *natural right* – and *religion* stand in an immediate connection; they influence one another. To be complete in our anticipation of them, we must touch upon them all.

[Schlegel now embarks upon a short metaphysical excursus dealing with the metaphysical problem of freedom (*KA* xii, pp. 52–4). He argues that both the voluntarist and determinist wrongly presuppose a mechanistic conception of nature. If we view nature as an organism, though, we can see freedom as part of nature with no danger of fatalism.]

Principles of Religion

We proceed here as we did with philosophy and morals, namely we seek two *basic concepts* and a *principle*.

We will find these concepts most easily in the opposition of *external life*. We seek, however, the principles of the philosophy of inner life. We proceed to consider inner life, because the external is only individual and does not satisfy us.

The higher life of the inner human being relates to the whole. This is the *criterion of religion*. One of the basic concepts is *nature*. It is *completely objective*.

We now have to search for that concept opposed to it; therefore, something that is *completely subjective* and that relates to the whole. This is *love*.

We have to search for the maxims of religion in opposition to morals, because we make deductions from the opposition of our concepts. In morals the principle is *individuality, naturalness*, or *independence* or *originality*.

Here it will be the opposite of that – therefore, *universality*. The individual viewpoint should be cancelled.

Everything conflicts with our viewpoint that does not have a relation to the whole, the infinite. Here it is opposed to the concept of *freedom of the will*, in so far as it, apart from other powers in a person, designates *a special capacity for an absolute beginning, a new causal series.*[7]

(This is Kant's concept of freedom of the will.)

But we can agree as little with the concept of freedom, which we find in Jacobi.

With Kant, freedom is of course the opposite of mechanism.

But Jacobi accepts a much higher mechanism. It is indifferent, he says, whether it is a mechanism of being or of consciousness (and here we agree with him).

Mechanism is certainly the evil principle in philosophy and reality. (Because in mechanism finitude is posited absolutely.) But if one wants to determine the opposing good principle as freedom, the kind of opposition is not properly characterized, namely when freedom is only the opposition of mechanism. It is also incorrect that this freedom is attributable only to man.

The causality of the whole cannot be thought otherwise than as they vaguely intuit; only not with the mechanism of our consciousness having an absolute causality.

We can attribute absolute causality to people only in the case of the *causality of love*. The world is still imperfect. A beginning always must be made, therefore, to perfect it. There must be causality in the whole, then, that of course coheres with the whole. This is no other than the *causality of love*. By *love* everything began, and by love it will be perfected. Who recognizes this principle within himself, and who has become a creator by doing so, he will make the original fact comprehensible to himself.

---

[7] Here Schlegel criticizes Kant's concept of freedom as spontaneity, the power to begin a series of causes. See *CPR*, B, pp. 561, 579, 580, 581, 582, 584.

Love is the indifference point,[8] the core of ourselves.

The two most important positive religions are the *mythology of the Greeks and Romans*, and *Christianity*. If we wish to relate them to our concepts of religion, the *mythical religions of antiquity* correspond to *nature*, and *Christianity to love*.

[Schlegel now begins a brief excursus on the nature of religion, considering such topics as how we know God, the relation between God and nature, and the nature of anthropomorphism. See *KA* xii, pp. 53–4.]

Remark concerning the maxim of religion, *universality*.

That it is not imaginary can be shown by appealing to the instinct that expresses itself everywhere when a new view of nature has become part of oneself. An inner force compels one to communicate it.

This maxim shows us most easily the connection between the principles of religion and politics. *Religion* is completely separated from *morals*; they are opposed to one another. But this opposition must be united in a higher synthesis, since a life without honour or love is pitiable.

The maxim of religion connects with *hierarchy*, just as the principles of morals do with the *family*.

Religion and morals also connect with politics through the negative elements. *Love* relates to the highest good, and so does *honour*.

The connection takes place only *one* element. In education there is nothing by which a person will be driven to contribute to humanity. There is more a reason for separating from it.

The unifying principle lies in the opposing element. *The principles and feelings of honour* carry objectivity in themselves and join a person with all humanity.

Through the connection of this concept, namely *honour, with the highest good*, and with the manner in which this appears in life, as the highest harmony, it assumes a new character. It becomes *positive*; one can call it *ambition*. This is therefore distinct from honour, which is merely negative.

---

[8] 'Indifference point' (*Indifferenzpunkt*): the point where opposites meet and become completely one. The term was made famous by Schelling, who used it to characterize the absolute. See his *Darstellung meines Systems der Philosophie*, *Werke*, iii, p. 11, no. 1.

If we look at history from a moral point of view, then we find that these two principles were also valid.

It is true of morals, as of religion and politics, that philosophy can sketch only their outlines. We must oppose, therefore, those moralists who wish to construct systems. Morals cannot be comprised in a system, because one can borrow only a limited number of concepts and principles.[*]

Among all moral doctrines, *stoicism* corresponds best with our principles. If one wants to say that Christian morals is purer, we answer that *Christ taught only love*. He did not want to establish a morals.

In *stoicism* the principle of *honour* is explained splendidly; and as far as moral education is concerned, there is probably no one greater than *Socrates*. One could say of him: *he discovered the art of moral education*. He was not the most educated person himself, but he knew how, as far as was practical, to educate others.

Just as *honour* is that which negates the separation of *morals and politics*, *education* is that which connects the *external* with the *internal* person – morals with religion.

The connection can be expressed in a *fact* and a *precept*.

The fact is: *moral education begins with love*.

(Love is regarded here not in its highest abstraction, but merely in its subjective origin, as the beginning of universal love.)

This is the most important fact. The *precept* is borrowed from nature, and says: *follow nature*. It is the only precept of moral education.

(The highest concept of nature is meant, as the whole, free, living, organic, individual.)

Follow nature therefore means: *just as nature is organized, so organize yourself*.

How that is to be done is obvious, but everyone can learn only from himself.

The principles of *politics* are also dependent on *morals* and *religion*. The developing person isolates himself, but in such a manner that he makes a *family*. The *hierarchy* cannot be thought

[*] The best morals is found in the annals of Sparta and Rome. Tacitus and Thucydides are the greatest moralists; if one is clear about the principles, one can learn much more from them than systematic moralists.

without activity and the formation of the inner power of a person – therefore without *religion*. The question arises whether *the principles of politics* are demonstrated like those of morals and religion? Certainly. Namely, the two basic concepts are *the family* and *hierarchy*. The *basic maxim* is *republicanism*. The basic concepts can be very exactly determined; they are completely absolute. There is no question with them of an approximation to the infinite.[9]

If a society relates to the inner person, and if a definite form is moulded on to it, then it is not what it should be. Either it is what it should be or it is not at all. It is the same with the *family*.

But the opposite case holds with the maxim *republicanism*. Here there is an approximation to the infinite. *Republicanism* is the principle of all societies; hence the approximation to the infinite occurs. Even in common states a tendency to approach republicanism is visible, even if the form is opposed to it. The first tendency of all states was probably always republican.

Just as now the principles of politics depend on morals and religion, so morals and religion would be nothing without politics. The principles of politics unite the whole. For just as it is necessary that the principles of morals, politics and religion be separated – for from not distinguishing them all kinds of confusion arose – it is also necessary that they be united again.

[Schlegel now embarks upon a long discussion of metaphysical and religious topics, such as the relation of freedom and necessity and the nature of faith. See *KA* xii, pp. 57–70.]

Criterion to prove the existence of love. All feelings and impulses, hence all sympathetic virtues, if they are beautiful, must be able to be referred to love. But from what can one see whether one can ascribe *love* to oneself or to someone else? From *whether one is capable of friendship*.

Morals and religion are connected with love. Love is what joins religion and politics. Love therefore must be applicable to the three concepts of politics. And that is indeed the case. A *republic* is unthinkable without *love of country*. It is obvious that love must take place in the *family*. And the hierarchy has no other material than *love*.

---

[9] Approximation to the infinite (*Annäherung ins Unendliche*): a reference to Kant's doctrine of regulative principles. Cf. *Oldest Systematic Programme*, note 3.

For the sympathetic virtues,*f* that are all to be related to love, that are not virtues of obligation,[10] and that therefore have something free and indeterminate (unlike virtues of obligation) – for these the criterion has been found, namely, *they are moral when they are beautiful.* True love must prove itself through deeds; hence the criterion of love can be established: whether someone is capable of friendship. Nowhere can the principle of love show itself so purely as in friendship.

[At this point (XII, p. 71), Schlegel again considers broader moral and metaphysical issues not strictly related to politics. The discussion of political matters does not begin again until XII, p. 84.]

Usually, the doctrine of right is considered as the positive, and politics is subordinate to it. But here it is the opposite. Politics (namely the science of society) is here the *positive*, and the doctrine of right is subordinate to it.

The categories of society are *freedom – equality – community.* To banish any misunderstanding, we will seek terms with a more definite meaning instead of these.

Practical philosophy began by *inquiring into the vocation of man.* This can be sought nowhere but in human nature. But the essence of man consists in *intellect* and *fantasy.*

Intellect is the highest power of consciousness joined with the *characteristic of lawfulness in the relation of the whole to the individual.*

The opposite will be that which *drives the finite into the infinite*, where all laws cease. That is *fantasy.* This definition will express what everyone feels.

One can say: intellect and fantasy are the elements of the form of humanity. Consequently, we still have to seek that which is common to them both. It will be visible in a person, but it will not be so definitely demonstrable as understanding and fantasy. This is *freedom*, but not freedom of the will or morality, but an absolute

---

f These virtues appear especially among the new moralists.

[10] Virtue of obligation (*Pflichttugend*): the virtue of acting upon some perfect duty, that is, where there is a specific duty to some definite person, for example honesty and trustworthiness. This is opposed to a sympathetic virtue (*sympathetische Tugend*), which acts upon some imperfect duty, that is, where there is not a specific duty to a definite person; a sympathetic virtue would be the sentiments of sympathy or charity. The modern moralists, to which Schlegel refers in his note, are most probably Hutcheson, Hume and Rousseau.

freedom, that which we call omnipotence. Namely, *it is freedom as the first condition of fantasy and the final goal of the pure understanding*. Understanding is the influence of the higher on the finite; the goal is to destroy illusion, or the finite. How this goal is attained leads us to *freedom*.

A society [formed] according to this concept of freedom will be *anarchy* – one may call it the *kingdom of God*, or the golden age. The essential point is that it will be always anarchy.

This freedom is the capacity of man; it is the final goal for everyone. It is *the highest good* – but it is an *ideal*, which can be found only through *approximation*. These conditions are to be found only in an opposition, not in an absolute but a relative opposition. Namely, freedom is the ideal; we approach it through lawfulness.

But does that [lawfulness] not conflict with freedom? The contradiction is resolved when lawfulness is decided by freedom, so that a relative freedom arises. Whoever gives himself laws is relatively free. And this is the condition of an approximation to absolute freedom.

———————

Philosophy is concerned with the universe, and therefore with *unity*. All philosophy is concerned with unity. But the *character of unity* is different. The unity of our philosophy is harmony, or the unity in the relation of the individual to the whole. This philosophy rests on the concept of the organism of nature. This concept also extends into practical philosophy. Here the first problem was the question of the vocation of man. According to our method, we also constructed concepts here. We could seek the vocation of man only in his essence, and there we found the concepts *fantasy*, *intellect* and *freedom*. Freedom is the only reality in wishing, willing, sensing and striving. The *highest good* is freedom, or at least it must be contained in it. One enquires into the highest end to be able to examine all ends according to it. The concept of freedom is not capable of any absolute presentation. Life is only an approximation to it. For practical purposes the detail of the approximation is more important than the pure concept. The condition of the approximation is relative freedom. This is found through lawfulness as what is opposed to absolute freedom; hence *autonomy* is found to be the first degree of approximation. This autonomy is coordinated with *isonomy*, namely that autonomy should be universal and not relate to the individual but the whole, for otherwise it would destroy itself. The product of both is *harmony*, which determines the relation of the individual to the whole. The first consequence of this: *that we cannot consider human beings individually*. The question of the vocation of man concerns, therefore, not the individual but the whole of humanity. We have constructed it as an organic concept. Practical philosophy should not construct therefore the ideal of an individual person, but the ideal of the whole, of society.

The middle term between morals and religion is politics. It was constructed through the family, hierarchy and republic.

The family has been established as relating to nature. Hierarchy has been left completely indeterminate; it is opposed to the family. The family rests upon absolute limitation, whereas hierarchy rests upon absolute extension, but not as in any republic. The republic comprehends always only the present; the hierarchy should comprehend also the past and future; this extension is based upon the fact that humanity is a whole.

The republic is the highest concept. Every society must be a republic, because it must rest upon the categories of autonomy, isonomy and harmony.

If we now want to construct the form of society, we must go back to what is real in society. The real is that which consists in the connection of part to whole in society, a *power – a political power*. This power must be so characterized that it relates to consciousness and can be explained from it. We must seek a concept that expresses the capacity of an *absolute decision*. This is the *constitutive power*, that part of the political power that contains absolute decisions.

Regarding the principles of politics, which are also principles of the reunification of religion and morals.

The whole of politics comprises the form of *how people can be one*. The further application can do nothing more than make the mediating concept clearer through new constructions. *Republicanism* is the chief concept of society.

The forms of the state are referred to by *democracy, aristocracy, monarchy.* To make these forms fruitful, we will first have to construct the matter for the forms; and the concepts of the forms must so attach to it that they become comprehensible.

We enquire into *political power,* which makes up the *political matter.*

The *executive power* is unthinkable without the *constitutive,* which has the right of *absolute decision* and *resolve.* But the constitutive is thinkable without the executive. In particular, we can think a constitutive power, which also had the executive power, though only negatively. Everything would happen only through its permission.

We can regard the constitutive power as a *negative element* of political power in general. The positive will now have to relate to the whole. That one could express with the concept of *representative* power. But one should distinguish that from what is usually meant; namely, one calls *representatives* those who can be regarded only as deputies, who do not present the whole but are only subordinates of it. That power can be called representative that presents the whole itself and is *positive;* for *the whole in relation to its parts* is positive.

In several states, as we know from history, it was a principle of *monarchy* that the whole was given over to one person as magistrate. But the question is not exactly of *unity of person,* still less that this is hereditary.

For the *constitutive power,* or the negative element, the converse case must arise. Here the principle of *democracy* becomes the essential element. It should be that kind of political power that reveals itself through absolute decision. This power should unite the sum of all individual wills.

The third concept that reveals itself as a mediator between the two previous ones should be referred to as the executive power. This is also generally recognized. It is the essence of *aristocracy.*

It follows 1) *that every republic is aristocratic.* Because it springs from both concepts. True aristocracy arises only through the opposition of the two elements of monarchy and democracy. 2) That what is essential in the construction of political power rests upon positive and negative power; the latter would not be if one did not refer it to the positive as a whole. The otherwise customary legislative power then lapses. For each of these three powers cannot be other than legislative.

Not only every state but every society and association is to be judged according to this schema.

But not only in the external, but also in the internal side of a person separation, and reunification, are demanded as a problem to be solved. All of these concepts are perfectly applicable to the inner person, since they are constructed from autonomy and isonomy, which are in the inner person.

With these constructions the principles of politics are completed.

The essential point was the separation of *religion* and *morals*, and their reunification through *politics*.

Philosophical fragments from the
Philosophical Apprenticeship (excerpts)
Friedrich Schlegel

First Epoch II

508 It is very improbable that the Revolution will ever cease; to all appearances it is eternal. One does not need to be in Paris; Burke is better than so many travellers.

538 Should there be a state only so that there are families? *Property* is a family concept. All property is property of the family. Here all the so-called *tituli*[1] are joined together. A healthy family must have a trade. Should children conduct the trade of their fathers? Certainly, that is better; the military caste can and should not be a trade. *Trade* is a concept that is inconceivable without the family. *Estate* is only a *legal* concept. Among themselves the peoples should not form a state, like under the Romans, nor a family, like the church, but a society. International law should be *vegetable*.[2] Constitution and representation are chimeras contrary to *honour* and *peace*.

539 Every genuine nation is a great family.

540 When corrupted, the power of the family turns into the urge to dominate. Priests and mandarins should rule – the philosophers according to Plato. Intellectuals should form themselves into a humanistic estate, like the Christians and the knights of the best times. There should be many institutions for the poor, criminals, the sick, children.

The fragments of the *Philosophical Apprenticeship* (*Philosophische Lehrjahre*) came from notebooks collected by Schlegel throughout his lifetime. Of the sixty-five notebooks devoted to philosophy, only thirteen survive. The fragments were ordered by Schlegel himself into 'epochs' (*Epochen*). These were conceived not only chronologically but also thematically, since material written at different times was sometimes placed into a single epoch. The approximate dates for the epochs excerpted here are as follows: First Epoch II, 1796–98; First Epoch III, 1797–1801; Second Epoch I, 1798–99; Second Epoch II, 1798–1801; and Epoch VII, 1802–03.

These fragments provide a glimpse into Schlegel's evolving political outlook. They reveal some of the germs of his later conservatism: a growing sympathy for the Middle Ages and Catholicism, and an increasing ambivalence about the legacy of the French Revolution. Although Schlegel attempts to fuse these new attitudes with his republicanism, the synthesis proved to be a fragile one. By 1808 Schlegel had converted to Catholicism.

The fragments translated here are the most important for Schlegel's political thought from 1796 to 1803. The translation is based upon *KA* XVIII, *Philosophische Lehrjahre* ed. E. Behler.

---

[1] *Tituli*: deeds to ownership.

[2] Vegetable: for Schlegel, vegetables, animals and minerals are the basic elements of the natural world. Vegetables are characterized by their gradual, unconscious growth. Schlegel implies that internal law should develop in a similar manner, and that it is fruitless attempting to establish a written constitution.

591 The most vulgar opponents of the Revolution, who detest it as a diabolical chaos, are much better than those who get involved with principles. The Revolution is the highest that the French possess; better than this it is not.

652 Love is a unification of moral and poetic feeling; it therefore has a place only in modern ethics, not in ancient.

697 A person can endure everything, even suffering, better than truth. One lives not to be happy, also not to fulfill duty, but to cultivate oneself.

732 *Catholicism* is politically and aesthetically more consistent than Lutheranism, whose contribution lies only in its philology and polemics.

956 *Robespierre* wanted to politicize the whole realm of free transactions; that was the maximum of his tyranny, and as a maximum it was always great. He is the apex of the French Revolution.

First Epoch III

49 Love is universal friendship, and friendship is abstract love, partial marriage.

73 The Middle Ages were like the epoch of crystallization of modern development. Then the European spirit was like a coral reef.

80 *Sparta*, *Rome* and *Athens* combined would give perhaps a perfect republic.

83 The administration should be monarchical, the directorate democratic, the representative aristocratic.

147 The highest virtue is to make one's individuality the final end. Divine egoism. People therefore have a right to be *egoists*, if they only know their ego, which one can do only if one has one. There is always some indication.

Second Epoch I

2 Against Candide one can counter with only an *aesthetic* optimism: that this world is the most *beautiful*.

8 Beauty lies in the manner of representation and perception; in the aesthetic view of the world one really sees all things in God.

Aesthetics has a centrepoint, and that is – humanity, beauty, art – the golden age is the centre of this centre.

40 If there should be equality, then women must possess all property. The desire for possessions would be naturally beautiful in their case. A family can crystallize around only a woman and mother. If all property is family property, then this [that women possess property] would also be just. Women should rule in the family as men do in the state.

41 In the morals of the critical philosophy there remains an eternal gap between theory and practice, even irresolveable knots, which can be filled or cut only through poetry and historical virtue.

123 *Diotima* [is] a necessary idea for Socratic philosophy, just as the Madonna is for the Catholic religion.

265 The state has the right to requisition from all citizens, but not to make citizens into soldiers or to ruin writers in their profession, or not to take account of it. The same holds for parents.

335 *Honour* and *peace* should be the spirit among contemporary international relations; property and contract are not applicable.

358 The goal of the state is as little merely [the protection of] right as the goal of marriage is utility.

$$\frac{\text{Minerality . Humanity}}{\text{o}}$$

is the goal of the state.[3] The kings are enthroned by God, namely through juristic genius.

359 A political Germany will go to ruin through incompetence.

375 Politics belongs to morals, religion and history, which are distinguishable only in their dignity.

391 The new Bible must be for the Germans what the Revolution was for the French.

403 The Revolution was the (anti-religious) religion of the French. Through its words it has worked miracles. It also has its mythology.

---

[3] $\dfrac{\text{Minerality . Humanity}}{\text{o}}$

Schlegel frequently expressed his ideas in mathematical equations. This one means pure humanity and minerality. What, precisely, Schlegel means by minerality in this context is unclear. But, elsewhere, he equates it with the legal system of a state. See *KA* XVIII, p. 228, no. 416.

531 The *hierarchy* must base itself upon mysteries and magic, especially upon the latter. Mysteries are independent of biblical art and mythology.

543 Every artificial constitution is worthless, even that based on an ephorat.[4] The hierarchy is the only just state.

544 The entire culture of this age is superficial; on the other hand, that of the Middle Ages was built from a solid foundation. There is probably more than one Middle Ages – any pause full of chaos in a culture.

595 The French Revolution began with the self-divinization of the nation and ended with it too. It has built many things, but no constitution.

603 The state is the whole life of man, something very sacred. This marriage is magnifiable to infinity.

704 A political constitution is something completely irrational. There is only one republic, that of all men. Economics is realistic, politics is idealistic. Perhaps only the family should have a constitution, the republic only representation. There always remains art and approximation [to ideals].

730 The basis of eternal revolution. (Christ always made war). The chaos that has been subconscious and passive in the modern world must come again so that it is active; eternal Revolution.

749 At the time of the republic even the artists will not be a special class.

771 The true reform of states must begin by *educating* masters and servants. The artist (priest) may not wish to rule anymore than serve.

790 The *Revolution* is the key to the whole of modern history. The Reformation and the partial civil wars in Europe were only precursors for it.

931 *Politics* must be as historical as poetry; only the latter concerns itself with the past as much as the former with the future. Even logic should be as historical as ethics.

1173 The *state* is something in the middle between the family and church. The goal of politics should be negative. There should

---

[4] *Ephorat*: in Fichte's *Grundlage des Naturrechts* (1796–7), the ephorat were a group of elders who supervised the executive power to ensure that its decisions conformed to the general will. See Fichte, *Werke*, III, pp. 150–87, no. 16.

be as many families and churches as possible as in the Middle Ages not fewer corporations, associations, states within states.

1255 Never was there more freedom, equality and fraternity than in the Middle Ages – and these were their best in Germany. The great alliances, the trials of the peasants, the Swiss, the Hansa, the free cities, the law of the club. The best in the state then was the masculinity, the friendship.

1291 Politics (as the art and science of the community of all human development) is for the periphery what religion is for the centre.

1294 Religion is the art of wisdom, the science of life, and that higher politics that I previously sought.

1358 After the great Middle Ages every nation in Europe has its own little Middle Ages or political chaos. Similarly, almost every nation, one after the other, has its fit of Roman world dominance.

1363 Politics is the proper art of wisdom – the science of the appropriate.

1366 All politics should become economics – a more effective use of all powers.

1376 Religion is the revolutionary principle in man.

1379 This age strives after a Revolution of the family as well as the republic. Only in the family should there be a free monarchy; all states must be a *republic*. Only through and in the family and republic does man raise his view *ad sidera*[5] and become like God.

1400 In the Roman republic and Middle Ages morals and religion were one and economics and politics were in the grand style.

1405 All politicans should be intellectuals.

1471 The essence of the modern consists in a *creation out of nothing*. Such a principle lay in Christianity – and something similar in the Revolution, and in Fichte's philosophy – and likewise in the new poetry. Only this can bring back the spirit of antiquity. Philology cannot do it.

1473 Cannot it be derived from the essence of humanity that there must be a higher species, men of genius, having greater powers, heroes . . . Their existence is that which constitutes religion and education, and to make them free is the goal of a true republic.

---

[5] *Ad sidera*: to the stars or heavens.

1475 To have genius, to be a daemon, is the natural condition of human beings. But it must emerge healthy from the hands of nature. In the golden age everyone had genius. That it has been lost is to be explained from the principle of corruption; but it has not completely disappeared from humanity.

1480 Artists should not have power; others may rule. But, free like gods, they should educate everyone standing in the centre.

1531 Ideas for a critique of religion. The Protestant and Catholic must be mixed in a new religion.

1538 The papal hierarchy will always remain an ideal for every society of priests and intellectuals.

Second Epoch II

68 The French Revolution will become universal only through the German.

101 Completion of community = love.

105 *Property* is a marriage of man with things.

123 Before a centre is found, German education cannot be applied. Freedom, equality and fraternity are the principles of all universality.

317 The genuine true Middle Ages is perhaps that of the Neoplatonic philosophy. Then and only then had mysticism manifested itself in great measure.

376 The hierarchy should be nothing more than a school for schools. Not academies and universities but councils are the true form of assembly for artists. Could the state not direct them? They could just be convened to decide political matters.

417 Europe should be united through religion; but Europe will exist for the next generation only in the German school.

505 Without *opinion publique*, no *volonté générale*; and no *opinion publique* without the ephorat of intellectuals and propaganda of reason.

580 The *highest* work of art for man is the state. Hence true technology must be based upon a *construction of the estates*. Thus *politics* is the height of aesthetics, which is as universal as history.

643 The history of humanity is nothing more than a presentation of the dualism between reason and unreason, i.e. love. Love is the *dark light*, and the positive in human beings.

666 *Republic of intellectuals*: a Protestant concept; *hierarchy of art*: a Catholic concept.

706 Universal eternal peace can take place only in the golden age. For just that reason it is from now on [our] goal. In the centre eternal war, as an end in itself, like in the Middle Ages; but [it should be] with intelligence and goals, like with the ancients. Peace must be the end of war, as theory of practice.

768 Religion needs a firm point for its external appearance; perhaps my ideas about the family and republic are just that.

822 Should there be a hierarchy, then it must appear externally and be presented [to the senses]. Only a republic of intellectuals is appropriate for that, because humanity must be put in contact with its ancestors and posterity.

876 Should there not be secret and learned societies? All morals seems to rest upon society.

916 The republic is only a middle state of fermentation, an expedient. *Family* and *hierarchy* are the only forms of true society. Hence Fichte was right – the republic should destroy itself. All contemporary, and generally modern states fumble around these two ideas.

925 The new Christianity must be *catholic* without any further ado, but old catholic, not the papacy.

932 It can be deduced not only that the church is possible only through artists, but that the fine arts are only that through the hierarchy, and should be called *catholic* arts.

946 Mere excommunication and limitation of freedom should be sufficient punishment – not pain or death – also not disgrace, except perhaps for commoners.

998 There is no republic without an ephorat, and only the spiritual class can execute this.

1207 To regard the republic as a contract is as bad as regarding it as property.

Epoch VII

201 The greatness of the feudal constitution was this: that in the freedom of assembly and club-law there was the idea that everyone should be king.

203 *State within a state*, an idea that should be raised to the power of the infinite. Intellectuals will be artists, artists will be intellectuals, and agriculture will be an art. The choice of a king will be left to intellectuals, not the *knights*. There will no longer be peasants and knights.

303 In a true Revolution one should confiscate the goods of not the clergy and aristocracy but the speculators. The other traders should all be put in the service of the state.

Monologues II and III
Friedrich Daniel Schleiermacher

II: Self-examination

People are afraid of looking into themselves. Many tremble slavishly when they can no longer escape the questions: What have I done, what have I become, and who am I? The whole business is frightening to them, and its outcome is uncertain. They think that a person can more easily judge others than oneself. They believe they show a respectable modesty when, after the most rigorous self-scrutiny, they admit they could have still made a mistake.

Yet it is only the will that conceals people from themselves. When they really turn their attention upon themselves, their judgement cannot err. It is just this, however, that people cannot or will not do. Life and the world completely binds them; deliberately confining their view to it so that they perceive nothing else, they see nothing but the disparate, deceptive reflections of themselves.

I can know another person only from his actions, for never does his inner life come directly before my view. What a person really wants I can never know immediately. I can only compare his various actions and make uncertain conjectures about the aim of their conduct and the spirit that guides them. Surely, though, it is a pity when one sees oneself only as one stranger does another, when one knows nothing of their inner life! How clever one fancies oneself for merely considering the last decision regarding some external action, and for comparing it with the feeling that accompanied it and the idea that preceded it. How

Schleiermacher wrote his *Monologues* (*Monologen*) in December 1799, and they were published in the Spring of 1800. Their melancholy and wistful tone gives expression to the alienation and *Weltschmerz* characteristic of the young romantic soul. Despite their personal and confessional form, the *Monologues* state some of the fundamental themes of early romantic political thought: the ethic of love, the need for community, the value of individuality, and the organic conception of the state. The work is also significant for its break with the ethics of Kant and Fichte.

The text appeared in four editions during Schleiermacher's lifetime, in 1800, 1810, 1822 and 1829. Schleiermacher made many changes in these later editions, sometimes adding whole passages. All these changes have been carefully noted in the critical edition of Friedrich Schiele, *Monologen, Kritische Ausgabe* (Hamburg: Meiner, 1902).

The following translation is based upon the Schiele edition and the *Kritische Gesamtausgabe*, 1/3, pp. 1–61, which reproduce the original 1800 text. In a few minor cases I have translated from later editions if doing so clarifies the meaning of the first edition. The translation comprises two of the five parts of the *Monologues*, parts II and III.

does such a person expect to know others or himself? What is to guide his shaky conjectures in inferring the internal from the external when it is not based on anything immediately certain in any clear case? A clear presentiment of error creates anxiety; a dark foreboding of guilt oppresses the heart; and the mind vacillates from the fear of that small portion of self-consciousness that has been degraded to the role of a disciplinarian and whose voice must be often ungladly heeded.[1]

People have indeed cause to be concerned when they honestly examine the inner deeds that are the basis of their life. Often they do not like to recognize the humanity in them, and they do not want to see their conscience, this consciousness of their humanity, deeply violated. For whoever has not examined his past actions cannot provide a guarantee that their future ones will still belong to humanity and prove worthy of it. If such a person has only once torn up the thread of self-consciousness, if he has once abandoned himself only to the consciousness and feelings that they share with animals, then how can he know that he has not completely sunk into the deepest animality?

To contemplate humanity in oneself, and when found never to divert one's gaze from it, is the only certain means never to stray from its sacred realm. This is the inner and necessary connection between action and contemplation,[2] which is inexplicable and mysterious only to the foolish and slow of heart.[3] A truly human action creates the clear consciousness of humanity in me, and such consciousness permits no other action than one worthy of humanity. Those who cannot raise themselves to this level of clarity are driven only by dark intuition. In vain are they educated and trained; they think of thousands of stratagems and make decisions to force their way back into the sacred realm of humanity. But the holy gates never open. They remain on unconsecrated ground and cannot escape the punishment of the offended deity, the disgraced feelings of banishment from the fatherland. It is always sheer folly and vain

---

[1] 'Small portion of self-consciousness' (*kleinen Antheil des Selbstbewusstseins*): a reference to conscience. See *Gedanken* III, *KGA* I/2, p. 126, no. 34: 'People all have a small fragment of divine reflection, and when it is degraded to a schoolmaster they call it conscience.'

[2] 'Contemplation': *Schauen*.

[3] Luke 24: 25.

trifling to lay down rules or to make experiments in the realm of freedom. What is required to be a human being is a single free decision. They who have made it once will forever remain a human being; whoever ceases to be one has never been one.

With proud joy, I still recall the time when I discovered humanity and knew that I would never again lose it.[4] This noble revelation came from within, produced by no doctrine of virtue or system of the wise. A lucid moment crowned a long search, which neither the doctrine nor system could satisfy. Through action freedom dispelled my dark doubts. I can say that, since then, I have never lost my true self. What they call conscience I do not recognize anymore; no qualm punishes me, none needs to warn me.[5] Since then I also do not strive after this or that virtue, nor am I especially pleased by this or that action, unlike those for whom a dubious ray of reason appears occasionally and singly in the flux of life. In peaceful silence, in unchanging simplicity, I preserve constantly within myself the consciousness of all humanity. Gladly and with an easy heart I see my actions in their context, certain that I will find nothing that humanity must repudiate.

Were this the only thing that I demand of myself! How long ago I could have rested and peacefully awaited the end of my days! For the certainty I have attained is unshakably firm, and it seems to me reprehensible cowardice, which is alien to my nature, were I to expect from a long life fuller confirmation of it, and were I to fear that something might happen to plunge me from the heights of reason to the depths of bestiality. But I too am still plagued with doubts. Another higher goal is set before me, just as the first has been achieved. Having it sometimes clearly and sometimes dimly in view, my self-reflection does not know how I should approach it, or at what point I now stand, and it hesitates in its judgement. Nevertheless, the goal becomes more certain and confirmed the more I return to my old self-examination. But even if I were far from attaining certainty, I would still seek only in silence and not complain; for stronger than any doubt is the joy to have found what

---

[4] An allusion to Schleiermacher's break with the religious community of the *Herrnhuter*, which took place in April 1787.

[5] An implied criticism of Kant's and Fichte's ethics, which regards conscience as the stern voice of duty. See Kant, *Metaphysics of Ethics Ak.* VI, p. 483, and Fichte, *System der Sittenlehre, Werke, IV*, pp. 173–4.

I seek, and to have escaped the common delusion that confuses many of the best for their whole life, preventing them from ascending to the real heights of humanity. For a long time,[6] I was content to have found only reason; and honouring the universality of one and the same being as its only and highest aspect, I believed that there is only one right thing to do in every circumstance, that action must be the same for everyone, and that it is only because of situation and place that people differ from one another. I thought that humanity reveals itself differently only in the multiplicity of external deeds, and that a person is not an individually formed being but made of one element that is the same everywhere.

So it is with people! If, by scorning the particularity of animal life, they attain consciousness of a universal humanity and throw themselves before duty, they are not immediately able to ascend also to the higher standpoint of the development of individuality and ethical life,[7] and to see and understand the sphere of nature that is chosen by freedom itself. Most people rise only halfway. They portray humanity only in its crude element, merely because they have not grasped the idea of their own higher existence. This idea has seized me.[8] The feeling of freedom alone has not satisfied me for long; personality, and the unity of my fleeting consciousness, seemed superfluous and I was compelled to search for something higher in ethics which would explain them. It did not satisfy me to see humanity in inchoate, crude masses, which internally are all alike, and which externally form fleeting phenomena from contact and friction.[9]

So dawned on me what is now my highest intuition. It has become clear to me that every person presents humanity in his own unique way, by his own mixture of its elements, so that humanity reveals itself in every possible manner, and so that everything

[6] A reference to the early Kantian phase of Schleiermacher's intellectual development.

[7] Ethical life: *Sittlichkeit*. There is no exact equivalent in English. *Moralität* designates the standpoint of Kant and Fichte that Schleiermacher wishes to overcome.

[8] Schleiermacher criticizes the opposition between reason and nature in Kant's and Fichte's ethics. Duty and inclination, reason and nature, are joined through the organic development of the individual.

[9] Fleeting phenomena (*flüchtige Phänomene*): a critique of Spinoza's principle of individuation. Schleiermacher maintains that Spinoza can distinguish the modes of his single universal substance only through their mechanical properties. See *Kurze Darstellung des Spinozistischen Systems, KGA* I/I, pp. 573–4.

diverse realizes itself in the fullness of infinitude. This idea alone
has elevated me and separated me from the vulgar and uncouth who
surround me; it has inspired me to a work of divinity, which should
be pleased to have its own unique form and development. The act
of freedom that accompanies this idea has gathered and joined
together the various elements of human nature into a unique existence. Had I always considered so persistently the uniqueness of my
actions as I viewed their humanity, were I properly aware of every
action and limitation that is the consequence of that free act, and
had I steadfastly observed the further development and every mani-
festation of nature, then I would have had no doubt what province
of humanity belongs to me, and where the common ground of my
expansion and limitation is to be sought. I should then have measured the whole extent of my being, recognized my limits at all
points, and known prophetically what I still am and could become.
But it is only late, and with difficulty, that a person attains complete
consciousness of his individuality.[10] One does not always dare to
regard it as an ideal, and focuses instead upon the common possession of humanity, which one has lovingly and thankfully
embraced. Indeed, one often doubts whether one has a right as
an individual to tear oneself away from this common possession.
Confusing the sensible with the spiritual, one fears sinking into the
old reprehensible limits of the narrow circle of the external personality. It is only late that one learns to cherish and use one's highest
privilege. Hence the retarded consciousness of individuality must
long remain vacillating; the most genuine striving of nature is often
not observed; and even if its limits reveal themselves most clearly,
the eye glances all too often upon the outlines of things, seeing only
the vague general features when the unique manifests itself only
through negation.[11] However, I may be pleased with how far the
will has tamed my laziness, and how practice has sharpened my
sight so that much less escapes it now. Whenever I act, however
that might be, according to my own spirit and disposition, the

---

[10] Individuality: *Eigenthümlichkeit*. In this context the term means what is unique
or distinctive of a person. The same term is used by Humboldt for his individualist
ethic. See *Ideen zu einem Versuch, die Gränzen der Wirksamkeit des Staats zu bestimmen, Werke*, I, pp. 63, 64–5.
[11] An allusion to Spinoza's maxim *Omnis determinitio est negatio*, all determination
is negation. See Spinoza, letter 50, *Opera*, ed. C Gebhardt (Heidelberg: Winter,
1925), IV, p. 240.

imagination gives the clearest proof of the free choice of a thousand other ways of acting according to a different spirit and disposition without violating the laws of humanity. I imagine myself in a thousand different forms so that I see my own form all the more clearly.

Yet, because the image of my individuality still stands incomplete before me, and because the unbroken connection of a clear self-consciousness still does not vouch for its truth, my self-reflection still cannot proceed at an even and calm pace. Often I must deliberately review all my actions and strivings, and recall my own history; and I may not ignore the opinion of friends, whom I have gladly permitted to look into my inner life, if they differ from my own judgement.[12] I still seem to be the same person I was when my better life began, only more resolute and determined. And, indeed, how should a person, having once attained an independent and individual character, suddenly take on a new nature in the middle of his growth and development? How should they grasp another side of humanity without having brought the first to perfection? How should he be able to want this side? How will he find it if he does not know what it is? Either I have never understood myself or I am still now who I always believed myself to be; and every apparent contradiction, when reflection has resolved it, must show me all the more clearly where and how the extremes of my nature have been concealed and how they can be bound together in harmony.

It still seems to me that the twofold vocation of man on earth marks the great dividing line between all its diverse natures. The two activities are much too distinct: to develop humanity in oneself to a definite form and to present it in many different kinds of action, or to portray it externally through artistic works so that everyone must recognize what one wants to show.[13] Only he who stays on the lowest level in the mere forecourt of individuality and does not want to define themselves from a fear of limitation, could want to unify both, only to achieve little in either of them. Whoever wants to

---

[12] 'Friends' (*Freunde*): a reference to the romantic circle in Berlin, which Schleiermacher joined in 1797.

[13] In the *Speeches*, *KGA* 1/2, pp. 193–4, Schleiermacher says that the soul is the product of two opposed drives: one is the striving to appropriate everything, to make it conform to the self; the other is the drive to extend oneself to everything, to expand and embody oneself in the world. The object of the first is enjoyment, while the end of the second is activity, power over things.

achieve something in one of them must renounce the other. Only at the end of the course is there a transition,[14] a perfection which humans rarely attain.

How could it seem doubtful to me which activity I chose?[15] I was so completely resolved to avoid troubling myself with the work of the artist, and I so passionately seized everything that benefited my own education and accelerated and strengthened its development. The artist chases after everything that can be a sign or symbol of humanity. He fumbles through the treasure of languages and forms the chaos of sounds into a world of his own; he seeks a secret meaning and harmony in the beautiful play of colours in nature; in every work he conceives the effect of all parts, the structure and law of the whole, pleased more with the beautiful container than the precious contents it offers. He then forms ideas for new works. Secretly, he nurtures them in his soul and they grow in quiet seclusion; his creative energy never rests, draft and execution following upon one another. Through constant practice his skill improves steadily; his maturer judgement disciplines and binds the imagination. Thus the artist's creative nature approaches the ideal of perfection.

But I observed all this only with my senses, for it remained foreign to my thoughts. The humanity portrayed in works of art strikes me much more clearly than the artistry of the creator. It is only with difficulty that I grasp his artistry, and then I understand but little of it. I abandon myself to free nature;[16] and when she shows me her beautiful suggestive signs they arouse all kinds of sensations and thoughts in me; but they do not impress me so strongly that I transform them into my own creation. I do not strive to form the material of my senses to perfection; hence I refrain from acquiring skill through practice; and if I put forth in action what is within me, I do not trouble myself to make the act more beautiful and clear.

---

[14] The third edition version of this sentence reads: 'Only at the extremes do the two directions appear to approach one another, so that to unite them a perfection is required that is seldom achieved.'

[15] In the immediately following paragraphs Schleiermacher settles his accounts with the aestheticism of the romantic circle. Although he does not care to be an artist himself, he places a high value upon art. In the *Speeches* he maintains that art is the sister of religion, *KGA* 1/2, p. 263.

[16] The 1800 version reads: *Ich lasse frei die freie Natur.* In the 1822 edition the passage runs: *Ich gebe frei mich hin der freien Natur.*

The free muse is my favourite goddess.[17] From leisure one learns how to understand and define oneself. Thought bases its power upon leisure, and it then easily governs everything if the world demands action from it. Hence I cannot develop myself in isolation, as the artist does. In isolation all the juices of my mind dry up, and the course of my thought is arrested. I must get out and join a community with other spirits, to see the many forms of humanity and what is alien to me, to know what can become of myself, and to determine more securely through give and take my own nature. My burning desire for greater self-realization does not allow me to give the expression of my innerness external perfection. I put forth my speech and action in the world, not bothering whether those who listen or look at it penetrate its crude shell, or whether they find their own inner thoughts and spirit in the imperfect form. I have neither time nor inclination to trouble myself about this. In this short life I have to move on and, as far as possible, perfect my individual nature through new thoughts and deeds. I hate to repeat anything even once, so little of the artist is there in me. For just this reason I like to do everything in company with others. In thinking, contemplating and learning I need the presence of some beloved person, so that communication immediately follows the inner deed, and so that I easily reconcile myself to the world through the sweet and gentle gift of friendship. So it has been, so it is now, and I am so distant from my goal I no longer expect ever to get beyond it. Indeed, I have the right, whatever my friends say, to exclude myself from the sacred domain of the artists. I will gladly renounce everything they gave me if, in the field in which I have placed myself, I find myself less imperfect than they fancy.

Reveal yourself once again to me, intuition of the far flung field of humanity! Here dwell those who strive only to develop themselves and, without producing a permanent work, to reveal themselves in varying actions. Reveal yourself once again, and let me see whether I can find my own place here, whether there is something in me that makes sense, or whether an inner contradiction prevents my design from coming to fruition, so that it dissolves into nothing-

---

[17] 'Free muse': *Die freie Musse*. In German there is an untranslatable affinity between *die Musse*, the muse, and *Müssigkeit*, idleness or leisure. The importance of idleness for self-realization was a favourite theme of the romantic circle. See Schlegel's novel *Lucinde*, 'Idylle über die Müsiggang', *KA* v, pp. 25–9.

ness rather than achieving perfection. Oh, no, I should not fear! No sad feeling emerges in the depths of my consciousness. I recognize how everything comes together to form a true whole; I feel no foreign element that oppresses me; and I am missing no part, no noble aspect of my own life. Whoever wants to form themselves into a determinate being must have a sense[18] open for everything that is not themselves. Here too in the sphere of the highest ethical life the same union of contemplation and action prevails. Only when someone is conscious of his uniqueness in his present actions can he be sure not to injure it in future ones; and only when he constantly requires himself to survey the whole of humanity, comparing all of its manifestations with one another and his own, can he maintain consciousness of his own selfhood. For only through contrast is individuality known.

In limited circumstances the highest condition of one's own perfection is a universal sense. And how could this exist without love? Without love the dreadful disproportion between giving and receiving will soon unhinge the mind in its first efforts at self-realization, driving it from its proper course. He who wants to be a person in his own right will be completely destroyed, if not degraded to the common level. Yes, love, you power of attraction of the spiritual world! No individual life or development is possible without you. Without you everything must degenerate into a crude, homogeneous mass! Those who do not desire to be anything in their own right do not need you; for them laws and duties, uniform action and justice are sufficient.[19] The holy feeling of love would be a useless ornament to them. Hence they neglect the little they get from you; not recognizing the sacred, they cast it among the common good of humanity, which should be directed by a single law. But, for us, you are the alpha and omega! There is no individual development without love; and without the development of

---

[18] Sense: *Sinn*. A technical term of Schleiermacher's epistemology, sense is the intuitive capacity to perceive an object as a unique whole, to grasp it for itself and not simply in relation to something else. Schleiermacher distinguishes it from the discursive understanding (*Verstand*) that analyses things into their parts and relations to other things. While the understanding is active, sense is passive, receiving the 'undivided impression of something whole'. See *Speeches, KGA* 1/2, pp. 253–5.

[19] Allusion to the ethics of Kant and Fichte. Schleiermacher suggests that their ethics of duty cannot explain the importance of love anymore than individuality.

one's individuality there is no perfection in love. When one comp-
lements the other, both grow together inseparably. I feel united
within me the two fundamental conditions of ethical life! I have
made sense and love part of myself. Both are ever growing within
me, a sure sign that my life is fresh and healthy, and that my own
development becomes still firmer.

Is there anything for which my sense is not open? Those who
would gladly elevate everyone to a virtuoso and artist in science
complain enough that they cannot get me to limit myself, and that
all their hopes prove delusory when it seems that I surrender myself
to everything serious. For when I attain one viewpoint, my fleeting
spirit rushes in its usual way to other objects. Oh, if they would
only leave me in peace! If they would only understand that I cannot
do anything else, and that I cannot perfect a science, for I am
resolved only to develop myself. If they only allowed me to keep
my mind open toward everything that they do, and if they only
considered worthy of their trouble what I develop in myself through
the contemplation of their actions.

With their complaints these friends only testify in my behalf. But
there are others, unlike me in nature but like me in striving to get
to the bottom of everything human, who accuse me of the opposite
failing. They complain that my sense is really too limited, that I
pass over many sacred things with indifference, and that I corrupt
the deeper more impartial view by some idle desire for dispute.[20]
Yes, it is true that I pass over many things; but it is not out of
indifference. It is indeed also true that I engage in dispute; but that
is only to keep my mind open. In this, and in no other way, I
must act, because I am concerned both to fill and expand my sense.
Whenever I have the feeling for something in the field of humanity
that has hitherto escaped me, my first reaction is not to contest that
it exists, but that it is that, and that alone, as the person who first
told me about it sees it. My late awakened spirit, recalling how long
it has borne an alien yoke,[21] fears becoming subject again to the
domination of foreign opinion. When a new subject shows it new

---

[20] Schleiermacher replies to some criticisms of his personality in Friedrich Schlegel's
   Lucinde. See Schlegel, *KA* v, pp. 74–8. Cf. Schleiermacher to Henriette Herz, 1
   July 1799, *KGA* v/3, pp. 133–7, esp. 135.
[21] Allusion to Schleiermacher's education in the Moravian seminary at Niesky, where
   he studied from 1783 to 1787.

life, my spirit arms itself, weapons in hand, ready to fight for freedom so that it does not lapse again into the servitude of some alien influence.[22] But once I have won my own point of view, the time for dispute is past. I allow everyone else their opinion, and I perfect the task of interpreting and understanding the viewpoint of others.

So it is that what often first appears to be a limitation of the sense is really only its first stirring. Of course, during this beautiful period of life, it often had to express itself when many new things touched it, and when many things appeared in a new bright light that previously I only darkly felt and had no preparation for. Often these first stirrings of my spirit must have negatively affected those who were the source of my new insights. I have calmly observed this, trusting that they too will sometime understand me when they have more deeply penetrated my nature. Even my friends have often misunderstood me in this way, especially when I unsympathetically passed over, though did not dispute, what they rashly embraced with warmth and naive passion. The mind cannot grasp all things at once; and it is pointless to try to finish its task in a single action. Its activity always goes infinitely in two directions,[23] and everyone must have their own way of uniting both to perfect the whole. When something new strikes my mind, I do not have the power immediately to penetrate to its very heart and to know it perfectly. Such a method does not suit my mental equilibrium, which is the keynote to the harmony of my being. To focus thus upon one thing alone would upset the balance of my life; by penetrating one thing I would alienate myself from another without having possessed the true properties of the first. Every new acquisition I must first lay down in the inner depths of my mind; and then carry on with the usual business of life in all its varied concerns, so that the new mixes with the old and comes into contact with everything that was once in me. Only thus do I succeed in preparing myself for a deeper and more intimate intuition of things. Before I have completely fathomed something, the interchange between contemplation and practice must be frequently repeated. Thus, and thus alone, do I have to proceed if my inner being is not to be violated, because in me self-development and the activity of the senses should be in

[22] Despite his later criticisms of the *Aufklärer*, Schleiermacher defends here the value of reason and intellectual autonomy.
[23] Cf. note 13.

every moment kept in a balance. Hence my progress is slow, and I must be granted a long life before I grasp all things equally. Nevertheless, whatever I have once comprehended bears my stamp, and however much my sense understands of the infinite sphere of humanity will be transformed by me and become part of my nature.

Oh, how much richer my life has become! What a happy self-consciousness of my inner worth, what a heightened feeling for my own life and existence, crowns my self-reflection now that I consider the rewards of so many beautiful days! Not in vain was my quiet activity, which externally seemed like idleness. It has nicely aided my inner development. This would not have succeeded so well if I had to contend with all the distracting business and affairs of everyday life, which do not suit my nature; and still less would it have done so with a more narrow sense. Oh, pity that the inner nature of a person is so neglected by those who can and deserve to understand it best, that so many of them confuse the external action with the internal deed, and that they think they can understand the deed and action only from torn fragments, seeing contradictions everywhere when everything is really in harmony.

Is, then, my individual character so difficult to recognize? Does this difficulty deny me forever the dearest wish of my heart: to reveal myself more and more to everyone who deserves it? Yes, even now, by looking deeply into my soul, I am confirmed anew in the conviction that this is the drive that moves me most. This is the truth, however often I am told that I am withdrawn, and that I coldly reject the sacred offerings of friendship and love. It is indeed the case that I never think it necessary to speak of what I have done or what has happened to me. But that is because I regard the worldly side of my life as too insignificant to dwell upon for those to whom I would rather reveal my inner nature. Also, I do not speak of that which lies dark and inchoate within me, and that lacks the clarity by which I make it my own. How can I show to a friend what still does not belong to me? Why hide from him what I already am? How can I hope to communicate without misunderstanding what I do not understand myself? Such caution is not reserve or lack of love. Rather, it is only sacred respect, without which love is nothing; it is only tender care not to desecrate or needlessly to entangle the highest. As soon as I learn something new and grow in my individuality and independence, do I not rush to announce it in word and deed to my friend, so that he shares my joy and, seeing the growth of my inner life, benefits from it? I love my friend as I do myself; as soon as I recognize something as mine I give it to him.

I do not have as much interest in what my friend does, or what happens to him, as most of those who call themselves his friends. His external actions leave me quite unconcerned and unperturbed when I understand the inner nature from which they flowed and know that they must be so and not otherwise because he is as he is. They neither nourish nor stimulate my love, and have little to do with it. These actions belong to the world, and they must comply with the laws of necessity and everything that flows from them. Whatever follows from these laws, or whatever happens to my friend, he will know how to treat in a manner worthy of his freedom. Nothing else concerns me here; I calmly regard his fate just as I do my own. Who will regard this as cold indifference? It is the clear consciousness of the opposition between the world and man that is the basis for my self-respect and the feeling of freedom. Should I bestow it less upon my friend than myself?

This is what I am so proud of: that my love and friendship are of such a noble origin in me; that it is never mixed with vulgar sensation; that it is never the product of habit or weakness; but that it is the purest deed of freedom, directed only to the proper inner being of people. I have always kept a distance from those common feelings. Never has kindness seduced my friendship, nor beauty my love; never has pity so blinded me that I abetted misfortune and represented the suffering person in a different or better light. Thus I left a space in my mind free for true love and friendship, and the urge to fill it with richer and more varied contents never abated. Wherever I notice an aptitude for individuality, because sensitivity and love, its highest guarantees, are present, there I also find an object for my love. I would like to embrace with love every individual being, from the naive youth, in whom freedom first blossoms, to the most mature perfection of humanity. Whenever I see such a person I give them the greeting of love, even though the deed is only suggested because nothing more than a fleeting meeting is granted to us. I also never measure things according to some worldly standard, judging friendship by some external appearance. My view transcends the world and time, searching for the inner greatness of a person. Whether someone has understood much or little, whether they have progressed far in their inner development, and whether they have many achievements to their credit, cannot sway me, and I can easily console myself if these are missing. What I am looking for is individuality and its relation to the whole of human nature. How much I find of the former and understand of the latter determines how much love I have for a person. But I can prove my love for him only to the extent that he understands me. Alas, how often for this reason it is misunderstood. The language of the heart is not heard, as if I were deaf and they thought so too.

People often travel along narrow paths, but still do not come near to one another. One senses a friendly presence and calls for a meeting. But it is in vain. The other does not hear. Those whose paths are far apart often approach one another; one of them thinks that it is forever, but it is only for a moment. Opposed movements tear them apart, and neither understands whither the other is going. So it has often been with my longing for love. Would it not be shameful if it had not grown mature, if my facile optimism had not disappeared and a rich wisdom taken its place? 'This person will understand so much of you, and that person so much; you may love this person in this way, but you should not do so to another.' This is how the voice of moderation often speaks to me. But usually it is in vain. The deeper urges of my heart have no place for prudence, and even less for the presumption that would set limits to people, their feelings for me, and my love for them. I always demand more and constantly strive anew. I am often punished for my possessiveness, losing what I had already gained.

Yet it cannot be otherwise for someone who develops their individuality. That it happens to me is the surest sign of my development. Only such people unify in their own manner the diverse elements of humanity. They belong to more than one world. How could one always remain in proximity to the other, developing along a similar path, when the other is also an individual? Like a comet, the self-realized individual traverses many systems and encircles many stars. Now a star happily sets her eyes upon him, strives to know him, and he swerves from his course to approach her. Then she sees him again in distant spaces. His appearance has altered and she doubts if he is still the same. But he returns again at a quick pace, greeting her again with love and friendship. Where is the idea of perfect union, the friendship that is equally perfect from both sides? Only when spirit and love have grown in equal measure almost beyond all measure. But then with their love they too are perfected, and the hour strikes for them that has already struck for all. It is time to give onself to infinity, returning to her womb from the world.

III: Worldview

'It is for dreary old age,' they say, 'only to complain about the world. It is excusable when we look back to a better time when we had the full strength of our living powers. Happy youth should smile upon the world. Ignoring all the defects, it should make the most of what is there and gladly trust the sweet delusions of hope. But only he sees the truth, and only he knows how to deal with the world, who knows how to steer the middle course, neither vainly lamenting nor naively hoping.'

Such peace of mind, however, is only the foolish transition from hope to contempt; and such wisdom is only the dull echo of the gladly retracted steps by which they stride from youth to age. Such complacency is only a perverse, polite self-deception, which does not want to appear to scorn the world it will soon leave, and which still less wants to admit itself wrong. Such praise is a vanity embarrassed of its errors, a forgetfulness that does not remember what it wanted the previous moment, and a cowardice that would rather be poor than take any trouble.

I have never flattered myself when I was young, and so I will now never flatter the world. He who expects nothing cannot be disappointed, so I cannot despise the world out of revenge. I have done nothing to change it, and hence have no need to find it improved. But I am disgusted by the base flattery that is heaped on it from all sides, so that once again the work praises its master.

This perverse generation talks so glibly of the improvement of the world only so that it can think better of itself and raise itself above its fathers.[24] If the first sweet fragrance now arose from the beautiful blossom of humanity, if in untold numbers the germs of individual development were flourishing free from all danger, if

---

[24] A criticism of the optimism and complacency of the *Aufklärer*.

everything breathed and enjoyed a sacred freedom, and if everyone embraced everything with love and brought forth in harmony new and wonderful fruits, this still would not match their praise for humanity.

As if the thundering voices of their powerful reason had broken the chains of ignorance! As if they had finally completed their beautiful portrait of human nature, which formerly had been painted in such gloomy dark colors so as to be scarcely recognizable, but which now appeared from above in a mysterious light that illuminated everything so that no healthy eye could mistake the whole outline or the individual details.[25] As if the music of their wisdom had tamed crude predatory egoism into a mild household pet and taught it the arts! Thus they speak of the modern world. It is as if every passing moment brought forth new wonders.

Oh, how deeply I despise this generation, which boasts more shamelessly than any preceding, which cannot endure the thought of a better future, and which basely reviles everyone who wants to work toward it. It does this only because the true goal of humanity, toward which it has not taken a single step, lies unknown to it in a dark, distant future!

Yes, indeed, whoever is content that only man governs the physical world; that he discovers its powers only for his needs; that space does not weaken the spirit but quickly executes any action that the will demands of it; that everything shows itself to be standing under the command of thought so that the spirit reveals its presence everywhere; that every crude piece of matter becomes animated; and that mankind enjoy its life through its feeling of mastery over the body; whoever thinks that this is the ultimate end of humanity should join in this loud song of praise of our time.[26] Man is right to be proud of his mastery over nature, which he has never enjoyed before. However much is still to be done, so much has now been achieved man must feel that he is the lord of the earth, that nothing may remain untried in his realm, and that the limit of impossibility is steadily shrinking.

[25] A criticism of the optimistic conception of human nature of the *Aufklärer*, who denied original sin.

[26] A critique of *inter alia* Fichte's doctrine of moral striving, which sees increasing domination over nature as central to morality. Fichte expounded this ethic in the third part of his popular *Bestimmung des Menschen*, *Werke*, II, pp. 278–319. Schleiermacher gave this work a critical review, *KGA* I/3, pp. 235–48.

Here at every moment I feel the community that connects me to everything as the complement of my own power. Everyone engages in their special task, completing the work of someone that they do not know, and preparing the way for someone else, who in turn will scarcely know what has been done for him. Thus the common work of humanity is promoted throughout the world. Everyone feels the effect of others as part of their own life. Like an electric charge, the ingenious machine of the community conducts the slightest movement of each individual along a chain of a thousand links to achieve a single goal, as if all were members of a whole, and everything they did were its work, executed in a moment. This feeling of a life enhanced by common effort is more vivid and beautiful in me than in those who boast of it. For I am not disturbed by their gloomy imagination, according to which everyone enjoys so unequally what they help to create and maintain.[27] Through thoughtlessness and through laziness of mind everyone loses something; custom exacts its toll from all of us; and whenever I compare a person's restrictions with their powers, I find everywhere the same formula,[28] expressed only differently; and the same amount of life spreads to all.

In any case, I have little regard for this feeling.[29] I do not wish the world only something better of this kind. It torments me to death to think that this should be the whole work of humanity and that it should squander its sacred gifts on such a profane task. My demands are much less modest and do not rest simply with the relation of man to the external world, even if this were already brought to the highest peak of perfection.[30] Is man only a sensible

---

[27] A critique of German radicals, such as Fichte and Georg Forster, who argued for a more equal distribution of property according to the principle that he who works more should receive more.

[28] The formula would be: the fewer social and economic restrictions, the greater the power; but also the greater the expectations and consequently disappointments. Hence the enjoyment of life does not depend upon social standing. See the early sermon *Neujahrspredigt von 1792*, Schiele, pp. 153–4.

[29] 'This whole feeling' (*dies ganze Gefühl*): the feeling of belonging to a community, of 'a life enhanced by common effort'.

[30] The 1822 edition adds this passage after this sentence and before the next: 'To what purpose is the higher power over matter if it does not promote the life of the spirit? Why praise the outer community if it does not aid the community of spirits themselves? Health and strength are indeed of great value; but does not everyone scorn them if they are only for empty show?'

being that the highest feelings of life, health and strength, are his highest good? Is it sufficient for the spirit that it inhabits only a body, that it continually and increasingly develop it, and that it becomes self-conscious of dominating it? But their whole striving is directed to that, their overweening pride is based upon it. So high have they raised themselves in their consciousness of humanity that they have ascended from the care of their own physical life and well-being to the care for the equal welfare of all. That is their virtue, justice and love; that is their cry of triumph over lower egoism; and that is the end of all wisdom for them. It is only these rings in the chain of ignorance that they care to break. They think that everyone should help in this task, and that every community is established for this end alone. Oh, the corrupt mentality that thinks the spirit should devote all its powers to acquire for others what it would itself reject for a higher price! Oh, the perverse sensibility that regards it as a virtue to sacrifice the highest for such base idolatry!

Accept your bitter fate, my soul, to have seen the light only in such dark and wretched times. From such a world you can hope for nothing for your strivings, nothing for your inner development. Your association with it will be felt not as an enhancement but as a restriction of your powers. So it is for everyone who knows and wants something better. Many a heart is starved for love. Many have a clear idea of the friend with whom they can exchange their thoughts and feelings for the sake of mutual development and greater self-awareness. Yet, unless they are lucky to find someone in the same circle of their outer life, they and their ideal partner will sigh in vain for their whole lives with the same wish.[31] What the earth gives me here and there thousands can describe; where something can be found that I need I can know in one moment and

[31] The 1822 edition adds this passage after this sentence and before the next: 'For, as always, the external estate of a person – the position that they cannot attain in their wretched community, or that is assigned them by others – enslaves them. A person clings to these bonds more than a plant does to the earth. But why? Because people think that it costs them little to oppress their higher spiritual life to enjoy more securely their lower physical life. For this reason a more spiritual community, a freer public life, still cannot prosper; for this reason they live cloistered in damp isolated cells, more *next to* rather than *with* one another; and for this reason they avoid every greater form of union, contriving only the miserable appearance of it by joining together many separate parts. Just as the fatherland is divided, so too is every individual society.'

possess it in the next. But there is no means to know where there is another spirit who is indispensable for my inner life. For that there is no community in the world; and there is no business to bring closer those who need one another. And do they know, those whose yearning hearts vainly pour forth love in all directions, where their friend and beloved dwells? Their external position; the position they have in that miserable community, enslaves them; and a person clings closer to these bonds than stones and plants to mother earth. The lamentable fate of the black, who is torn from his loved ones in his native land and condemned to servitude in a distant unknown place,[32] is also imposed upon his betters,[33] who, prevented from reaching their homeland and compatriots, must waste away their inner lives in barren surroundings that forever remain alien to them.[34]

The minds of many are open enough to grasp the inner essence of humanity, to intuit intelligently its various forms and to find what is common to them. Yet this takes place in a desolate wilderness or in a barren luxury, where eternal monotony gives no nourishment to the needs of the spirit. Turned upon itself, the imagination grows sick; it consumes the spirit in dreamy delusions, and exhausts its creative power in abortive efforts. For the world offers no assistance; and it is no one's vocation to give nourishment to the wretched or to carry them lovingly to better climes. Many have the impulse to create works of art; but no opportunity to sift through the material, to weed out what is not useful, or, should the sketch be complete, to give the right polish and perfection to every part. Does anyone give him what he is missing, freely offer him materials, or complete what he has not finished? Everyone must stand alone and undertake what they cannot do by themselves! Neither in art nor in the realization of human perfection is there any community of talent like that which was established long ago for the service of our external needs. It is only painfully that the artist becomes aware of the existence of others, when their judgement finds fault with

---

[32] A critique of slavery.

[33] Betters (*Bessern*): in this context this phrase means those who are normally regarded as better off or more fortunate.

[34] A reference to German emigration to America, perhaps also to mercenaries there during the War of Independence. The need to emigrate, and subsequent depopulation, had become a political issue in Germany by the close of the eighteenth century.

what is alien to his genius, and when the alien and critical inhibits beauty and his own work.

Thus a person searches in vain for relief or help from the community in what is most important to them. Indeed, to the sons of our time, to demand these things would be merely a nuisance and foolishness. They think that it is idle dreaming to imagine, or to want to promote, in spite of ignorance and prejudice, a higher and more intimate community of spirits. They claim that it is immoderate desire, not poverty, that makes us feel the limits that oppress us. They say that it is a contemptible laziness, not the lack of community, that makes a person unhappy with the world, and that makes him roam about in the realm of impossibilities with his empty wishes. But these are impossibilities only for those whose view, pinned to the lower plains of the present, only sees a low horizon. How I must despair of humanity ever coming closer to its goals if my foolish imagination had to limit itself only to the present and its immediate consequences!

All who belong to a better world must languish under a dismal servitude. Whatever now exists of a spiritual community is degraded to serve an earthly one. Only of use to the earthly community, the spiritual community limits the spirit and does violence to our inner life. When friends extend the hand of friendship to each other, their bond should create deeds greater than each could achieve alone. Everyone should allow everyone else to go where their spirit leads them, and help others only when they need it, never imposing ideas upon a friend. In this manner everyone will find life and sustenance from others; and what each can become that he will become completely.

But how are things done in this world? One person is always ready to serve the earthly needs of another, and is even prepared to sacrifice his own well-being. What is most valued is communicating one's ideas and experience, and sympathizing with others and diminishing their pain. But even in friendship there is an antipathy to one's inner nature. People want to erase a friend's failings from his nature, and what is a failing in themselves they see in him too. Thus one friend sacrifices his individuality to the other, and both are untrue to themselves by becoming only like one another. This will continue unless a strong will calls short the corruption, or the false friendship weakens and dissolves from the constant harmony and discord. Woe to the person with a soft heart if a friend becomes attached to him! The poor wretch dreams of a new and stronger life; and he rejoices in the happy hours that pass. But little does he see how his spirit becomes indebted to, and dissipated in, his false felicity; until finally, oppressed and paralysed from every side, his inner life disappears. So it happens to many of the better sort, who hardly know the outlines of their own individuality because it is carved out by a friend and then plastered over with his detritus.

Sweet love joins man and wife, who go to build their own home. Just as new creatures spring from the womb of their love, so a new common will should come from the harmony of their nature. The peaceful home, with all its activities, routines and pleasures, should reveal this will in action. Alas, how I must see this most beautiful bond of humanity desecrated everywhere. It remains a mystery why they joined together; each wants his or her own way now as in the past. Now one person, then the other, dominates; and each sadly reckons in silence whether the gain outweighs the loss in freedom. The fate of one finally becomes that of the other; and in the recognition of cold necessity the glow of love dies out. In the last analysis, everyone brings the same account to the same result: nothing. Every home should be the beautiful body, the beautiful work of one's own soul, having its own form and characteristics. Yet almost all of them degenerate into a dull uniformity, the desolate grave of freedom and true life. Does she make him happy, does she devote herself to him? Does he make her happy, is he completely obliging? Are both made happiest when the other completely sacrifices him or herself? Oh, do not torment me, image of misery that lies hid beneath their bliss, the sign of impending death, which plays its old game by painting before me the last semblance of life!

What has become nowadays of the state described in the ancient fables of the wise?[35] Where is the power that this highest form of existence gives to a person, the consciousness that everyone should have of being part of its reason, fantasy and strength? Where is the love for this new self-created being, which would rather sacrifice its own individual consciousness than lose this being, and which would rather risk its own life than the fatherland be murdered? Where is the concern that carefully watches, so that the fatherland is

---

[35] Probably an allusion to Plato's *Republic* and Aristotle's *Politics*.

not seduced and its soul corrupted? Where, indeed, is the individual character of each state, and the works by which it makes itself known? The present generation is so far from having an inkling of what this side of humanity means that it imagines the better organization of the state, like an ideal human being, will be such that whoever lives in the state, be it in the old or new form, will gladly impose their mould upon everything, that the sage will lay down a model for all future generations in his works and hope that all humanity will be saved by honoring it as a symbol. It holds that the best state is that which one feels the least, and that which can least feel the need for its own existence.[36] Whoever thus regards the most splendid work of art of humanity, which elevates it to the highest level of its being, as merely a necessary evil, as an indispensable mechanism to prevent and control crime, must feel as only a restriction that which is designed to secure him the highest degree of life.

The vile source of this great evil is that people have a sense only for the external community of the sensible world, according to which they want to measure and model everything. In the community of the sensible world there must be always limitation; one person who wants to preserve and enlarge the sphere of their physical well-being must permit another the space to do the same. Where one stands is the limit for the other; and they suffer it resignedly only because they cannot possess the whole world themselves, and because they can make use of the other persons and their possessions. Everything is directed to these ends: increasing possession of things and knowledge; security and aid against fate and misfortune; increased power through the community to limit others. This is all that people now seek and find, whether in friendship, marriage or the fatherland; they do not seek and find help to complete the development of their individuality, or to enrich their inner life. In these ends every community binds the individual with the first ties of education. From an early age, the young spirit is burdened with alien ideas and accustomed to a life of servitude, rather than getting space for itself and the opportunity to explore the full extent of the world and humanity.

[36] A critique of the liberal theory of the state, already prevalent in German physiocratic circles in the 1780s. In the 1790s this doctrine was defended by Humboldt, Dohm, Schiller and Forster.

Oh, what lamentable poverty in the midst of wealth! How hopeless is the struggle of the noble spirit, who seeks morality and culture, with this world, which recognizes only laws and commands, and which loves rules and customs rather than free actions. It boasts of its higher wisdom when it abolishes some antiquated form and gives birth to a new form, which, though it appears to have life in it, all too quickly degenerates into a mere formula and dead custom. What could save me if you, divine fantasy, did not exist, and if you did not give me a presentiment of a better future?

Yes, culture will develop out of barbarism, and life from the sleep of the dead! The elements of a new world are already present. The higher powers will not slumber forever; sooner or later the spirit that animates humanity will awaken them. Just as the cultivation of the earth for man's benefit is now far superior to that wild dominion by nature when people timidly fled before every expression of her powers: so the blessed time of the true community of spirits cannot be far removed from the present childhood of humanity. The slave of nature never dreamed of future lordship over it, and still less did he understand what a prophet meant when he foretold it; for he was lacking the very idea of a condition for which he felt no longing. Similarly, the person of today does not comprehend when someone describes other goals to him, when he hears of other relationships between people and a new form of community; for he does not understand that one can want something higher and better, and does not fear that something can happen that must deeply shame his pride and lazy complacency. When the present state of culture sprang forth from a wretched barbarism, which barely revealed the first germs of a better condition to a trained eye, why should not the sublime kingdom of culture and morality not arise from our present confused chaos, especially when the eye already discerns the rudiments of a better world through the sinking mists? It will come, this better world! Why should I count the hours that pass by, the generations that pass away? Why should time concern me when my inner being is not attached to it?

A person belongs to the world that he helps to create. This world absorbs the whole of his thought and will; and only outside its boundaries are they a stranger. Whoever lives content with the present and desires nothing more is a contemporary of those early semi-barbarians who laid the foundation for our world. His life is the sequel to theirs; he enjoys contentedly the fulfilment of what they wanted; and he does not conceive the better world that they could not conceive. I, for my part, am a stranger to the mode of thought and life of the present generation.[37] I am a prophet of the future world, to which I am drawn by a lively imagination and a strong faith, and to which I belong in every thought and deed. I am indifferent to what the present world does or suffers. Lying deep below me, it seems very small; and at a glance I can survey the confused cycle of its life.

Returning to the same point and maintaining the same form after all the convulsions in the spheres of life and science,[38] this world shows its limitations and the narrow scope of its striving. What it creates it cannot develop further; everything just revolves in the same old circles. I take no pleasure in its creations; and every favourable sign does not deceive me because of some empty expectations. But whenever I find a spark of that hidden fire that will sooner or later consume the old and create the new, I am drawn to it with love and hope, regarding it as a sign of my distant home. And from where I now stand one should see the holy flames burn in a new light, testimony to the initiated of the power of the spirit. In love and hope those, like myself, who belong to the future draw closer; and through every deed and word the beautiful, free alliance of the initiated becomes closer and expands in anticipation of a better age.

But even this the world hinders as much as it can. It prevents all knowledge of kindred spirits, and conspires to ruin the seeds of a better future. A deed that has sprung from the purest of intentions gives room for a thousand misinterpretations. What is done in the most innocent moral spirit is inevitably associated with worldly motives. Too many adorn themselves with false appearances for everyone to be trusted; and he who seeks a kindred spirit is rightfully sceptical of first impressions. Because time and the world undermine the boldness of trust, it often happens that kindred spir-

---

[37] On the theme of a stranger, see Novalis' early poem 'Der Fremdling', *Schriften*, I, p. 399.
[38] 'Convulsions in the spheres of life and science' (*Erschütterungen im Gebiete des Lebens und der Wissenschaft*): a reference to the French Revolution and the Kantian Copernican Revolution.

its pass by one another. So have courage and hope! Not only you have roots in that deeper soil that will be the surface of some future age. Everywhere the seeds of a better future germinate! Continue to look for it whenever possible. You will still find many friends, and many of them will be among those that you have long misjudged. And you too will be recognized by many. In spite of the world, mistrust and suspicion will eventually disappear, if you only show constancy in action and your intuition often warns your fraternal heart. Boldly stamp your spirit upon every action, so that those who are near find you! Boldly go out in the world speaking your mind, so that others hear you!

Of course, the magic of language serves only the world, not us. It has exact signs and a beautiful abundance for everything that is thought and felt in the sense of the world. It is the clearest mirror of the times, a work of art in which its spirit comes to self-knowledge. But, for us, language is still crude and inchoate, a poor instrument for the formation of a community. How long it hinders the spirit so that it cannot attain an intuition of itself! Thanks to the mesh of language the spirit belongs to the world before it finds itself; only gradually does it free itself from these entanglements. And if in spite of all the errors and corruptions introduced by words the spirit finally penetrates the truth, language then changes the rules of engagment and lays siege to the spirit, so that it cannot communicate to others or receive sustenance from them. The spirit must search for a long time in the great abundance of words before it finds a trustworthy sign, so that under its protection it can transmit its innermost thoughts. Quickly, though, the enemy snatches it away, giving the sign a foreign meaning, so that a listener will doubt from whom it originally came. Probably many replies will come from afar to the lonely spirit; but he must question their meaning, not knowing whether they come from a friend or enemy. If only language were the common possession of the sons of the spirit and the children of the world! If they only were so curious about higher wisdom! No, they cannot succeed in confusing or intimidating us! This is the great struggle for the sacred banner of humanity, which we must preserve for a better future and following generations. This is the struggle that decides everything. But it is also a certain victory, which, unaffected by luck or chance, is to be won only through the power of spirit and true art.

Morals should be the dress and covering of individuality, delicately and suggestively clinging to its noble form, revealing its proportions and gracefully accompanying its movements. If this noble garment is treated with respect, if it is more transparently and finely woven and more tightly worn, then artful deceipt must end; and it will soon be revealed when a profane, common nature tries to appear in a noble, higher form. The wise observer will detect with every movement the true shape and strength of the concealed parts; the magical costume will lie loose over empty space so that it easily flutters away to reveal the inner disproportion. Thus constancy and harmony of morals should and will become a sign of the spirit's inner essence, and the secret greeting of all the initiated.

Language too should portray the spirit's innermost thoughts. It should reproduce its highest intuition, its most secret contemplation of its actions; and its wonderful music should signify the worth that it lays upon everything, the hierarchy of its love. Of course, others can abuse the signs that we consecrate for the highest things; and they can impose their petty thoughts and limited perceptions onto the sacred things these signs should signify. Still, the manner of speech of the worldling is different from that of the initiated. The slaves of the age arrange the signs of their thought to a different melody than the wise. They ascend to their first principles, and draw conclusions remote from them, in a different manner. If only everyone formed their own language, making it their property and an aesthetic whole, so that derivation and transition, connection and consequence, exactly mirrored the structure of their spirit, and so that its harmony precisely reproduced the ascent of their heart and the keynote of their thought. If we only do this, then there will be, even in the vulgar tongue, a holy and secret language that the uninitiated will not know to interpret or imitate,[39] for only in the inner disposition is there a key to its characters. A few phrases of his thought, a few notes of his discourse, will betray the outsider.

Oh, if the wise and good would only recognize one another merely from their morals and speech! If the present confusion were

---

[39] Cf. Novalis, *Faith and Love*, Preface, nos. 1–2, p. 35.

only dissolved, the barriers torn down! If only the inner dispute finally broke out! Then the victory would be near, the beautiful sun would dawn. For the free judgement and impartial sense of the younger generation would inevitably incline to the better side. But only significant actions can reveal the spirit's presence, only miracles testify to a divine origin. Someone is lacking in consciousness of the inner spirit if there is no beautiful unity in their morals, or if there is only a cold pretension of morals to conceal an inner deformity. Someone knows nothing of their inner development, and has never felt the depths of humanity in themselves, if the foundation stones of their language have crumbled into dust, if the power of their speech has dissolved into empty phrases and superficial polish, and if their loftiest rhetoric degenerates into an idle play of sounds. No one can live harmoniously according to a simple beautiful morals than he who strives after his inner development, and so belongs to a future world. No one can become a true artist in the use of language than he who has looked into himself with a free view and taken possession of the inner essence of humanity.

From this feeling of peaceful omnipotence, not from the criminal violence of vain experiments,[40] must respect for the highest, the beginning of a better age, go forth. To promote this age is my aspiration in the world! Thus will I discharge my debt to her, and thus will I satisfy my vocation. And thus will my free powers combine with the efforts of all the elect, so that my actions will help humanity to progress on the right path to its goal.

---

[40] A critique of the French Revolution, and in particular all its failed attempts to establish a stable constitution for France.

Index of names

Index of names

Hülsen, A. L., 134
Humboldt, Wilhelm von, xxiii, 116 n3, 175 n10, 192 n36

Imle, Fanny, xxxviii

Jacobi, F. H., xvi, xx, xxi, xxiii, 150

Kant, Immanuel: critique of his concepts: of democracy, 102, 107; of political reform, 111; of Enlightenment, 69, 126; of freedom, 55–6, 136, 150; of morality, 83, 110, 128, 173–4, 179; of peace, 39, 48, 108–9; of a republic, 48, 95–9, 102; of revolution, 111–12; influence of, 3–5, 9, 17, 78, 79, 86, 87, 95, 100, 101, 111, 143, 144, 146
Kepler, Johannes, 136, 137
Kirchner, Erwin, xxxvi
Kluckhohn, Paul, xxxvi
Kurzke, Hermann, xxxviii

Lessing, Gottphraim, xvi, xxi, 24 n42, 79 n46, 133 n6, 146b, 146 n5
Linden, Walter, xxxvii
Locke, John, 31
Loyola, Ignaz, 67
Luther, Martin, xx, 65, 66, 68, 136

Mähl, Hans Joachim, ix, xxxviii
Malsch, Wilfried, xxxviii
Meinecke, Friedrich, xxxvii
Mendelssohn, Moses, xx, 126 n1
Mirabeau, Comte de, 121
Möser, Justus, xvi, xxix
Müller, Adam, xii, xviii
Müller, Andreas, xxxvii
Müller, Johannes, xxix

Napoleon, 61, 73
Newton, Isaac, 70 n21
Novalis: on aesthetics, 18, 19, 85; on aristocracy, 37, 84; critique of atomism, 45–6, 55–6; on Christianity, 61–3, 78–9; on Enlightenment, xvi, 69–71; on epistemology, 9, 10, 16, 17; on history, 10, 27, 38; on human nature, xxv, 19, 77; on law, 26, 38; on love, 35–6, 54, 86; on monarchy, 38–40, 41, 56–7, 84, 86; on the mystical, 10, 12, 15, 17, 27, 35; on

poetry, 21, 85, 86; on religion, 22, 75; republicanism of, 41, 57, 77, 86; on revolution, xiv, 37–8, 41, 53, 65; on sciences, 20, 26, 27, 35–6, 76; on poetic state, 24, 48, 84

Pius VI, 61, 78 n42
Plato, 127, 191
Pope, Alexander, 21
Pufendorf, Samuel, xxii, 45 n27

Rehberg, A. W., 104 n21
Richelieu, Armand Jean, 122
Robespierre, Maximilien, 73, 99 n9, 121, 162
Rousseau, Jean Jacques, 55 n6, 56 n8, 90, 121

Schanze, Helmut, xxxvii
Schelling, F. W. J., vii, xi, xii, 9 n1, 76, 85 n4
Schiller, Friedrich, xv, xxiii, 83 n1
Schlegel, A. W., 9, 115
Schlegel, Friedrich: on the artist, 126, 129, 130; on democracy, 102, 104, 157; on family, 147, 153, 156, 165, 167; on freedom, 96–7, 150, 154–5; on French Revolution, xiv, 118, 119, 121, 122, 128, 133, 161, 162, 163, 164; on human nature, 143–7; on insurrection, 111–12; on love, 132, 134, 149, 150, 151, 152, 153, 162; on Middle Ages, 162, 165; on monarchy, xxiv, 106–7, 120; on mysticism, 120, 121, 126, 131, 139; on peace, 109–10; on philosophy, 127, 128, 129, 155; on poetry, 116, 128, 129, 155; on religion, xviii, 119, 125, 126, 127, 128, 129, 149–52, 165; on republic, 95–105, 118, 143, 147, 153, 156–7; on women, 116, 121, 163
Schleiermacher, Friedrich: on art: 177, 189–90; on community, 189–90, 192; critique of Enlightenment, xix, xxiv, 185–8; critique of Kantian ethics, 173–6; on individuality, 173–6, 184; on language, 195–7; on love, 179–80, 183; on mysticism, xix, 179, 180; on self-knowledge, 171–2; on state, xxiv–v, 191–2
Schmitt, Carl, xxxvii
Schubert, Gotthilf Heinrich, xii

Index of subjects

Cambridge Texts in the History of Political Thought

Titles published in the series thus far

Aristotle *The Politics* (edited by Stephen Everson)

Arnold *Culture and Anarchy and Other Writings* (edited by Stefan Collini)

Austin *The Province of Jurisprudence Determined* (edited by Wilfrid E. Rumble)

Bakunin *Statism and Anarchy* (edited by Marshall Shatz)

Baxter *A Holy Commonwealth* (edited by William Lamont)

Beccaria *On Crimes and Punishments and Other Writings* (edited by Richard Bellamy)

Bentham *A Fragment on Government* (introduction by Ross Harrison)

Bernstein *The Preconditions of Socialism* (edited by Henry Tudor)

Bodin *On Sovereignty* (edited by Julian H. Franklin)

Bossuet *Politics Drawn from the Very Words of Holy Scripture* (edited by Patrick Riley)

Burke *Pre-Revolutionary Writings* (edited by Ian Harris)

Christine de Pizan *The Book of the Body Politic* (edited by Kate Langdon Forhan)

Cicero *On Duties* (edited by M. T. Griffin and E. M. Atkins)

Constant *Political Writings* (edited by Biancamaria Fontana)

Diderot *Political Writings* (edited by John Hope Mason and Robert Wokler)

The Dutch Revolt (edited by Martin van Gelderen)

Early Greek Political Thought from Homer to the Sophists (edited by Michael Gagarin and Paul Woodruff)

Ferguson *An Essay on the History of Civil Society* (edited by Fania Oz-Salzberger)

Filmer *Patriarcha and Other Writings* (edited by Johann P. Sommerville)

Fourier *The Theory of the Four Movements* (edited by Gareth Stedman Jones and Ian Patterson)

Gramsci *Pre-Prison Writings* (edited by Richard Bellamy)

Guicciardini *Dialogue on the Government of Florence* (edited by Alison Brown)

Harrington *A Commonwealth of Oceana* and *A System of Politics* (edited by J. G. A. Pocock)

Hegel *Elements of the Philosophy of Right* (edited by Allen W. Wood and H. B. Nisbet)

Hobbes *Leviathan* (edited by Richard Tuck)

Hobhouse *Liberalism and Other Writings* (edited by James Meadowcroft)

Hooker *Of the Laws of Ecclesiastical Polity* (edited by A. S. McGrade)

Hume *Political Essays* (edited by Knud Haakonssen)

King James VI and I *Political Writings* (edited by Johann P. Sommerville)

John of Salisbury *Policraticus* (edited by Cary Nederman)

Kant *Political Writings* (edited by H. S. Reiss and H. B. Nisbet)

Knox *On Rebellion* (edited by Roger A. Mason)

Kropotkin *The Conquest of Bread and Other Writings* (edited by Marshall Shatz)

Lawson *Politica sacra et civilis* (edited by Conal Condren)

Leibniz *Political Writings* (edited by Patrick Riley)

Locke *Two Treatises of Government* (edited by Peter Laslett)

Loyseau *A Treatise of Orders and Plain Dignities* (edited by Howell A. Lloyd)

Luther and Calvin on Secular Authority (edited by Harro Höpfl)

Machiavelli *The Prince* (edited by Quentin Skinner and Russell Price)

de Maistre *Considerations on France* (edited by Isaiah Berlin and Richard Lebrun)

Malthus *An Essay on the Principle of Population* (edited by Donald Winch)

Marsiglio of Padua *Defensor minor* and *De translatione imperii* (edited by Cary Nederman)

Marx *Early Political Writings* (edited by Joseph O'Malley)

Marx *Later Political Writings* (edited by Terrell Carver)

James Mill *Political Writings* (edited by Terence Ball)

J. S. Mill *On Liberty*, with *The Subjection of Women* and *Chapters on Socialism* (edited by Stefan Collini)

Milton *Political Writings* (edited by Martin Dzelzainis)

Montesquieu *The Spirit of the Laws* (edited by Anne M. Cohler, Basia Carolyn Miller and Harold Samuel Stone)

More *Utopia* (edited by George M. Logan and Robert M. Adams)

Morris *News from Nowhere* (edited by Krishan Kumar)

Nicholas of Cusa *The Catholic Concordance* (edited by Paul E. Sigmund)

Nietzsche *On the Genealogy of Morality* (edited by Keith Ansell-Pearson)

Paine *Political Writings* (edited by Bruce Kuklick)

Plato *The Statesman* (edited by Julia Annas and Robin Waterfield)

Price *Political Writings* (edited by D. O. Thomas)

Priestley *Political Writings* (edited by Peter Miller)

Proudhon *What is Property?* (edited by Donald R. Kelley and Bonnie G. Smith)

Pufendorf *On the Duty of Man and Citizen according to Natural Law* (edited by James Tully)

The Radical Reformation (edited by Michael G. Baylor)

Seneca *Moral and Political Essays* (edited by John Cooper and John Procope)

Spencer *The Man versus the State* and *The Proper Sphere of Government* (edited by John Offer)

Stirner *The Ego and Its Own* (edited by David Leopold)

Thoreau *Political Writings* (edited by Nancy Rosenblum)

Utopias of the British Enlightenment (edited by Gregory Claeys)

Vitoria *Political Writings* (edited by Anthony Pagden and Jeremy Lawrance)

Voltaire *Political Writings* (edited by David Williams)

Weber *Political Writings* (edited by Peter Lassman and Ronald Speirs)

William of Ockham *A Short Discourse on Tyrannical Government* (edited by A. S. McGrade and John Kilcullen)

William of Ockham *A Letter to the Friars Minor and Other Writings* (edited by A. S. McGrade and John Kilcullen)

Wollstonecraft *A Vindication of the Rights of Men* and *A Vindication of the Rights of Woman* (edited by Sylvana Tomaselli)